The Art of Craft Winemaking

Dr. R.J.Harris

Contents:

Foreword	iii
Chapter 1. The Experience of Making Wine at Home	1
Chapter 2. The Basics of Home Winemaking	10
Chapter 3. Making Wine from Kits	53
Chapter 4. The Process for Making Basic Craft Wines	64
Chapter 5. Making Mead	80
Chapter 6. Making Sparkling Wines	84
Chapter 7. Making Cider	92
Chapter 8. Blending Wines	96
Chapter 9. Ageing and Maturing Wine	108
Chapter 10. Bottling and Labelling your Wine	111
Chapter 11. Advanced Winemaking Techniques & Equipment	116
Chapter 12. Troubleshooting Common Issues	131
Chapter 13. Serving Wine	142
Chapter 14. Making Spirit Based Drinks and Liqueurs	145
Chapter 15. Sustainability and Biodiversity in Winemaking	160
Chapter 16. Prizewinning Craft Wine Recipes	165
Chapter 17. Top 30 Cocktail and Mixer Recipes	314
Glossary of Winemaking Terms	349
Scales and Conversion Tables	358
Index	365

The Art of Craft Winemaking at Home

Foreword:

This book provides a comprehensive guide for both beginners, and those that have progressed on their journey into winemaking. It is also a useful guide for advanced winemakers, offering practical advice, and a wide range of recipes to make delicious wines.

During the 1960's and 70's home winemaking developed into a thriving cottage industry and many readers will remember their parents' making wines from fruits picked from hedgerows and their gardens, with varying degrees of success. The equipment and necessary supplies were often quite basic, but there were a range of books to support the hobby, such as First Steps in Winemaking. This became a best seller and adorned most winemakers' shelves. These books provided the key knowledge needed to become fully immersed in the rewarding and exciting hobby of home winemaking.

Jump forward fifty years and the landscape is completely different. Our knowledge and appreciation of commercial wines from all corners of the world is greater and we have the internet at our finger tips to acquire a myriad of information. Furthermore, the equipment and supplies available to home winemakers is of a much higher quality, and on a par with commercial craft wineries. Wine kits are now sold in specialist winemaking shops that cost over a hundred pounds and produce stunning wines, which are equivalent to commercial wines costing £15-£20 per bottle. However, it is still possible to make a delicious fruit wine at home for less than £1 per bottle.

The recipes outlined in this book have been developed by the author through fifty years of specialist retail experience and have been tried and tested by thousands of home winemakers. They have won many prizes in national winemaking competitions, so you can be sure that they will produce delicious wines. This book aims to modernise the information available to winemakers and integrates dried ingredients into recipes, to supplement fresh fruits. The recipes also incorporate the latest grape concentrates to ensure consistent results of the highest quality are achieved.

The information provided, together with troubleshooting advice, comes from decades of experience in supporting retail customers, and providing solutions to their problems. Many issues that arise in winemaking can be easily circumvented by having the correct knowledge and skills in place. This book aims to provide that knowledge and to allow you to quickly develop the skills to ensure you make prizewinning wines that will impress your friends.

So, whether you are a curious beginner or a seasoned enthusiast, "The Art of Craft Winemaking at Home" invites you to embark on a delicious and rewarding journey into the world of Home Winemaking,

Cheers.

Chapter 1. The Experience of Making Wine at Home:

Home winemaking is an exciting hobby which allows you to produce wonderful wines at amazing prices. There are numerous reasons why making wine at home can be a fulfilling and enriching endeavour. From the joy of creating something with your own hands to the opportunity to explore your creativity. From selecting unique ingredients to experimenting with different fermentation techniques, home winemaking allows you to express yourself and tailor your creations to suit your tastes and preferences. Whether you dream of crafting a bold red wine or a delicate rosé, the possibilities are endless, and the only limit is your imagination.

Witnessing the transformation of humble ingredients into a delicious bottle of wine is truly magical. Through the process of fermentation and ageing, flavours develop, aromas evolve, and complexity emerges, turning simple grapes or fruit into a sophisticated finished drink. Engaging in home winemaking allows you to experience this journey firsthand, deepening your appreciation for the art and science of winemaking.

When you make wine at home, you have complete control over the ingredients used and the quality of the final product. You can select the finest grapes, grape concentrate, or fruit available, ensuring that your wine is made from the freshest, highest-quality ingredients. Additionally, you can avoid the use of additives or preservatives commonly found in commercial wines, allowing you to create wines that are pure, natural, and tailored to your preferences.

Home winemaking can be a highly cost-effective and sustainable alternative to purchasing wine from a store. This is a welcome benefit in times where high energy costs and the economic squeeze put a serious dent in consumer spending power. By making your own wine, you can save money on expensive bottles while reducing your carbon footprint by minimising packaging and transportation emissions. Furthermore, you can repurpose glass bottles and corks, minimising waste and contributing to a more environmentally friendly lifestyle.

Making wine at home is a social activity that brings people together. Whether you're collaborating with family members, friends, or neighbours, home winemaking provides an opportunity to bond over a shared passion and create lasting memories together. From harvesting grapes to bottling the finished wine, each step of the winemaking process can be enjoyed as a collective experience, fostering a sense of connection and camaraderie.

Homemade wine makes a thoughtful and memorable gift for special occasions. Whether you're celebrating a birthday, anniversary, or holiday, presenting a bottle of wine that you've crafted yourself adds a personal touch and demonstrates the time and effort you've invested in creating something special. Additionally, homemade wine can be enjoyed during celebrations, serving as a centrepiece for shared moments of joy and laughter.

Therefore, making wine at home offers a multitude of benefits that extend far beyond the final product in your glass. From unleashing your creativity to fostering connections with loved ones, home winemaking is a rewarding and fulfilling endeavour that enriches both the body and the soul. So why wait? Embrace the opportunity to embark on your own winemaking journey and discover the countless joys that await you.

History of Winemaking at Home:

The history of winemaking begins thousands of years ago, in the cradle of civilization. Ancient civilizations such as the Mesopotamians, Egyptians, Greeks, and Romans were among the first to cultivate grapes and ferment them into wine. In these early societies, winemaking was often a household activity, with families producing small batches of wine for personal consumption and religious ceremonies.

Throughout history, home winemaking has held profound cultural significance, serving as a symbol of hospitality, celebration, and communion. From the intimate gatherings of family and friends to the grand feasts of royalty, wine has been a constant companion, enriching moments both ordinary and extraordinary. Today, the tradition of home winemaking continues to thrive, preserving ancient techniques while embracing new technologies and trends.

During the Middle Ages, monasteries played a crucial role in preserving the art of winemaking. Monks meticulously tended to vineyards and developed innovative techniques for producing wine, laying the foundation for modern viticulture and oenology. Home winemaking continued to thrive within monastic communities, with monks sharing their knowledge and expertise with the wider populace.

The Renaissance brought about a renewed interest in the arts and sciences, including winemaking. Wealthy aristocrats and merchants began to establish vineyards on their estates, further popularising the cultivation of grapes and the production of wine. As trade routes expanded and colonies were established, the practice of home winemaking spread to new regions, from the hills of Tuscany to the vineyards of the New World.

The early 20th century saw a significant disruption to the tradition of home winemaking with the enactment of Prohibition in the United States and other countries. Despite the ban on alcohol production and sales, resourceful individuals continued to make wine at home, often using clandestine methods to evade authorities. This is where the term "Bathtub Gin" emerged from, as alcoholic spirits were made in back house bathtubs to evade the law. After Prohibition was repealed, home winemaking experienced a resurgence in popularity, fuelled by renewed interest in artisanal crafts and DIY culture.

The UK introduced home brewing licenses as part of the Licensing Act 1964. This act allowed individuals to brew beer and make wine for personal consumption without requiring a license, as long as it was not for sale. However, there were restrictions on the quantity that could be produced without a license. In 1976, the law was further relaxed with the Intoxicating Liquor Act, which allowed individuals to produce beer and wine for personal use without any restrictions on quantity, effectively legalizing homebrewing in the UK. Since then, homebrewing has become a popular hobby for many people across the country.

Home winemaking in the 1960s and 1970s experienced a surge of interest, particularly in countries such as the United Kingdom and United States. This period saw an increase in the availability of equipment and supplies for home winemaking. Specialty stores began to stock a variety of winemaking equipment, including fermentation vessels, airlocks, corks, and bottles. This made it easier for enthusiasts to get started with winemaking at home. Furthermore, key retail chains such as Boots PLC championed the industry, which increased the availability of supplies.

During the 1970's and 80's, there was a growing appreciation for wine in Western societies. Wine consumption was no longer limited to the elite, and more people were interested in exploring different varieties and styles of wine. Wine bars emerged offering (what was back then) sophisticated German styles such as Piersporter, Hock. Mosel, and the infamous Liebfraumilch! This cultural shift contributed to the popularity of home winemaking as hobbyists sought to replicate their favourite wines or experiment with unique flavours.

Home winemaking kits and concentrates became increasingly popular in the 1980s and 90s. These kits typically included grape juice concentrate, yeast, and additives, along with instructions for making wine at home. Wine kits offered convenience and consistency, making it easier for beginners to produce drinkable wine without the need for extensive equipment or expertise. The quality of some early kits was "average" but as time went on kits started to deliver results which were comparable to commercial wines at a fraction of the cost.

Home winemaking clubs and associations began to form during this period, providing enthusiasts with opportunities to connect, share knowledge, and exchange recipes and techniques. These clubs often organised events such as tastings, competitions, and educational workshops, fostering a sense of community among home winemakers.

Overall, the 1960's through to the 1990s marked a period of growth and innovation in the world of home winemaking. With increased access to equipment and supplies, growing interest in wine culture, and a supportive regulatory environment, more people than ever before were able to enjoy the pleasures of making wine at home. The number of independent specialist home brew shops continued to grow to support this flourishing hobby.

During the 1990s and into the new Millennium interest in home winemaking waned as cheap commercial wine from Europe flooded the market. This reduced the cost advantage of making wine at home. The core base of enthusiasts remained but the industry struggled to maintain the level of supply and some retailers were forced to close. Furthermore, the internet provided a new e-commerce platform for winemakers to buy on line.

Over the last 15 years there has been a huge growth in craft beer, which has supported new interest in home brewing. However, home winemaking interest remained static, failing to keep pace with its beer brewing counterpart. That was until the COVID-19 lockdown, when everything changed, literally overnight! Demand for home winemaking kits exploded and retailers were initially unable to meet that demand. New and returning winemakers suddenly realised that the quality of contemporary wine kits was significantly better than the early ones and they were easily able to make commercial quality wines at home in only a few weeks.

The COVID-19 lockdown had a significant impact on various aspects of daily life, including home winemaking. An increased interest in home hobbies was observed. With restrictions on social activities and limited options for entertainment outside the home, many people turned to hobbies as a way to pass the time and alleviate boredom. Home winemaking experienced a surge in popularity as individuals sought out creative and productive activities to occupy their time during lockdown periods. This inevitably created Supply Chain disruptions. The lockdown disrupted supply chains worldwide, leading to shortages of certain winemaking supplies and ingredients. Home winemakers faced challenges in sourcing grape juice, yeast, fermentation vessels, and other essential equipment and additives. This prompted some enthusiasts to adapt their recipes or experiment with alternative ingredients based on what was available.

A major disruptor to the home winemaking industry was a shift to Online Purchasing. As bricks-and-mortar stores closed or operated with reduced hours during lockdowns, many home winemakers shifted to online purchasing for their supplies. Online retailers experienced increased demand for winemaking kits, equipment, and ingredients, leading to delays in shipping and fulfilment. However, the convenience and accessibility of online shopping allowed enthusiasts to continue their winemaking pursuits despite the restrictions. This shift in buying behaviour continued beyond lockdown. Many retailers have experienced significant reductions in shop footfall and increased online sales.

Home winemaking clubs and associations adapted to the new reality of social distancing by transitioning their meetings and events to virtual platforms. Online workshops, webinars, and forums provided opportunities for home winemakers to connect, share knowledge, and exchange ideas with fellow enthusiasts from the safety of their homes. This digital shift fostered a sense of community and camaraderie among home winemakers, even during periods of isolation.

The lockdown provided an opportunity for home winemakers to explore new techniques and experiment with different styles of wine. With more time spent at home, enthusiasts had the freedom to devote additional attention to their winemaking projects, fine-tuning recipes, and honing their skills. Some individuals took advantage of the situation to embark on ambitious projects such as barrel ageing, wild fermentation, or fruit wine experiments.

Engaging in home winemaking served as a therapeutic outlet for many individuals during the stressful and uncertain times of lockdown. The process of nurturing fermenting batches, monitoring progress, and witnessing the transformation of ingredients into wine provided a sense of purpose, accomplishment, and fulfilment. Home winemaking offered a creative outlet for self-expression and a source of joy and satisfaction amidst the challenges of the pandemic.

The COVID-19 lockdown period put home winemaking back on the map and the interest in the hobby has continued. It introduced a new audience of Millennials to take the hobby forward. Their expectations and buying behaviour is changing the direction of the industry. Preferences for online shopping, responsible manufacturing, and sustainability, will shape the industry. Millennials are more health conscious and are averse to food additives. The opportunity to craft wines without additives and using natural ingredients means the winemaker has full control over the process, which appeals to many younger people.

Advances in technology and international accessibility will continue to revolutionise the world of home winemaking. Enthusiasts now have access to a wide range of equipment, ingredients, and resources to support their winemaking. From beginner-friendly kits, and commercial yeast strains, to sophisticated fermentation vessels, modern innovations are making it easier than ever for individuals to craft high-quality wine in the comfort of their own homes.

Furthermore, the interest in commercial craft beer continues to grow and small-scale brew houses and tap rooms are in great demand. These tap rooms are increasingly showcasing craft wines and meads to align with a growing interest in homebrewing and do-it-yourself (DIY) craft culture. This is reshaping the home winemaking industry and while some traditional homebrew shops are facing challenges from online competitors, others are adapting by offering unique products, educational workshops, or community events to attract customers.

The existence of specialist (bricks and mortar) home beer and winemaking shops will continue to be important for the development of the hobby. These guys offer excellent advice and are a catalyst for new products and the development of winemaking. Your homebrew shop offers an experience that cannot be replicated online so please support them where possible, they are an important part of the fabric of the hobby.

The Benefits of Making Wine at Home:

Making wine at home offers a multitude of benefits, ranging from creative expression to personal satisfaction. Home winemaking allows you to unleash your creativity and experiment with different grape varieties, fruit combinations, fermentation techniques, and ageing processes. You have complete control over the ingredients and can tailor your recipes to suit your taste preferences, resulting in unique and personalised wines that reflect your individual style.

Cost saving is a major benefit of home winemaking. Making wine at home can be a cost-effective alternative to purchasing wine from a store, especially if you're able to source ingredients locally or grow your own grapes or fruit. While there is an initial investment in equipment and supplies, the long-term savings can be significant, particularly if you're producing wine in large quantities or experimenting with high-end ingredients. Even the more expensive wine kits will produce fantastic wine for under £3 a bottle. The quality is equally as good as commercial equivalents costing over £10.

When you make wine at home, you have control over the quality of the ingredients used and the entire winemaking process. You can select the freshest, highest-quality grapes or fruit available, ensuring that your wine is made from premium ingredients. Additionally, you can avoid the use of additives or preservatives commonly found in commercial wines, producing wines that are pure, natural, and free from unwanted chemicals.

Home winemaking provides an opportunity to learn about the art and science of winemaking firsthand. You'll gain valuable knowledge about fermentation, yeast strains, pH levels, acidity, and other aspects of the winemaking process. Through trial and error, you'll develop a deeper understanding of how different factors impact the flavour, aroma, and texture of wine, honing your skills as a winemaker with each batch you produce. You will also gain an understanding of food pairing to compliment the flavours of your wine.

There is a profound sense of satisfaction that comes from creating something with your own hands, and home winemaking is no exception. As you watch your grapes or fruit transform into wine over time, you will experience a deep sense of accomplishment and pride in your work. Whether you're sharing your homemade wine with friends and family or enjoying it on your own, every sip becomes a testament to your skill and dedication as a winemaker.

The skills you develop will enhance the experience and many are transferable to other areas. Many home winemakers apply their skills to making other craft products, such as beer, spirits and liqueurs, mead, kombucha, and fermented fruits. There are many opportunities to widen your field of interest.

Home winemaking has a long history of bringing people together, fostering connections, and preserving cultural traditions. Whether you're participating in a winemaking club, attending a wine tasting event, visiting a craft fayre, or sharing bottles of homemade wine with loved ones, home winemaking provides opportunities for social interaction, cultural exchange, and the celebration of shared experiences.

Overall, making wine at home offers a rewarding and enriching experience that combines creativity, education, and enjoyment. Whether you're a novice or an experienced winemaker, the benefits of home winemaking extend far beyond the final product in your glass, enriching your life with every batch you produce.

Chapter 2. The Basics of Home Winemaking:

Home winemaking is a fascinating process that transforms grapes or other fruits into delicious wine in the comfort of your own home. The specifics may vary depending on factors such as the type of wine being made and personal preferences, and it is possible to supplement fresh fruits and flowers with dried ingredients. This will extend the time that you can make wines outside of the normal season for fruits and flowers. Furthermore, it is possible to swap natural grapes for grape concentrate so that the winemaking season can be extended throughout the year. It is important when purchasing grape juices to avoid those that contain preservatives. This could prevent fermentation from taking place.

Specialist wine kits are available in a wide range of styles, which will enhance your experience. These kits are supplied with yeast and chemical packs and many only require water, in addition to the ingredients. Wine kits are available in a wide range of styles, and many focus on one grape variety. They are a great way to start your hobby and most winemakers begin with a kit. Wine kits are a good way to maintain your stocks as your hobby develops. Don't consider them as cheating, most experienced winemakers make both kit wines, and craft wines (country wines made from fresh fruits, vegetables, and flowers). As a general rule, wines made from kits will mature faster than craft wines. Having a mixture of styles will mean you are not tempted to drink a country wine too early!

If you are making craft wines, then selecting the right ingredients is an important consideration. Begin by selecting high-quality grapes or fruit for your winemaking project. Consider factors such as ripeness, acidity, and sugar content when choosing ingredients. You can also experiment with different grape varieties or fruit combinations to create unique flavours and styles of wine. If you are making a wine from fresh flowers (such as Rose Petal or Elderflower), then it is important to avoid picking them from busy roadsides, where exhaust pollutants will affect the flowers. The recipes in this book will provide alternative dried ingredient weights. These can be used as a substitute for fresh equivalents, where appropriate. This is useful as it will allow you to make country wines out of season if required.

Once you have chosen your ingredients, the next step is to prepare them for fermentation. Grapes may need to be crushed and destemmed, while other fruits may require peeling, pitting, or chopping. An olive or cherry pitter is a very useful gadget for quickly removing stones from fruits. It is important to remove stones as they can introduce a bitter or almond flavour to the final wine. Some fruits such as Elderberries need to be stripped from their stalks to prevent similar bitter flavours from developing.

A useful tip when using fruits and grapes is to freeze them before use. This not only means you can schedule the winemaking process, but once rethawed, the fruit becomes naturally mushy and can be more easily crushed. Freeze-thawing opens up the fruits and subsequently allows the fermentation process to extract more flavour.

The fermentation process is a fundamental part of the winemaking process. Depending on the technique being followed, there may be a primary and secondary process. Grape concentrates can be fermented directly in a fermenter or demijohn (a one-gallon glass or plastic fermentation vessel), fitted with an airlock. This type of fermentation is known as anaerobic fermentation (without air). However, fruits need to be fermented aerobically (with air) for around five days in an open bucket covered with a cloth. This allows the flavours and colours of the fruits to be extracted. This is known as the primary fermentation. Once completed the liquid (referred to as wine "must") is strained into a secondary fermenter fitted with an airlock. During the primary fermentation, flavour extraction takes place, and during the secondary fermentation stage, alcohol is produced.

Wine yeast is added to the grape concentrate or fruit mix to initiate fermentation, which converts the sugars in the fruit into alcohol and carbon dioxide. The airlock allows carbon dioxide to escape while preventing oxygen from entering.

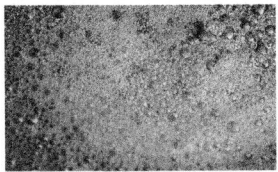

Throughout the fermentation process, it is important to monitor the temperature, sugar levels, and acidity of your wine. Adjustments may need to be made, such as adding nutrients or controlling the temperature, to ensure a healthy and successful fermentation. Regularly check for signs of fermentation activity, such as bubbles or foam on the surface of the wine.

Once fermentation is complete, the wine is syphoned or transferred to a clean vessel to separate it from the sediment or lees. This process is known as "Racking" and helps clarify the wine by removing any unwanted solids or sediment. Some winemakers choose to perform multiple rackings and most use fining agents to further clarify the wine.

The final stage of the production process is filtering. You should filter your wine through a wine filter to ensure that it achieves a commercial clarity. Filtering removes all minute suspended particles which could otherwise render the wine with a dull finish. It ensures that when poured into a glass, your wine is indistinguishable from a commercial wine.

After clarification, the wine is aged to develop its flavour, aroma, and complexity. Your wine can be transferred into ageing vessels such as barrels or carboys and stored in a cool, dark place for several months or even years, depending on the type of wine. Alternatively, you may choose to bottle your wine and allow it to mature in its final bottles. The options will be explored later. During ageing, your wine will undergo chemical changes that soften tannins, integrate flavours, and improve overall its quality.

When bottling it is important to Sanitise and prepare clean bottles, corks, and other bottling equipment. Carefully syphon the wine into bottles, leaving behind any sediment or impurities. Seal the bottles with corks or screw caps and label them with the wine's year, type, and any other relevant information.

The basic process of winemaking is easy to follow and the recipes in this book are designed to be straightforward and foolproof. The two areas where most failures arise are from a lack of sanitisation or exposure of the wine to the air.

It is important that all equipment and fermenters are meticulously cleaned and sanitised prior to use. The golden rule is that if anything comes into contact with your wine it should be sanitised beforehand. There is a difference between sanitisation and sterilisation. Sanitisation typically reduces the number of microorganisms by a certain percentage, such as 99.9%, depending on the specific sanitising agent used and the duration of exposure. While sanitisation significantly reduces microbial populations, it may not eliminate all microorganisms present. Sterilisation, on the other hand, achieves a much higher level of microbial destruction, effectively eliminating all viable microorganisms from surfaces or objects. Sterilisation processes such as autoclaving, dry heat, or chemical sterilant are capable of achieving a sterility assurance level (SAL) of 10^{-6}, meaning there is only one chance in a million of a viable microorganism remaining. We will explore the range of sanitisers and sterilisers available to you later in this book but generally speaking sanitisers are all that is needed for everyday use. Sterilisers are useful to have on stand by for one-off deep cleans and where infections may have been experienced.

When you first introduce yeast into the wine must it requires a good supply oxygen to start the fermentation process. If you are making a country wine, the yeast also needs access to oxygen for the first few days until it is strained into the fermenter. After that point you should restrict air contact as much as possible. Air can introduce bacteria into the wine and cause it to spoil so avoid opening lids unnecessarily and once fermentation has completed, finish the process as soon as possible. Try to control the environment where your wine is kept as far as you possibly can. This includes the ambient temperature.

Wine Chemistry:

Understanding the fundamental principles of wine chemistry is the key to making consistently good wines. By gaining an insight into wine chemistry basics, you will be better equipped to make informed decisions throughout the winemaking process and achieve the optimum characteristics in your wines.

pH and acidity play a crucial role in shaping the fundamental characteristics and stability of wine. pH is a measure of the acidity or alkalinity of a solution, with lower pH values indicating higher acidity. Wine with higher acidity tends to have a crisper, more refreshing taste, while lower acidity can lead to a flatter, less vibrant wine.

Acidity in wine is primarily derived from organic acids present in grapes and other fruits, such as tartaric, malic, and citric acids. During fermentation, yeast metabolises sugars into alcohol and carbon dioxide, producing additional acids and influencing the overall acidity of the wine. Winemakers can adjust acidity levels through various techniques, including blending, acidulation, or acid removal, to achieve the correct balance and flavour profile.

Sugar Content and Fermentation are vital elements to consider. The sugar content of wine, measured in degrees Brix (°Bx), determines the potential alcohol level (ABV) and sweetness of the finished wine. Grape juice contains natural sugars, primarily glucose and fructose, which are converted into alcohol by yeast during fermentation.

Fermentation is the biochemical process by which yeast converts sugars into alcohol and carbon dioxide. This process is initiated by inoculating the grape juice with selected yeast strains, which metabolise sugars into ethanol and other byproducts. The rate and completeness of fermentation depend on factors such as yeast strain, fermentation temperature, nutrient availability, and sugar concentration.

Yeast is a vital component in the winemaking process. Yeast are single-celled microorganisms responsible for fermenting grape sugars into alcohol and carbon dioxide. Saccharomyces cerevisiae is the primary yeast species used in winemaking due to its ability to tolerate high alcohol levels and produce desirable flavours and aromas.

During fermentation, yeast undergoes several metabolic processes, including glycolysis, the Krebs cycle, and alcoholic fermentation, to convert sugars into ethanol and other compounds. Yeast also produces secondary metabolites, such as glycerol, esters, and volatile sulphur compounds, which contribute to the aroma and flavour complexity of wine.

Winemakers need to consider techniques to preserve their wines and keep them in perfect condition during the ageing process. Sulphur dioxide (SO_2) is a naturally occurring compound used in winemaking as a preservative and antioxidant. SO_2 inhibits microbial growth, oxidation, and enzymatic browning, helping to maintain the freshness, colour, and flavour stability of wine.

Winemakers can add SO_2 to grapes, juice, fruits, or wine at various stages of the winemaking process to prevent spoilage and protect against oxidation. However, excessive use of SO_2 can lead to undesirable sensory effects, such as sulphur off-flavours or allergic reactions in sensitive individuals. Therefore, it is important to monitor and manage SO_2 levels carefully to ensure wine quality and safety.

By understanding the basics of wine chemistry, you will gain valuable insights into the factors that influence wine composition, fermentation, and stability. Armed with this knowledge, you'll be better equipped to make informed decisions throughout the winemaking process and create wines that showcase the best of your grapes and your craftsmanship. Specific skills and techniques relating to wine chemistry will be introduced throughout this book.

The Equipment Required to Make Wine:

There are a few essentials that you will need to make wine. The basic equipment will allow you to make both craft (country) wines and wine from kits. As you progress with the hobby and develop your skills, you can add further accessories and build your resource base. This is an exciting part of winemaking and there are new innovations constantly entering the market space. The quality and specification of some equipment matches that available to commercial winemakers. Don't be tempted to rush into buying as much as you can at the start. Gather more advanced items as you gain experience. If possible, visit your local homebrew shop or telephone an online supplier for advice before purchasing equipment. There are a good range of winemaking starter kits available, which include everything you need to get started at a value price. Some of the premium starter kits also include a filter kit and a heat mat, which are useful accessories to ensure perfect results every time.

You will need to decide what quantity of wine you wish to make as this will impact on the size of fermenters required. Generally, home winemakers choose either 5 litres (one gallon) or 22.5 litres (five gallons) batch sizes. The industry is geared to these quantities. In the 1970s and 80s most winemakers made small one-gallon batches and larger five-gallon quantities were less common. However, as the range of wine kits increased, there was a gradual move towards five-gallon sizes as they were more cost effective and produced 33 bottles (rather than 6 bottles for a one-gallon batch). Therefore, this offered a greater opportunity to allow wines to mature better. There was a saying "a 5-gallon batch will produce five times as much wine as a 1-gallon batch and will last twice as long!"

The vast majority of wine kits sold are now 22.5 litres (5 gallons). There are only a comparatively small number of 5 litres (1 gallon) kits available to buy. Smaller sizes are favoured by people who have mobility issues and prefer the lighter more manageable sizes, or those with limited space at home. Some winemakers start with a small 1-gallon batch to try out the hobby and when they realise how good the results are, they usually scale up. If you are planning to make craft wines It is worth considering buying buckets that can accommodate larger quantities as it is possible to start a 1-gallon batch in a 5-gallon bucket, but you cannot work the other way around!

The basic equipment that you will need to make wine is listed below. Most of this equipment should be available as a bundled starter kit:

Fermentation Vessel:

A food-grade plastic bucket is an essential piece of equipment. It will allow you to mix water with other ingredients. A bucket is necessary for primary fermenting fruit pulp if you are making a craft wine. If the bucket is fitted with a rubber grommet and an airlock it can also be used to ferment wine kits. Some wine makers prefer to ferment their wine in a glass or plastic carboy, or a demijohn fitted with a bung and airlock to complete fermentation. The final choice is yours, but it is useful to have a second vessel of the correct volume to strain the must from any fruit, or for transferring wine from the sediment at the end of fermentation. A second vessel will also be necessary for filtering the wine at the end of the process. Make sure to choose a vessel with a capacity that matches your batch size to allow sufficient space for the bubbling fermentation process.

Make sure you choose a bucket with a little extra capacity than the volume of wine you are making. This will allow space for the yeast head which will form during fermentation. In the first few days the head may be quite large but will die down as fermentation progresses. Extra volume in the bucket will prevent the head from spilling over the top of the bucket. Buckets for 22.5 litres (5 gallons) batches normally have a 25 litres capacity. If you are making 5 litres (1 gallon) batches choose a 10-litre bucket.

Demijohn:

A 5 litre (1-gallon) glass or plastic container for fermenting wine. Some winemakers prefer this size to a larger fermenter as it is easier to handle. It is possible to make a 22.5 litre (5-gallon) batch in a bucket and then split it into 5 demijohns for ease of use. Plastic demijohns have a grommet fitted to the cap which takes an airlock. Glass demijohns require a cork or rubber bung to fit an airlock. Some winemakers store wine to age in glass demijohns fitted with a solid bung or safety cork.

Airlock and Bung:

To maintain a controlled anaerobic fermentation environment, invest in an airlock and bung. The airlock allows carbon dioxide to escape while preventing outside air from entering the fermenter. An airlock half-filled with water is essential to prevent contamination and ensure a smooth fermentation process.

Sanitisation Supplies:

Sanitisation is paramount in wine making. Purchase a quality sanitiser to clean all your equipment thoroughly. Suresan and Chemsan are popular choices among homebrewers for routine everyday use and they do a god job. Putting some solution into a spray bottle is useful and makes it easy to sanitise surfaces on the fly. No Rinse sanitisers are effective for regular use, but they need to be made up fresh as their power only lasts around one hour. It is important that any equipment that comes into contact with your wine is sanitised before use. Poor hygiene is the main cause of problems associated with spoiled wine. Even spoons need to be sanitised before use.

It is worth keeping a supply of a more powerful steriliser in stock, such as Steri-Cleen, Deep-Cleen, VWP, or Enzybrew 10. These are useful for the occasional deep clean but be careful as they contain chemicals which can bleach clothes! Caustic Soda is often used for deep cleaning commercial breweries and wineries, but extreme care needs to be taken as it highly irritant and can damage clothes and some materials. It is therefore, not recommended for home winemaking. Milton and Sodium Metabisulphite were used in days gone by as sterilisers, but they are not as effective as contemporary products, so are also not recommended.

Syphoning Equipment:

Transferring your wine from one vessel to another requires a syphon or racking cane. This minimises the risk of oxygen exposure during the transfer, preserving the delicate flavours of your wine. Consider using an auto-syphon for added convenience.

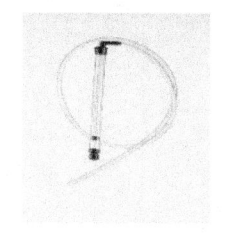

Hydrometer and Test Jar:

Monitoring the progress of fermentation and determining the alcohol content of your wine is made possible with a hydrometer. The test jar allows you to take small samples without exposing the entire batch to unnecessary risks. This tool is indispensable for achieving consistent and predictable results.

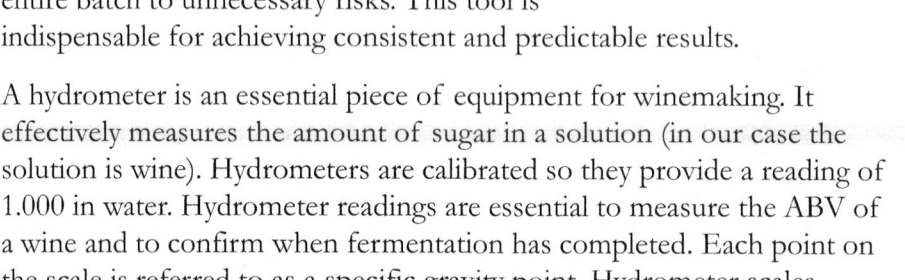

A hydrometer is an essential piece of equipment for winemaking. It effectively measures the amount of sugar in a solution (in our case the solution is wine). Hydrometers are calibrated so they provide a reading of 1.000 in water. Hydrometer readings are essential to measure the ABV of a wine and to confirm when fermentation has completed. Each point on the scale is referred to as a specific gravity point. Hydrometer scales typically range from 0.980 – 1.150. The Specific Gravity of a liquid is that liquid's density compared to water. For example. a liquid with a Specific Gravity of 1.085 is 1.085 times the density of water.

Wine hydrometers are typically calibrated to measure specific gravity and related parameters at a standard temperature of 20 degrees Celsius (68 degrees Fahrenheit). This temperature is considered the reference point for most hydrometer measurements in winemaking and is commonly used in wine laboratories and production facilities.

It should be noted that variations in temperature can affect the accuracy of hydrometer readings. Therefore, if the wine being tested is at a different temperature than the standard calibration temperature of 20°C (68°F), slight adjustments may be necessary to correct for temperature differences. Digital hydrometers often include temperature compensation features to ensure accurate measurements regardless of the sample temperature. The use of digital hydrometers and refractometers is discussed later, in the advanced winemaking techniques/equipment section of this book.

When using a wine hydrometer, follow the manufacturer's instructions regarding calibration, temperature compensation, and sample handling, to obtain accurate and reliable measurements.

Using a Hydrometer:

To take a hydrometer reading, put a sample of the wine into a trial jar and lower the hydrometer into it. Position it vertically and read the level of the wine at eye level. You will note that the liquid seems to curve up a little at the edges where it meets the hydrometer. Try to read at the base line of the liquid (referred to as the meniscus).

Tip: If bubbles collect around the hydrometer, try spinning it between your thumb and forefinger to push the bubbles away.

A hydrometer reading a specific gravity (SG) of 1.000

If you are returning the wine to the batch or are putting the hydrometer directly into the fermenter, make sure the equipment has been pre-sanitised. Try to avoid taking too many hydrometer readings as fermentation progresses, as this increases the opportunity for airborne bacteria to be introduced into the batch.

Take an initial reading at the point when you are about to introduce the yeast into the wine (referred to as must at this stage). Ensure the must is at fermentation temperature. This reading is called the original gravity (OG). Make a note of the reading for later use.

You should take another hydrometer reading when the fermentation process is complete. This is the point where CO2 has stopped bubbling through the airlock (alcohol will have been generated at this point, so the batch is now referred to as wine not must). This reading is called the final gravity (FG) and should be close to 0.996 for s dry wine. Take care when opening the fermenter lid to take readings and undertake the process as quickly as possible to minimise air contact. If a high reading is obtained (above 1.005) then this may indicate that the fermentation has not yet finished, or it has stuck.

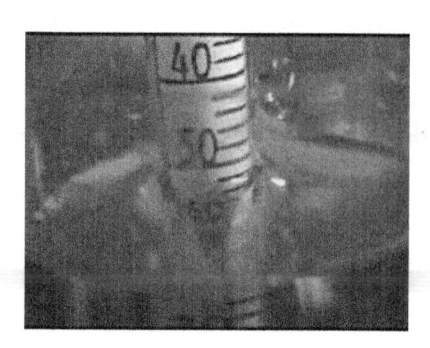

A hydrometer reading an SG of 1.052 in a wine that shows no visible signs of fermentation. This indicates a stuck fermentation.

Thermometer:

Maintaining the right temperature during fermentation is crucial. A stick-on thermometer fitted to your fermentation vessel provides real-time temperature monitoring during fermentation. It is also worth acquiring a glass or digital dip-in thermometer to ensure the correct temperature of the must prior to adding yeast. Yeast is sensitive to temperature fluctuations, and maintaining a consistent range is essential for a successful fermentation.

Measuring Utensils:

Precision is key in wine making. Accurate measurements of water, and other ingredients are vital for achieving the desired flavour profile. Invest in a quality set of measuring spoons, jugs, and a digital scale to ensure your recipes are followed precisely.

Large Spoon or Paddle:

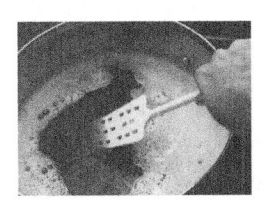

Mixing your ingredients thoroughly is essential to ensure an even distribution of flavours and nutrients. A large spoon or aeration paddle (like a spoon but with slots) made of food-grade material is perfect for stirring your wine must during the initial stages of brewing. A paddle will help to oxygenate the must. This is important to promote a healthy fermentation.

Nylon Straining Bag:

To filter fruit and other particles from your craft wine, use a nylon straining bag or muslin bag during the primary fermentation stage. This helps achieve a clean taste and a polished final product. A straining bag will not be necessary if you are restricting your winemaking to kit wines.

Filter Kit:

Although your wine will partly clear on its own after it is syphoned from the sediment (especially if finings are added), it will not look like a commercial equivalent unless it is filtered. Filtering is the last stage of the winemaking process and removes all suspended particles and dead yeast cells. This will ensure the cleanest taste and a commercial clarity.

For small batches (1-5 gallons) a gravity-based wine filter is the ideal choice, offering excellent results and affording great value. The Harris Vinbrite Filter is the world's best-selling wine filter and is recommended for all wine styles.

Heat Pad:

A heating pad simply plugs into an electric socket and sits under the fermenter. It is efficient to use and raises the temperature of your wine by 8C. It ensures an even temperature for fermentation and allows you to make wine throughout the year. To achieve the best possible taste, it is important to avoid fluctuations and spikes in temperature. This may occur because of domestic heating being switched on during the evening and off during the day. The heat pad avoids these issues and enables a constant temperature to be achieved to promote a healthy fermentation and avoid 'stuck fermentation'. Some premium starter kits will include a heat pad. They can also be purchased with a thermostat to precisely regulate the temperature during fermentation.

Ageing Vessels:

All wines will benefit from ageing, and some craft wines, such as Elderberry may take over a year to reach their best. You can mature wine in bottles fitted with a cork, but you may wish to invest in an oak barrel, or glass/plastic carboys to mature your wine in bulk. These vessels, particularly oak casks, contribute to the development of complex flavours over time. It is important that storage vessels have a secure cap as any air ingress may spoil the wine. Try to fill containers as full as possible then add half a Campden tablet before sealing. Campden tablets release sulphur dioxide which will sit on top of the wine and preserve it. Avoid opening the vessels during maturing as it is important to keep oxygen out. Ageing vessels are not included in starter kits but can be purchased from specialist home brew shops. For short-term ageing and dispensing you may wish to consider a bag in the box style wine dispenser. These are convenient to use and can be cleaned and re-used for later batches.

Wine Press:

Whilst not being an essential item, a wine press will make the process of making craft wines much easier and more efficient. A wine press is an indispensable tool for craft winemakers, providing the means to extract juice from grapes or fruit efficiently and effectively. It is used to extract juice from crushed grapes or other fruits. By pressing the fruit, you can separate the liquid (juice) from the solids (skins, seeds, and pulp), allowing you to ferment the juice into wine. It helps maximise the yield of juice from the fruit, ensuring that you extract as much liquid as possible. This is important for optimising the quantity of wine produced from your grapes or fruit. Pressing also helps control the extraction of tannins from grape skins and seeds. By adjusting the pressure and duration of pressing, you can manage the level of tannins in the juice, which influences the structure and mouthfeel of the finished wine. Pressing also affects the extraction of flavour compounds from the fruit. Gentle pressing techniques can help preserve delicate aromas and flavours, while more aggressive pressing may extract more robust flavours and aromatics. Pressing techniques can, therefore, contribute to the overall quality of the wine. By efficiently extracting juice and controlling extraction parameters, you can produce wines with better balance, clarity, and complexity. Wine presses are available in a range of sizes. 6 litres, 12 litres, and 18 litres are the most common sizes used by home winemakers.

Using a Wine Press:

All fruits ideally need to be prepared for pressing. The skins of grapes will need to be broken and apples must be crushed to give pomace (a grated consistency). Grapes can be crushed by pounding them in a bucket with length of clean timber or, if large quantities are to be pressed a purpose-built grape crusher can be used. Apples can be crushed in the same way although this is a much more vigorous process. Freezing and then thawing the apples before pounding will make the job easier. Crushing is essential because a body of unbroken fruit presents a great resistance to pressure (even hydraulically powered commercial cider presses are fed with finely milled apples). Cutting apples into slices is not sufficient. At the opposite extreme, food processors and liquidisers produce too fine a puree for pressing.

Once crushed, the fruit can be pressed. Fruit is poured into the cage of the press (the barrel-like part) and pressed by a wooden piston. The piston is pushed down, putting pressure on the fruit, forcing juice out through the gaps in the cage staves. The staves are positioned closely to reduce the escape of pomace, pips and skin and a press liner bag can used (not included with a press but can be obtained separately) to further reduce the amount of solids in the juice. The juice flows onto the base plate of the press and out through the lip or drain hole into a jug, bowl, or bucket. Once the pomace has been pressed dry the mechanism is unwound, the cage lifted off the base plate and the cake of dry pomace pushed out. Modern presses require minimal maintenance, A rinse with fresh water and a touch of vegetable oil to the screw thread is all that is required. The pressed pomace can be composted.

With practice you should be able to complete three or more pressings in an hour. Apples will yield up to 50% (or more) juice by weight and grapes considerably more. As a rough guide, 16-20 lbs of apples will yield up to about one gallon of juice.

Equipping yourself with the right tools is a fundamental step towards becoming a proficient wine maker. These essential items will not only make your brewing process more efficient but will also contribute to the overall quality and success of your wines. As you hone your skills and experiment with different recipes, you can buy additional equipment from your specialist home brew shop. You will also need to collect some chemicals and ingredients to support your activities if you are making craft wines. These are consumables which can be added to and re-stocked as you move forward with your hobby.

Your Essential Inventory:

The heart of a fine craft wine lies in your choice of ingredients and some necessary additions. Always choose high-quality fruits, flowers, or vegetables, as they will heavily influence the flavour. Also consider the water you will be using as this makes up the bulk of your wines' volume.

Water should preferably be free from chlorine or chloramine, but water authorities add this as standard to tap water. Fortunately, there is a product called Pure Brew which will eliminate chlorine and chloramine from tap water, avoiding the potential for off-flavours. Pure Brew does not contain sulphites but uses health friendly high-quality nutrients, zinc, and vitamin C to ensure a suitable water composition and support fermentation.
Pure Brew is added at the same time as a suitable yeast strain based on

your desired wine style. Pure Brew can also be added to kit wines to neutralise the effects of chlorine/chloramine and produce a purer final taste.

There are a few items that you should keep in stock, especially if you are intending to make craft wines. These are available from your local home brew shop:

Yeast:

The choice of yeast is an important decision in craft winemaking, as it directly influences the flavour, aroma, and character of the final product. In days gone by wild strains of yeast were used but these were unreliable and produced off-flavours and low alcohol yields. Later, winemakers progressed to using bakers' yeasts and then general-purpose wine yeasts, but these also produced lower ABV's and less clean flavours. Contemporary winemakers are fortunate in that specialist home brew shops carry a variety of technical yeast strains that are suitable for different wine styles. These strains provide better attenuation and healthier fermentations. They effectively contribute to the final quality by adding subtle flavours. You can also buy a general-purpose wine yeast and yeast nutrient mix, which is suitable for a wide range of craft wine recipes. Your specialist home brew shop will provide guidance on the most appropriate yeasts for your wines and help you to understand their unique characteristics. The key suppliers of yeast in USA are Lallemand (Lalvin), Red Star, White Labs, and Wyeast. In the UK the main suppliers are Fermentis, Lallemand (Lalvin), Mangrove Jack, Gervin, and Harris.

Wine yeasts have a relatively long shelf life (typically around 12 months) and are sold in 5g sachets. Sachets are resilient to moisture and humidity but should be stored in a cool dry place prior to use. Each sachet contains a great number of yeast cells, and some sachets include a small amount of nutrient to help the yeast start when rehydrated. Although the number of viable cells decreases the longer sachets are kept over a year, the viability of the yeast can be extended if the packet is stored in the fridge. A useful tip is to use the yeast as soon as possible after purchasing and stockpiling yeasts for over a year should be avoided.

Factors that should be considered when choosing and pitching a yeast are temperature, pitching method, attenuation, and flocculation.

Yeasts will function effectively within specific temperature ranges. These will be indicated on the sachet and will vary according to the strain. You should consider the location where your wine will be fermented. Wherever possible try to maintain a stable temperature as fluctuations can result in subtle flavours being affected. Attempting to use a yeast in conditions outside of the temperature range may result in a stuck fermentation or possibly the production of unwanted compounds that could alter the flavour. In colder months when ambient temperatures are low a heating pad can help to maintain an effective fermentation. Heating pads are inexpensive to operate and are available from good home brew shops.

Yeast pitching is the process of introducing a specific amount of yeast into the must to initiate fermentation. It is also referred to as Inoculation. Yeast plays a pivotal role in converting sugars into alcohol and carbon dioxide, transforming your sweet must into the final wine. Proper yeast pitching ensures a healthy and vigorous fermentation process, contributing to the development of desirable flavours and aromas.

The timing of yeast pitching is important for a successful fermentation. It is important to pitch yeast into must that is at the correct temperature and has been properly prepared. Ideally, pitch your yeast when the must is in the temperature range specified by the yeast manufacturer, typically between 20°C to 24°C (68°F to 75°F). Ensure that the must is free from any preservatives, and if you are making a yeast starter, it is a good practice to use a sanitiser to clean all equipment involved in the process. Pitching yeast too early or too late can impact the fermentation speed and the final flavour profile of your wine.

Yeast experiences a 'lag phase' which means that the visible signs of fermentation will not be seen immediately. When yeast cells are pitched into wine they begin a process of acclimation to the environment. During the lag phase yeast begin to uptake minerals and amino acids from wort. Amino acids are used to build proteins. Yeast growth follows four phases, the lag phase; the growth phase: the fermentation phase; and the sedimentation phase. During the lag phase, the cell count does not change. During the growth phase, cell division occurs and at this point they rapidly reproduce new cells. Therefore, it could be between 8 and 24 hours after pitching the yeast before you see active signs of fermentation.

Dried yeasts can usually be sprinkled from their sachet directly into the must. However, you may wish to make a yeast starter so that your yeast can 'hit the ground running'. To prepare a general yeast starter involves six stages:

1. Rehydrating the Yeast: Before pitching, rehydrate your yeast in a small amount (around 50-75ml) of warm water (about 40°C/105°F) in a clean glass with a teaspoon of sugar and a squeeze of lemon juice. This process helps wake up the yeast cells and prepare them for the fermentation journey. Stir the mix well and loosely cover with a cloth. Leave for approximately 30 minutes in a warm place (around 24C/75F) to activate. You will see a head form when the yeast is activated.

2. Checking Temperature: Ensure that the temperature of your rehydrated yeast is close to the temperature of the must before adding. A drastic temperature difference can shock the yeast cells and affect their performance.

3. Adding Nutrients or Pure Brew: The must needs essential nutrients for yeast health, and to achieve effective performance. If your yeast does not contain a nutrient, you should add a teaspoonful of yeast nutrient or energiser. This is important as some musts may have a low nitrogen content. Ideally add a dose of Pure Brew. This not only contains an effective nutrient, but it also includes zinc and vitamin C to eliminate chlorine and chloramine in the brewing water. These chemicals are added to tap water but can react with yeast to produce chlorophenols, which can adversely affect the final flavour of your wine.

4. Pitching the Yeast: Gently stir the rehydrated yeast in the glass, then evenly pour over the surface of the must. Avoid dumping the yeast directly into the centre of the must, as this can create an uneven distribution.

5. Mixing and Aerating: After pitching, stir the must vigorously for two minutes with a sanitised paddle or spoon to ensure an even distribution of the yeast. This step also introduces oxygen, which is beneficial at the beginning of fermentation. When yeast is pitched it is important to get as much oxygen as possible infused into the must. This will support the fermentation. However, once the airlock is fitted to your fermenter oxygen becomes an enemy and should be kept out as far as possible. Allowing air into the wine towards the end of the process can introduce bacteria or oxidise it (the wine may darken or taste flat).

6. Sealing the Fermentation Vessel (Kit Wines) or Covering the Bucket with a Cloth (Craft Wines): When making wines from kits, Seal the fermentation vessel lid and fit an airlock half-filled with water to allow carbon dioxide to escape while preventing outside air and contaminants from entering. Carbon dioxide is a biproduct of fermentation and must be allowed to escape from the fermenter (indicated by bubbles emerging from the airlock with a plopping sound). At the start of fermentation there will be a lot of activity through the airlock, but this will slow down after a few days. If any yeast emerges through the airlock, simply remove the airlock, clean under a tap and refit. When making craft wines cover the bucket with a cloth or loose lid and allow the primary fermentation to take place.

Attenuation is the degree to which yeast ferments the sugar in the must. A 50% attenuation means that 50% of the sugars have been converted into alcohol and CO2 by yeast. If you have 100% attenuation, all the sugars have been consumed by yeast. A high attenuating yeast indicates that the strain ferments more of the sugars available in a must relative to other yeast strains. This results in a drier finish in the final wine and/or a higher ABV. It is relatively easy to calculate the attenuation of your wine. Using a hydrometer take a specific gravity reading of the must prior to adding the yeast. The value known as the original gravity (OG) indicates the amount of available sugar in the must, which can be converted to alcohol by fermentation. Make a note of this value then take another hydrometer reading at the end of fermentation. This value, known as the final gravity (FG) indicates how much sugar is remaining in the must after fermentation. A calculation can be made to identify the attenuation which is (OG-FG)/OG.

Adding Pure Brew to your wine at the same time as the yeast will maximise the yeasts performance and attenuation as well as eliminating problems associated with chlorine and chloramine in brewing water.

Flocculation is the term used to describe the ability of the yeast to clump together and fall to the bottom of the fermentation vessel as a sediment. This sediment is also known as 'Lees'. The higher the flocculation, the clearer will be the final wine. Adding wine finings at the end of fermentation will make the lees more compact and easier to rack off since the sediment will not be disturbed as easily by the syphon.

To ensure consistent success in your winemaking, always use a reliable yeast strain. Choose a yeast strain that complements the desired wine style. Closely follow the manufacturers guidelines regarding rehydration, pitching rates, and fermentation temperatures. Finally, monitor fermentation closely. Keep a close eye on the fermentation process by checking airlock activity and using a hydrometer to measure sugar levels. This will help you to ascertain when fermentation has completed and will also allow you to intervene if any issues arise. Finally, patience is key. Allow the yeast sufficient time to complete its fermentation. Rushing the process can result in off-flavours and an incomplete fermentation.

If you are making craft wines, take time to choose an appropriate yeast for the selected recipe. Effective yeast strains to consider include:

Harris Premium Wine Yeast: A premium all-purpose wine yeast that is effective for any type of craft wine. Low foaming robust yeast.

Profile: Neutral aroma, ABV tolerance up to 18%, fermentation range 10-30C (50-86F), vigorous fermentation, fast starting and strong attenuation. This is the ideal general purpose wine yeast which is renowned for its robust and reliable fermentation kinetics. Suitable for most styles of wine. Harris Wine Yeast is widely available and receives excellent feedback from winemakers.

Ideal for: General winemaking,

Harris Vinkwik Restart Yeast: Saccharomyces Cerevisiae Var Cerevisiae (Ex Bayanus). This is the yeast to use when fermentation reliability is a key factor.

Profile: High tolerance to ethanol, making it the perfect choice when trying to re-start a stuck fermentation. ABV tolerance is up to 18%, and the fermentation range is 10-35C (50-95F).

Ideal for: re-starting stuck fermentations, Higher ABV red and white wines.

Harris Mead Yeast: A high ester-producing strain providing fresh, floral notes. For best results, ferment at 10-25C (50-77F). Alcohol Tolerance is 18% ABV.

Profile: High alcohol tolerance, and light floral esters makes this yeast the perfect choice for a wide range of mead styles.

Ideal for: Traditional Meads, Sack Meads, Melomels, and Sparkling Mead.

Gervin GV1 General Purpose Wine Yeast: Ferments up to 18% ABV. Temperature range 15-25C (59-77F)

Profile: Quick starting, settles well, produces a clean bouquet.

Ideal for: General winemaking, fruit wines, vegetable wines

Gervin GV2 Robust Wine Yeast: Ferments up to 15% ABV. Temperature range 15-25C (59-77F). Saccharomyces Cerevisiae (French Strain)

Profile: Quick starting, rapidly ferments, produces low foam

Ideal for: Full bodied red and white wines

Gervin GV3 Sparkling Wine Yeast: Ferments up to 18% ABV. Temperature range 15-25C (59-77F)

Profile: Quick starting, settles well, produces a clean bouquet.

Ideal for: Sparkling wines, higher ABV wines.

Lalvin EC-1118 Yeast: Saccharomyces Bayanus strain. Has a high alcohol tolerance, resulting in a dry and crisp finish. Lalvin EC-1118 has a voracious capability for eating sugar and producing up to 18% ABV. It can destroy finer, subtle flavours however, so is sometimes introduced later into the fermentation. It is an excellent yeast for sparkling wines. Temperature range is 10-30C (50-86F)

Profile: Known for its robust and reliable fermentation kinetics.

Ideal for: Sparkling wines, full bodied white and red wines, fruit ciders

Lalvin K1V-1116 (Montpellier Wine Yeast):

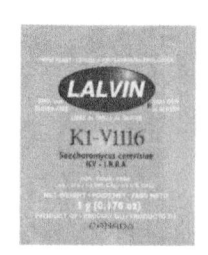

Profile: All-purpose wine yeast known for its ability to ferment in a broad temperature range from 10-35C(50-95F). K1V-1116 produces wines with a clean profile and enhances fruity and floral

notes. It is a reliable choice for various wine styles.

Ideal For: Ice wines, flower-based wines, aromatic white wines, rose wines, lighter red wines, late harvest wines.

Lalvin D-47 White Wine Yeast: Ferments from 15-30C (59-86F). Alcohol tolerance is 15%ABV.

Profile: Renowned for producing excellent white wines. It enhances honey aromas in mead and contributes to a well-rounded flavour profile. Some winemakers report D-47 having a temperamental temperature range.

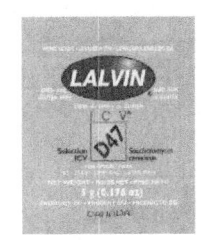

Ideal For: Complex white and Rose wines with citrus and floral notes.

Lalvin 71B-1122 (Narbonne Wine Yeast): The perfect choice to create young, fresh, and fruity red, rose and white wines that are easy to drink. Ferments from 15-30C (59-86F). Alcohol tolerance is 14% ABV.

Profile: Renowned for its ability to produce wines with enhanced fruity and estery notes, 71B-1122 is an excellent choice for fruit wines as it has a smooth tannin structure.

Ideal For: Young wines

Mangrove Jack's R56 Wine Yeast: A strain suitable for red wines which enhances body and mouthfeel, develops complex fruit flavours/aromas, and promotes structure and longevity. For best results, ferment at 18 - 28°C (64 - 82°F). Alcohol Tolerance is 15% ABV.

Profile: This moderate fermenting yeast is ideal for both new and old-world styles, producing complex and interesting fruit-driven red wines.

Ideal For: Merlot, Malbec, Nebbiolo, and Red Fruit wines.

Mangrove Jack's CR51 Wine Yeast: A strain suitable for red wines, especially those intended to be light, fresh and fruity. No rehydration required, add direct to grape must and stir well. For best results, ferment at 16 - 24°C (61 - 75°F). Alcohol Tolerance is 14% ABV.

Profile: This moderate fermenting strain produces soft, velvety-smooth wines, with aromatic enhancement of red berry fruits notes.

Ideal For: Pinot Noir, Gamay and craft wines from berries.

Mangrove Jack's MA33 Wine Yeast: This strain has the ability to reduce malic acid by up to 30-35%, and reduce total titratable acidity, making it perfect for young wines intended for early consumption, and for use with fruits high in acid. For best results, ferment at 18 - 28°C (64 - 82°F). Alcohol Tolerance is 14% ABV.

Profile: This moderate fermenting yeast will soften the palate but also contribute significant esters, conferring a fresh and fruity character to the wine.

Ideal For: Zinfandel, Fruit wines and more.

Mangrove Jack's CL23 Wine Yeast: A multi-purpose strain with a very neutral sensory impact, this fast-fermenting yeast is highly robust, tolerating difficult fermentation conditions and alcohol levels up to 18% ABV. Ferments at 14 - 32°C (57 - 90°F).

Profile: Suitable for most wine style but especially white, blush and sparkling wines.

Ideal For: Cabernet Sauvignon, Chardonnay, Vegetable wines

Wild Yeast Strains:

Profile: For those seeking a truly unique and artisanal approach, wild yeast strains can be used. This may include capturing wild yeast from the environment or using specific strains like Wyeast 3763 Roeselare Ale Blend. Be careful, however, as wild yeast strains may be less reliable and final ABV's may vary considerably.

Ideal For: Experimental wines, barrel-aged wines, and complex blends.

The dedicated wine yeasts listed above are available from specialist home brew shops and will ensure a healthy and progressive fermentation in your craft wines. You can experiment with high alcohol yeasts and specialist yeasts, to adjust the final flavour and strength of your wine.

Wine Kits are provided with a dedicated wine yeast which is matched to the kit to provide optimum performance. If the yeast in a wine kit fails to start, then you should introduce a restart yeast to get the fermentation going. This will not be necessary in the vast majority of cases as the yeast provided should get the job done.

Some of the yeasts listed may have limited availability but there should be sufficient choice for you to experiment with yeast strains. Remember that the yeast you choose is a key player in the final flavour of your wine and each yeast strain brings its own nuances. Your selection should align with the desired taste, sweetness level, and the overall style of your wine. Experimenting with different yeast strains allows you to discover the endless possibilities of winemaking, unlocking a world of flavours that reflects your creativity and craftsmanship.

Feeding the Yeast:

Yeast cells need oxygen and nitrogen to enable them to grow and thrive. Nitrogen is an essential nutrient for yeast metabolism, playing a crucial role in protein synthesis and cellular growth. Some nitrogen is contained in fresh fruits, but this is diluted when water is added to the must. Grape concentrate also contains some nitrogen, which can contribute to yeast growth during fermentation. However, the exact concentration of nitrogen in grape concentrate can vary depending on factors such as grape variety, processing methods, and storage conditions.

During the winemaking process, yeast requires nitrogen for optimal fermentation performance, particularly during the early stages of fermentation when yeast cells are actively multiplying. Nitrogen deficiency can lead to sluggish or stuck fermentations, resulting in incomplete fermentation, off-flavours, and other undesirable outcomes.

Winemakers usually add commercial yeast nutrients or yeast energisers, which typically contain nitrogen compounds such as diammonium phosphate (DAP) or yeast extract. These additives provide a readily available source of nitrogen to support yeast growth and fermentation. Wine kits will always include yeast nutrients, but craft winemakers must ensure they are included in recipes.

Yeast Nutrients, such as Diammonium Phosphate (DAP) and Ammonium Sulphate are commonly used to feed the yeast, and these should be considered on your inventory list:

Diammonium Phosphate (DAP):

Diammonium phosphate (DAP) is a commonly used yeast nutrient in winemaking, brewing, and other fermentation processes. It is a water-soluble salt that consists of ammonium ions (NH_4^+) and phosphate ions (PO_4^{3-}). DAP serves as a source of nitrogen and phosphorus, both of which are essential nutrients for yeast metabolism during fermentation.

DAP provides yeast with a readily available source of nitrogen, which is essential for protein synthesis, cell growth, and fermentation activity. Nitrogen is a crucial nutrient for yeast metabolism, and its availability can impact on fermentation, yeast viability, and the production of desirable fermentation by-products such as aroma compounds and glycerol.

In addition to nitrogen, DAP also supplies phosphorus, which plays a role in cellular energy metabolism, membrane integrity, and the synthesis of nucleic acids and ATP (adenosine triphosphate). Phosphorus is another essential nutrient for yeast growth and fermentation performance, and its availability can influence yeast viability and fermentation kinetics.

DAP can also contribute to the adjustment of pH levels during fermentation. When added to the must, DAP reacts with acids present in the solution, releasing ammonium ions and phosphate ions. The release of ammonium ions can increase the pH of the solution, thereby reducing acidity and buffering pH fluctuations during fermentation.

By providing essential nutrients such as nitrogen and phosphorus, DAP promotes yeast health and enhances fermentation performance. Adequate nitrogen levels can help prevent nutrient deficiencies and promote robust yeast growth, reducing the risk of stuck or sluggish fermentations and off-flavour production. Phosphorus also contributes to yeast vitality and metabolic activity, further supporting fermentation kinetics and wine quality.

In winemaking, DAP is typically added to the must at the beginning of fermentation or during yeast rehydration to provide yeast with essential nutrients for optimal fermentation performance. However, it is important to use DAP judiciously and in accordance with recommended dosage rates, as excessive nitrogen supplementation can lead to negative impacts such as increased volatile acidity, reduced aroma complexity, and potential fermentation problems. Winemakers should carefully consider factors such as grape composition, yeast strain, fermentation conditions, and nutrient requirements when using DAP in winemaking. On its own Diammonium Phosphate (DAP) is ineffective beyond 9% ABV levels so it is often used in a mix with other nutrient salts.

Ammonium Sulphate:

Ammonium sulphate is a salt compound commonly used in winemaking. It consists of ammonium ions (NH_4^+) and sulphate ions (SO_4^{2-}), and it is highly soluble in water. Ammonium sulphate serves primarily as a nitrogen source for yeast metabolism during fermentation. It supports cell growth, protein synthesis, and fermentation activity. Adequate nitrogen levels are crucial for ensuring healthy yeast populations and optimal fermentation performance.

Ammonium sulphate is often combined with DAP to provide yeast with a readily available source of nitrogen, which is essential for cell growth and fermentation activity. It can prevent sluggish or stuck fermentations, off-flavour production, and other fermentation problems. By supplementing the must with ammonium sulphate, winemakers can ensure that yeast has access to sufficient nitrogen to support a robust fermentation and ensure a good wine quality.

Ammonium sulphate can also contribute to pH adjustment during winemaking. When added to the must, it dissociates into ammonium ions (NH_4^+) and sulphate ions (SO_4^{2-}). The release of ammonium ions can increase the pH of the solution, thereby reducing acidity and buffering pH fluctuations during fermentation. This can be particularly useful in acidic grape musts or wines where pH adjustment is needed to achieve optimal fermentation conditions.

In addition to providing nitrogen, ammonium sulphate also serves as a source of sulphur, which is important for yeast metabolism and the production of sulphur-containing compounds during fermentation. Sulphur compounds contribute to the aroma and flavour profile of wine, and adequate sulphur levels can help enhance wine complexity and character.

It is important to use ammonium sulphate in accordance with recommended dosage rates, as excessive nitrogen supplementation can lead to negative impacts such as increased volatile acidity, reduced aroma complexity, and potential fermentation problems. Overall, ammonium sulphate plays a valuable role in supporting yeast health and fermentation performance in winemaking, helping to ensure successful fermentations and the production of high-quality wines.

Yeast Nutrient Mix:

Yeast nutrient mixes are formulations designed to provide essential nutrients to yeast during the fermentation process in winemaking. These nutrients are crucial for yeast metabolism, growth, and fermentation performance. While the specific composition of yeast nutrient mixes may vary depending on the manufacturer and intended application, they typically contain a combination of nitrogen sources, vitamins, minerals, and other additives that support yeast health and fermentation.

Yeast requires nitrogen for protein synthesis and cell growth during fermentation. Inorganic nitrogen sources such as diammonium phosphate

(DAP) and ammonium sulphate are the common basis in yeast nutrient mixes to provide readily available nitrogen to yeast cells.

Organic nitrogen compounds such as yeast hulls, autolysate, or amino acids may also be included in yeast nutrient mixes to supplement inorganic nitrogen sources and provide additional nutrients to yeast. These organic compounds can enhance yeast vitality, fermentation, and the production of desirable fermentation by-products.

Nutrient mixes often contain vitamins and minerals that are essential for yeast metabolism and enzyme activity. These may include vitamins such as thiamine (vitamin B1), riboflavin (vitamin B2), and pantothenic acid (vitamin B5), as well as minerals such as magnesium, zinc, and potassium. These micronutrients play important roles in energy metabolism, enzyme cofactors, and cell membrane function.

Some yeast nutrient mixes may contain other trace elements such as copper, manganese, or iron, which are required in small amounts for various enzymatic reactions and cellular processes in yeast. These trace elements can help optimise fermentation conditions and support yeast health and viability.

Antioxidants such as ascorbic acid (vitamin C) may be included in yeast nutrient mixes to protect yeast cells from oxidative stress and reduce the risk of oxidation during fermentation. This can help preserve wine freshness, aroma, and colour, particularly in challenging fermentation conditions.

Buffering agents such as potassium bicarbonate or calcium carbonate may also be included to help maintain optimal pH levels during fermentation. Buffering agents can prevent excessive pH fluctuations, which can inhibit yeast growth and fermentation activity.

Yeast nutrient mixes are typically added to the must at the beginning of fermentation or during yeast rehydration to provide yeast with essential nutrients for optimal fermentation performance. An additional dose may be added later in the fermentation, particular for higher ABV wines, in order to maintain yeast performance.

Pure Brew:

Harris Pure Brew® works to eliminate Chloramine and Chlorine from your brewing water, which could otherwise react with the yeast during fermentation to produce unwanted phenol flavours, also known as the "homebrew" taste.

This product also feeds the yeast to support a healthy, strong fermentation under restricted oxygen conditions, and promotes a clean pure final taste. This product removes the homebrew taste in Beer, Wine, and Cider, whilst at the same time providing an effective blend of nutrients to support yeast growth and a healthy fermentation. Pure Brew contains Yeast Hulls, Zinc. Magnesium Sulphate, Diammonium Phosphate, Vitamin C, Vitamin B1, Calcium Pantothenate, Folic Acid, and Niacin. It is available as a single dose sachet or a 5-dose pot.

Wine Tannin:

Wine tannin is a natural compound found in fruit and grapes, particularly in the skins, seeds, and stems. It is also found to a lesser extent in vegetables and flowers as well as in oak barrels used for maturing wine. Tannins are polyphenolic compounds that contribute to the taste, structure, and ageing potential of wine. They are responsible for the sensation of astringency and bitterness often associated with red wines, although they can also be found in white wines to a lesser extent.

Tannins bind to proteins in saliva, causing a dry, puckering sensation in the mouth known as astringency. This tactile sensation is often described as a feeling of "dryness" or "roughness" on the palate. A moderate level of tannins can contribute to the complexity and balance of wine, while excessive tannins can lead to an overly astringent or harsh mouthfeel.

Tannins play a crucial role in providing structure and backbone to wine. They interact with other components such as acids, sugars, and phenolic compounds to create a well-balanced and harmonious wine. Tannins contribute to the wine's body, mouthfeel, and texture, giving it depth and complexity.

They also contribute to the flavour profile of wine, adding notes of bitterness, astringency, and complexity. In red wines, tannins are often associated with flavours of black tea, leather, tobacco, and dark chocolate. In white wines, tannins are typically less pronounced but can still contribute to the wine's overall flavour and structure.

Tannins are important for the ageing potential of wine, particularly in red wines. Over time, tannins undergo polymerisation and oxidation reactions, softening and integrating into the wine. This process can lead to a smoother, more rounded wine with enhanced complexity and aromatic development. Wines with high levels of tannins, such as Cabernet Sauvignon and Nebbiolo, often benefit from extended ageing to allow the tannins to mellow and become more integrated.

Winemakers can add tannin powder (extracts derived from grape seeds or oak) to adjust the tannin levels in wine, particularly when the ingredients used are low in natural tannin. Some fruits, such as Elderberries, have a notoriously high tannin content and require a long maturation process to soften them.

Wine tannin is, therefore, a critical component that contributes to the taste, structure, and ageing potential of wine. While tannins are most commonly associated with red wines, they play a role in shaping the character and quality of both red and white wines, adding complexity, texture, and maturation to the finished product.

Citric Acid:

Citric acid is a naturally occurring organic acid found in citrus fruits such as lemons, limes, oranges, and grapefruits. It is used as an additive to adjust the acidity of a must, enhance flavour, and inhibit microbial growth.

Citric acid is most commonly used in winemaking to increase the acidity of grape must or wine, particularly where grapes have low natural acidity. Adding citric acid can help balance the acidity levels, improve flavour balance, and achieve the desired pH for fermentation. It can be particularly useful in white wines, where acidity is important for freshness and balance. Citric acid is also used for the same purpose in fruit, vegetable, and flower-based wines, where natural acidity of the ingredients is low. In days gone by winemakers used to add the juice of lemons instead of citric acid, but it is more difficult to achieve accurate acidity levels using that approach.

Citric acid can contribute to the flavour profile of wine, adding bright, citrusy notes and enhancing fruitiness. It can help accentuate the natural flavours of grapes and create a more vibrant and complex wine. However, excessive use of citric acid can lead to a pronounced citrus flavour that may overpower other characteristics of the wine. It should, therefore, be used in accordance with the recipe being followed.

Citric acid also has antioxidant properties that can help protect wine from oxidation and spoilage. It acts as a chelating agent, binding to metal ions that can promote oxidation and inhibit the growth of spoilage microorganisms such as bacteria and mould. Adding citric acid to wine can help preserve freshness, colour, and aroma, particularly in wines that are susceptible to oxidation.

It can also be used as a microbial stabiliser in winemaking to inhibit the growth of unwanted microorganisms such as bacteria and yeast. By lowering the pH of the wine and creating an acidic environment, citric acid can help prevent microbial spoilage and ensure the microbiological stability of the wine during storage and ageing.

When using citric acid in winemaking, it is important to carefully measure and adjust the acidity levels based on the specific characteristics of the grapes, fruits, vegetables, or flowers. Winemakers typically add citric acid in small increments, tasting and testing the acidity levels regularly to achieve the desired balance and flavour profile.

Tartaric Acid:

Tartaric acid and citric acid are both common acids used in winemaking, and each has its own distinct characteristics and applications. While both acids can be used to adjust acidity in wine, there are several reasons why winemakers might choose tartaric acid over citric acid.

Tartaric acid is a natural component of grapes and is the primary acid found in wine grapes. Its presence in grapes makes it a logical choice for acid adjustment in grape winemaking, as it maintains the natural acidity and flavour profile of the grapes.

Citric acid, on the other hand, is not typically found in grapes at significant levels. While it is naturally occurring in citrus fruits, it is not as closely associated with wine grapes as tartaric acid. Some winemakers, therefore, prefer to use tartaric acid for acid adjustment to maintain the authentic character of the wine.

Tartaric acid contributes to the flavour profile of wine, adding crispness, brightness, and acidity to the palate. It is often associated with flavours of citrus fruits, green apples, and stone fruits.

Tartaric acid plays a role in stabilising wine by preventing the formation of tartrate crystals, also known as wine diamonds. These crystals can precipitate out of wine during storage or chilling, causing aesthetic concerns for consumers. Tartaric acid helps keep these crystals in solution, improving the visual clarity of the wine.

Citric acid does not provide the same level of stability as tartaric acid and may not be as effective in preventing tartrate precipitation. Winemakers may prefer to use tartaric acid for this reason, particularly in wines that are intended for ageing or long-term storage.

Lactic Acid:

Lactic acid contributes to the overall acidity of wine. While it is typically less acidic than tartaric or malic acid, its presence influences the wine's pH and acidity balance. In wines that undergo MLF, the conversion of malic acid to lactic acid leads to a reduction in overall acidity. This can be beneficial for wines with high levels of malic acid, helping to achieve a smoother, more rounded flavour profile. It is naturally generated during malolactic fermentation and is sometimes used at the end of the winemaking process to adjust a wine's final acidity.

Malic Acid:

Malic acid is another naturally occurring organic acid found in grapes and many other fruits. In winemaking, it is one of the primary acids used in winemaking and contributes to the overall acidity of wine. It provides a tart, sour taste and helps balance sweetness, enhancing the overall flavour profile and freshness of the wine. Malic acid levels vary depending on grape variety, ripeness, and growing conditions.

Malic acid is abundant in many fruits, including apples, cherries, and grapes. It is particularly prevalent in unripe or under-ripe grapes and decreases as grapes ripen. It is typically found in higher concentrations in grape juice and young wines.

Malic acid affects the pH of wine, although its impact is less significant compared to tartaric acid. It contributes to the overall acidity of wine, helping to create a pH level that is conducive to fermentation, stability, and microbial control.

It influences the flavour profile of wine by adding crispness and tartness to the palate. Wines with higher levels of malic acid may exhibit flavours of green apple, tart citrus, or sour cherry. Some winemakers prefer to retain some malic acid in wine to enhance its freshness and fruitiness.

Malic acid is often converted into lactic acid through malolactic fermentation, a secondary fermentation process that occurs in many wines after primary alcoholic fermentation. During malolactic fermentation, lactic acid bacteria metabolise malic acid, producing lactic acid and carbon dioxide. This process can help reduce acidity, soften harsh flavours, and impart a smoother mouthfeel to the wine.

Malic acid is primarily added to wines for acid adjustment: Levels may be adjusted to achieve the desired acidity and balance in the wines and cider. Winemakers may choose to either supplement malic acid or encourage malolactic fermentation to reduce malic acid levels, depending on the style of wine they wish to produce.

Acid Blend:

Acid blend refers to a mixture of different acids used to adjust the acidity levels of wine. Acid blends typically combine tartaric acid, malic acid, and citric acid in calculated ratios. A blend of these acids mixed in the correct proportions will increase the quality of a finished wine and will be better than just using one type of acid.

It is possible to swap a recommended dose of any of the single acids with the same quantity of acid blend, to achieve a more rounded effect. In the USA, acid blend is preferred to single source acids. Modern recipes in the UK are increasingly recommending acid blend to achieve a more rounded flavour profile. Acidity is a critical component in winemaking, as it contributes to the wine's freshness, structure, and stability. Acid blends allow winemakers to fine-tune the acidity levels to match the style of wine they wish to produce.

Succinic Acid:

During alcoholic fermentation, yeast converts sugars present in grape juice into alcohol and carbon dioxide. As a byproduct of this process, yeast also produces organic acids, including succinic acid, through metabolic pathways. Succinic acid contributes to the overall acidity of the wine. Succinic used to be sold for winemaking but required longer maturation times. It is not often used in modern home winemaking.

Acid Reducer:

An acid reducer is a substance used to decrease the acidity levels of grape must or wine. Calcium Carbonate (Precipitated Chalk) is a natural mineral that is commonly used to reduce acidity in wine. When added to wine, calcium carbonate reacts with tartaric acid to form calcium tartrate crystals, which precipitate out of the wine. This process, known as cold stabilisation, reduces the acidity of the wine while also improving its clarity and stability.

Calcium carbonate is usually added at a rate of 7g per gallon, which will reduce the acidity by approximately 1.5ppt (parts per thousand). When added, it will release carbon dioxide as it neutralises the acid and it may also foam up. Therefore, ensure there is sufficient head space in your container before application. Sometimes the process can also produce sediment as the acid is neutralised, so if added to a finished wine or cider, leave it in a cold place for a week to allow any acid crystals to fall out as a sediment.

Pectolytic Enzyme:

Pectolytic enzymes, also known as pectinases or pectic enzymes, are a group of enzymes that play a crucial role in winemaking and fruit processing. These enzymes help with the breakdown of pectin, a complex polysaccharide found in the cell walls of plants, particularly in fruits.

Pectolytic enzymes are used primarily to extract juice from fruit and to facilitate the clarification and filtration of wine. They used to break down the pectin in fruit cell walls, helping to release juice from the fruit during the crushing and maceration process. By breaking down the pectin matrix, these enzymes increase the yield of juice extraction and improve the efficiency of juice pressing.

Their principal purpose is to clarify wine by breaking down pectin and other colloidal particles that can cause haze or cloudiness. During fermentation, pectolytic enzymes help to break down the pectin present in grape skins, seeds, and fruit pulp, releasing trapped solids and facilitating their settlement or filtration. They aid in the filtration of wine by promoting the sedimentation of suspended solids and facilitating the formation of compact lees (sediment). This helps to improve the clarity and stability of the wine, improving the effectiveness of filtration and fining agents.

In red winemaking, pectolytic enzymes can also contribute to the extraction of colour and phenolic compounds from grape skins. By breaking down the pectin matrix in the grape skins, these enzymes help to release pigments and tannins into the wine, enhancing its colour, flavour, and mouthfeel.

Pectolytic enzymes (such as Pectinaze), are typically added to the must at a rate of 10 drops per gallon, at the beginning of fermentation or during maceration. The dosage and application of pectolytic enzymes depend on factors such as grape/fruit variety and ripeness. Some fruits, such as damsons, and plums, are notoriously high in pectin. It is not possible to overdose with Pectinaze so you should consider increasing the dose rate when using high pectin content fruits. Pectin related issues are not such an issue in flower and vegetable wines. Root vegetables such as carrots, beets, and potatoes do contain some pectin, particularly in their skins and outer layers. However, the levels are lower than in many fruits.

Amylaze (Starch Reducing Enzyme):

Amylase is an enzyme used in winemaking to facilitate the breakdown of starches into simpler sugars, thereby aiding in the fermentation process. Typically derived from various natural sources such as malted barley or fungal cultures, amylase plays a crucial role in converting complex carbohydrates present in grains, vegetables, and fruit, into fermentable sugars such as glucose and maltose. The presence of Amylase ensures a more efficient fermentation process, leading to higher alcohol content in the resulting wine. Additionally, it can contribute to the development of desirable flavours and aromas, as well as improving the clarity and stability of the final product.

Some craft winemaking ingredients contain high levels of starch, which could contribute to a starch haze in the final wine if not treated. Starch is a type of carbohydrate. Its molecules are made up of large numbers of carbon, hydrogen, and oxygen atoms. Starch is a white solid at room temperature and does not dissolve in cold water. Most plants, including rice, potatoes, and wheat, store their energy as starch. This explains why these foods – and anything made from wheat flour – are high in starch. The starch in the ingredients used will make your wine cloudy. Finings work by attaching to haze particles, making them heavier and therefore fall down quicker. If the finings cannot attach to the particles, they will not work. By adding Amylase, excess starch will be destroyed so the wine will be able to clear.

The dose rate Is 10 drops per 5 litres (1 gallon). It does not matter If you add too much, you cannot overdose on this enzyme, in fact, the more you use the faster it works.

Campden Tablets:

Campden tablets are a commonly used additive in winemaking and brewing. They contain potassium metabisulphite, a compound that releases sulphur dioxide (SO2) when dissolved in water or wine. Sodium metabisulphite is a powder version of Campden tablets. They share similarities in their chemical composition and functions. They are routinely used to kill off the yeast at the end of fermentation. While Campden tablets will control yeast populations in wine, they may not entirely eliminate all yeast cells. Residual yeast may remain in the wine, especially if the Campden treatment is insufficient or if yeast strains are particularly resilient. Therefore, Campden tablets are typically used in conjunction with potassium sorbate, to ensure successful stability in wine production. Most wine kits will include a sachet of wine stabiliser containing a mix of potassium metabisulphite and potassium sorbate.

Campden tablets can also be used to preserve wine by inhibiting the growth of spoilage microorganisms, such as bacteria and wild yeast. Adding Campden tablets to wine before bottling or barrel ageing helps to create an environment that is hostile to microbial growth, extending the shelf life and stability of the wine. The usual dose rate is ½ a crushed tablet per gallon.

They are also used to treat craft wine musts before fermentation. Adding a crushed tablet to must helps to sterilise it, eliminating wild yeast and bacteria that may be present on the fruit or other ingredients. This allows winemakers to control fermentation with selected yeast strains and minimise the risk of spoilage.

Campden tablets and sodium metabisulphite powder used to be a common choice for sanitising equipment. However, commercial sanitisers available today are much more effective and have replaced them as the first choice for most winemakers.

Potassium Sorbate:

Potassium sorbate is commonly used as a stabiliser to inhibit the re-fermentation of residual sugars and to prevent refermentation in wines.

After fermentation is complete, residual sugars may remain in the wine. If potassium sorbate is not added, there is a risk that any remaining yeast in the wine could ferment these sugars, resulting in unwanted carbonation or even bursting bottles. Potassium sorbate helps prevent this refermentation by inhibiting the yeast's ability to multiply and ferment sugars.

Potassium sorbate is added after fermentation is complete and in conjunction with sulphites (Campden tablets or potassium metabisulphite). It is essential to add potassium sorbate only after fermentation has stopped. If you add it early by mistake, then it cannot be extracted and will prevent the yeast from working. The usual dose rate is ½ a level teaspoon per gallon of wine.

Potassium sorbate should be dissolved in a small amount of wine before being added to the entire batch. This ensures even distribution throughout the wine and maximises its effectiveness.

While potassium sorbate is effective at preventing refermentation, it is not a substitute for proper sulphite use. Sulphites are still necessary for stabilising wine and inhibiting microbial growth. Potassium sorbate should be used in conjunction with sulphites for comprehensive wine stabilisation.

When used correctly and at appropriate dosages, potassium sorbate should not significantly impact the flavour or aroma of the wine. However, excessive use or improper mixing may lead to off-flavours or aromas, so it is important to avoid overdosing.

Sugar:

Most craft wines and basic wine kits will require the addition of sugar to achieve the correct alcohol content (ABV). Various types of sugar are available, and your final choice will depend on various factors, including the type of wine being made, desired sweetness level, cost, and personal preference. Some common types of sugars used in home winemaking include:

Granulated Sugar (Sucrose): Granulated sugar, also known as household, or table sugar, is a readily available and inexpensive option for home winemaking. It is derived from sugar cane or sugar beets and is commonly used to increase the fermentable sugar content of the must and achieve higher alcohol levels in the finished wine. It is suitable for most types of wine, including dry, semi-sweet, and sweet wines.

Granulated sugar primarily consists of sucrose, a disaccharide composed of two monosaccharides. Sucrose (a crystalline substance) is the primary component of ordinary sugar, constituting nearly 100% of its composition. It is a disaccharide molecule composed of one molecule of glucose and one molecule of fructose bonded together.

Glucose is a monosaccharide, also known as dextrose or blood sugar. It is a simple sugar that serves as a primary source of energy for the body's cells and is essential for various metabolic processes. Glucose contributes to the sweet taste of sugar and is readily metabolised by the body.

Fructose is another monosaccharide, often referred to as fruit sugar. It is naturally found in fruits, honey, and some vegetables. Fructose is sweeter than glucose and contributes to the overall sweetness of sugar. Like glucose, fructose is easily metabolised by the body and provides energy.

Before fermentation starts the combination has to be split into these two component parts. The yeast excretes an enzyme called invertase, which inverts the sugar. This creates a delay in the fermentation process and is one reason many winemakers prefer to use brewing sugar or invert sugar.

Brewing Sugar (Dextrose Monohydrate): Also known as corn sugar or glucose, dextrose monohydrate is a simple sugar that is completely fermentable by yeast. Unlike some other sugars, such as sucrose (table sugar), which consists of glucose and fructose molecules bonded together, dextrose is already in its simplest form and can be readily metabolised by yeast during fermentation. This means that dextrose will ferment out completely, leaving minimal residual sweetness in the finished wine if fermented to dryness.

It Is a highly consistent sugar source, with known fermentability rates and predictable outcomes. This consistency allows winemakers to accurately calculate and control the sugar content of their musts, enabling them to achieve the desired alcohol levels and sweetness profiles in their wines.

Dextrose monohydrate has a neutral flavour profile, which means it won't significantly impact the taste or aroma of the finished wine. This neutrality makes it a versatile sugar source that can be used in a wide range of wine styles without affecting the wine's character or balance.

It is easily metabolised by yeast, leading to rapid and efficient fermentation. This can be particularly advantageous in winemaking scenarios where a quick fermentation is desired, such as when making white wines or fruit wines that are intended to be consumed young.

In addition to its use as a fermentable sugar, dextrose monohydrate is often used in winemaking to carbonate sparkling wines. When added to wine just prior to bottling, dextrose provides fermentable sugars for refermentation in the bottle, resulting in natural carbonation and the formation of bubbles.

Overall, dextrose monohydrate is the most popular choice for winemakers looking for a reliable, fermentable sugar source that can be used to achieve specific alcohol levels and sweetness profiles in their wines. Its consistency, fermentability, neutral flavour, and versatility make it a valuable tool in the winemaker's arsenal.

Honey: Honey is a natural form of sugar, produced by bees from the nectar of flowers. It consists primarily of glucose and fructose, with small amounts of other sugars and organic compounds. Honey adds a distinct flavour and aroma to wine, making it an excellent choice for Mead or Melomel (fruit mead) production. The floral characteristics of honey can complement certain wine styles, but it may overpower delicate flavours in other wines.

Fruit Juices: Fruit juices, such as grape juice, apple juice, or berry juice, can be used as sources of fermentable sugars in winemaking. They provide additional flavour complexity and can contribute to the overall character of the wine. Fruit juices should be free from preservatives and additives to ensure successful fermentation. Grape concentrate is often added to craft wine recipes to add extra sugar, whilst at the same time providing more body to the wine.

Invert Sugar: Invert sugar is a mixture of glucose and fructose formed when sucrose (a disaccharide consisting of glucose and fructose molecules bonded together), is hydrolysed, or broken down into its component sugars. This hydrolysis process can occur naturally over time, such as in ripe fruits, or it can be induced by heating sucrose in the presence of an acid or enzyme catalyst. Invert sugar is sweeter than sucrose and is more soluble in water. It can be added to musts or wines to increase fermentable sugars, boost alcohol content, and enhance flavour and mouthfeel. Invert sugar can be made at home by gently boiling 1kg of household sugar in ½ litre of water containing a teaspoon of acid blend (or citric acid). It is ready to use once cooled.

Golden Syrup: A thick, amber-coloured syrup with a distinctive caramelised flavour. It is not commonly used in winemaking due to its high sugar content and unique flavour profile. However, it is possible to incorporate golden syrup into certain types of fruit wines or meads for added sweetness and flavour complexity. It is essential to monitor fermentation carefully to prevent over-sweetening or fermentation issues. Excessive sugar levels can stress yeast or lead to fermentation problems, such as stuck fermentation or off-flavours.

Specialty Sugars: Other specialty sugars, such as demerara sugar, soft brown sugar, molasses, maple syrup, Barbados sugar, and muscovado sugar, can be used in winemaking to impart unique flavours and aromas to the finished wine. These sugars may have more complex compositions and flavours compared to granulated sugar, so they should be used carefully. Demerara sugar has a higher level of unfermentable sugars, for example, so will provide residual sweetness. Barbados and muscovado sugars will impart a caramel flavour, so they can be useful when making madeira or sherry styles.

Lactose: Lactose is a two-unit sugar, but unlike sucrose it cannot be fermented by yeast since yeast does not produce the enzyme necessary to digest it. Therefore, lactose cannot be used as primary sugar for winemaking. Lactose can, however, be used to sweeten wines that have completed fermentation and are too dry for the desired taste profile. Since lactose is a non-fermentable sugar, it can be added to wine to increase sweetness without the risk of re-fermentation. This can be useful for balancing acidity or adding sweetness to dessert wines or fruit wines. Lactose provides a third as much sweetness than sugar will. It can also be used as a stabilising agent in winemaking to prevent the growth of spoilage microorganisms, such as bacteria or yeast, particularly in sweet or fortified wines.

In certain styles of wine, particularly dessert wines or fortified wines, lactose can contribute to a smoother, creamier mouthfeel and texture. This can add complexity and richness to the wine's overall sensory profile.

Lactose is sourced from milk so beware of potential allergen issues. In practice, it is used more in beer making than winemaking, and is a key element in making Milk Stouts.

Experimentation with different sugars and sugar sources can lead to unique and enjoyable wines that reflect your creativity and preferences.

Chapter 3. Making Wines from Kits:

The basis of all wine kits is grape concentrate. Grape concentrate for home winemaking is a product derived from grapes that have been processed to extract and concentrate their natural juices. It serves as a convenient and versatile basis for making wine at home, offering several advantages for home winemakers:

Convenience: Grape concentrate provides a convenient alternative to using fresh grapes for winemaking. It eliminates the need for harvesting, crushing, and pressing grapes, saving time and effort in the winemaking process. Home winemakers can simply reconstitute the concentrated juice with water and begin fermentation, streamlining the process of making wine at home.

Consistency: Grape concentrate offers consistency in flavour, aroma, and quality, as it is produced from carefully selected grapes and processed under controlled conditions. This ensures that home winemakers can achieve predictable results with each batch of wine they produce, regardless of variations in grape availability or quality.

Variety: Grape concentrate is available in a variety of styles and grape varieties, allowing home winemakers to experiment with different flavours and styles of wine. Whether you prefer red, white, or rosé wine, or wish to explore varietals such as Cabernet Sauvignon, Chardonnay, or Merlot, there is likely a grape concentrate available to suit your preferences.

Accessibility: Grape concentrate is often readily available at homebrew shops, online retailers, and winemaking shops, making it easily accessible to home winemakers regardless of their location or grape-growing climate. This accessibility enables enthusiasts to pursue their passion for winemaking year-round, even in regions where fresh grapes may not be readily available.

Cost-Effectiveness: Grape concentrate can be a cost-effective option for home winemakers, especially in regions where fresh grapes are expensive or difficult to obtain. It allows enthusiasts to produce high-quality wine at a fraction of the cost of purchasing bottled wine from a store, making winemaking a more accessible hobby for individuals with budget constraints.

To use grape concentrate for home winemaking, home winemakers typically reconstitute the concentrated juice with water according to the instructions provided by the manufacturer. Although wine kits are usually made out of the box, home winemakers can adjust the acidity, sugar levels, and other parameters of the juice, to achieve a desired flavour profile and style of wine. The key benefit with grape concentrate, is that winemakers can enjoy the satisfaction of crafting delicious wine at home with ease and consistency.

The modern winemaker is fortunate in that there is an ever-increasing choice of wine kits available through specialist home winemaking stores. At the most basic level these are classified as White, Red, and Rosé. Some commercial winemakers have become worried that the quality of contemporary home-made wines is as good as their commercial equivalents. They have sought to protect their investments by ring fencing generic names and preventing wine kit producers from using them. Therefore, you may notice that a Rosé wine kit may be referred to as a Blush or White Zinfandel; a Rioja as a Rojo; Chateauneuf-du-Pape as a Vieux Chateau du Roi; Barolo as Nebbiolo.

When selecting a wine kit, imagine you are selecting from an escalator based on quality and cost. All kits will be supplied with a quantity of grape concentrate and a pack containing yeast, nutrients, finings, and chemicals to kill the yeast and stop fermentation at the end of the process. The quality and quantity of grape concentrate supplied will depend on the price of the kit. At the lower level there are the basic kits. These are normally sold as White, Red, and Rosé (Blush) styles. They may be classified as sweet, or dry but do not identify the types of grapes included. Basic kits will require sugar to be added to reach their target alcohol level (ABV). Often basic kits are sold as 7-day wines, meaning that they will typically ferment out in a week. They will only require minimal ageing so can be consumed young.

The next level up the escalator will include kits that still require additional sugar but will focus on a grape style. The SG Gold range of kits is a popular choice in this category. The wines will still ferment out in 7-days and are designed to be consumed young. They are a good choice for people that want a wine to be ready quickly and with minimal fuss.

The most popular point on the escalator is the premium range of kits. These are aligned to a grape style and do not require additional sugar. In these kits the grape concentrate is of a higher quality, containing a greater amount of natural sugar. Manufacturers will differ in the quantity of grape concentrate supplied in their kits. The greater the quantity, the higher the price. Some manufacturers quote quantities in weight and others by volume. These range from 5 litres (7kg) to 14 litres (16.4 kg). The costs vary from under £40 to over £120. The way to assess these kits is that a kit supplied with 5 litres of juice will produce a wine that is equivalent to a £7 bottle of commercial wine. It will normally ferment out within 14 days and ideally should be left to mature for a month before consumption.

In contrast, a super-premium kit containing 14 litres of juice will produce a wine comparable to a £15-£20 commercial equivalent. It will take up to three weeks to ferment out and to be at its best should be left to mature for 6-12 months.

The more expensive super-premium kits are often selected for special events and celebrations. However, even the most expensive kit will produce wine for less than £3.75 per bottle, which represents fantastic value.

Popular choices include Dark Rock Wines, SG Wines, Beaverdale, On the House, and Wine Expert kits. Wine Expert supply three ranges of kits- Classic (8 litres), Reserve (10 litres) and Private Reserve (14 litres). They also release limited editions from time to time. All these kits make 22.5

litres (5 gallons). Beaverdale, Wine Expert, and SG Wines also produce 5 litres (1 gallon) kits in limited styles.

How to Make a Wine Kit:

Most kits follow a similar method for making their wines. The only difference is that basic kits will require extra sugar to be added. Some of the super-premium kits may include grape skins that are added into the fermenter, but all will follow an anaerobic fermentation method. This means that the wine will be made directly in a fermenter under airlock protection. There is no requirement to ferment in an open bucket covered by a cloth as with craft (country) wines.

As mentioned earlier, there are two areas to focus on to ensure that you get consistently great results from your winemaking. Firstly, sanitise everything prior to use. By far the biggest failure of wines is through poor sanitisation of equipment. The second important area to focus on is temperature and monitoring the fermentation. It is important to store the wine in a room at an appropriate constant temperature to ensure a healthy fermentation. The kit instructions or yeast pack provided will state the correct fermentation temperature (this may vary according to the yeast). If your room is under 20C you may need to put a heat pad under the fermenter. If the room temperature is higher than 24C you may need to find a cooler place. When the fermentation is finished and the wine is clearing, try to complete the process by filtering and bottling (or storing in a wine box) as soon as possible. Whilst fermentation is progressing the wine will produce a layer of CO_2 which will keep airborne bacteria at bay. Once fermentation finishes this will stop, so it is advisable then to complete the process as soon as possible to avoid the subsequent risk of airborne contamination. Try to avoid frequently lifting off the lid of your fermenter during fermentation as this can introduce airborne bacteria into the wine.

Before starting to make your wine kit it is important to sanitise all equipment and the fermenter with a no-rinse sanitiser such as Suresan. This is a very kind routine sanitiser that can be used on all equipment including glass and stainless steel. It is a contact sanitiser. Simply mix a spoonful of Suresan into a litre of warm water. Then swill the solution around your fermenter and immerse other equipment such as spoons, syphon tubes etc in the solution. You may wish to use a sponge to ensure all surfaces that will be in contact with the wine are sanitised. Discard the solution after use as it is neutralised after 1 hour. Drain the solution from the equipment (many winemakers give equipment a quick rinse under the tap to remove all the sanitiser, but this is not necessary). Your equipment is now ready for immediate use.

Next, pour the grape concentrate into a sanitised fermenter. Then top up to the 23-litre mark (5 gallons) with water. Add a little boiling water to the mix in order to try to achieve a final temperature of 24C (75F). (Note: If you are using a basic kit which requires extra sugar then this would be dissolved into 2-3 litres of boiling water and added to the fermenter at this stage). Most winemakers use tap water. However, the quality of your final wine will be improved by using bottled spring water. I would certainly recommend using bottled spring water when making Reserve or Ultra-Premium wines. If using tap water, the addition of a dose of Harris Pure Brew will eliminate any problems associated with chlorine or chloramine in the water supply.

The next step Is to sprinkle the contents of the yeast and yeast nutrient sachet(s) onto the surface of the wine and stir well with a long-handled spoon for two minutes, backwards and forwards, to aerate the wine. Note that some manufacturers combine the yeast and nutrient in a single sachet.

Seal the fermenter and fit an airlock (filled with a little tap water). Then leave in a warm place (around 22-24C) to ferment. After one or two days you should notice CO2 escaping through the airlock and a foam should have developed on the surface of the wine. The fermentation will be vigorous initially and then calm down after a few days. When there are no signs of CO2 emerging through the airlock, this is an indication that fermentation has finished. Take a hydrometer reading at this stage. The reading should be between 0.996 and 1.000.

If fermentation has completed, carefully syphon the wine from the sediment that will have formed at the bottom, into another sanitised fermenter. One end of your syphon kit should have a tap or flow control clip which you can use to reduce or stop the flow. The other end should have a rigid tube with a sediment trap at the bottom. This prevents yeast sediment from being sucked from the bottom of the fermenter. There should also be a bucket clip fitted, which conveniently attaches the rigid end of the tube to the fermenter. Sanitise the syphon before use. Then place the fermenter on a higher-level work surface and your sanitised second fermenter underneath. Fit the rigid end of the tube with sediment trap into the bucket and suck the wine to prime the tube. Once filled close the control valve then position the open end over the second fermenter. Release the clip to start filling (it can be quickly reclosed if necessary). Carefully syphon out all the wine avoiding disturbing the sediment. Towards the bottom, carefully tilt the bucket to retrieve as much of the wine as possible. The final sediment can be discarded.

Add the contents of the wine stabiliser sachet to the wine and stir thoroughly backwards and forwards for 2-3 minutes to degas the wine. This will release any trapped CO_2 molecules and help clearing. Then add the finings sachet (s). Most wine kits provide a finings sachet with two parts. Pour the contents of the first part of the finings sachet into the wine and leave for 2 hours. Then add the second part and stir gently for 15 seconds to mix it into the wine. Note: the finings sachet may be a single pack with two separate pockets. Your wine should then be left in a cool room to clear for 7 days.

After 7 days, filter the wine through a Vinbrite Wine Filter to remove any remaining suspended particles (yeast and proteins). The wine should then have a commercial clarity and a pure taste. Taste the wine at this stage. If you prefer a sweeter wine, you can add a little glycerine or wine sweetener, which is available from all good home brew retailers. Be careful to add this in small stages and taste between additions. If you add too much and the wine becomes too sweet, it is not possible to subsequently make it drier except by blending with another drier wine.

Your wine should now be bottled as soon as possible. Fill bottles to within 2 cm of the top, either by using the syphon kit or a bottling stick fitted to the fermenter tap (this is available as an accessory or is included as standard with the deluxe starter kit). Bottling sticks are a quick and convenient way to fill bottles. Simply push the spring-loaded end onto the bottom of the bottle and it will start to fill. When the wine reaches the top lower the bottle. This will stop the flow and ensure the correct air space is maintained at the top of the bottle. Once filled, bottles should be secured with a cork, and a shrink seal to give a professional finish. If you are using screw topped wine bottles, then fit a Novatwist cap (these also contain a plastic bottle seal so no shrink seal will be necessary). Novatwist caps are available from your specialist home winemaking shop. They can be reused so they represent good value.

Finally apply a bottle label to complete the appearance and then store your wine in a cool place to mature. As a rule, the more expensive the kit, the more the wine will benefit from maturing for a longer period of time. It is recommended that basic kits are left to age for 3-4 weeks (although many winemakers drink them immediately). Premium kits should be left for 3 months ideally, and ultra-premium kits will continue maturing for 6-12 months (although they can be consumed earlier).

Adapting Wine Kits:

Winemaking kits offer a convenient and accessible way to produce high-quality wines at home, providing all the necessary ingredients and instructions for a successful batch. However, as you develop your skills, you may wish to experiment and adapt kits. Experimenting with extra additions, tweaking recipes, and adding personal touches will allow you to customise the flavour profile and characteristics of your wines.

The basis for success is to choose a wine kit that aligns with your desired flavour profile and style. You may wish to start off by blending two or more wines made from kits. This can be done in a wine glass, using a pipette or syringe. Once the preferred taste is achieved, it is then a simple matter of scaling up the ratios.

Wine Circles frequently encourage their members to make a standard 22.5 litres (5 gallon) wine kit. Then once made it is separated out into five smaller 5 litres (1 gallon) demijohns. Each demijohn is then customised by adding extra ingredients and additives. The result is the production of five completely different wines from one standard kit. For example, start by making a 22 litres (5 gallons) Dark Rock Sauvignon Blanc kit in a large fermenter. Mix in the wine yeast and nutrient sachets and stir well. Then syphon the must into five demijohns. This is the base from which to adapt:

Wine 1: Allow the first batch to ferment out as usual. Once fermentation is complete and the gravity reading is 0.996 add 1 crushed Campden tablet and ½ teaspoon of Potassium Sorbate. Leave in a cool place for 24 hours then add a dose of wine finings. Leave for a further 5 days in a cool place then carefully syphon the wine off the sediment. Your wine should finally be filtered through a Vinbrite Filter to achieve a commercial clarity. Bottle the wine and leave to mature for around 2-3 months in a cool room before drinking. This wine makes 6 bottles of classic Sauvignon Blanc.

Wine 2: Put the must into a bucket and add 1.4kg (3lbs) Strawberries. Ferment on the pulp for 5 days then strain into a demijohn and continue the fermentation. Once complete add 1 crushed Campden tablet and ½ teaspoon of Potassium Sorbate. Leave in a cool place for 24 hours then add a dose of wine finings. Leave for a further 5 days in a cool place then carefully syphon the wine off the sediment. Your wine should finally be filtered through a Vinbrite Filter to achieve a commercial clarity. Bottle the wine and leave to mature for around 2-3 months in a cool room before drinking This will make a delicious Rose wine.

Wine 3: Put the must into a bucket and add ½ oz of dried elderflowers (or ½ pint of fresh elderflowers). Ferment on the flowers for 5 days then strain into a demijohn and continue the fermentation. Once fermentation is complete and the gravity reading is 0.996 add 1 crushed Campden tablet and ½ teaspoon of Potassium Sorbate. Leave in a cool place for 24 hours then add a dose of wine finings. Leave for a further 5 days in a cool place then carefully syphon the wine off the sediment. Your wine should finally be filtered through a Vinbrite Filter to achieve a commercial clarity. Bottle the wine and leave to mature for around 2-3 months in a cool room before drinking. This will make a German style white wine. The subtle fragrance and taste of the elderflowers will provide a Rhine style addition to the wine.

Wine 4: Allow the batch to ferment out as usual. Once fermentation is complete and the gravity reading is 0.996 add 1 crushed Campden tablet and ½ teaspoon of Potassium Sorbate. Leave in a cool place for 24 hours then add a dose of wine finings. Leave for a further 5 days in a cool place then carefully syphon the wine off the sediment. Then add a Harris Martini Style Vermouth Pack. Leave to infuse for 2 weeks then remove the bag. Your wine should finally be filtered through a Vinbrite Filter to achieve a commercial clarity. Bottle the wine and leave to mature for around 2-3 months in a cool room before drinking. This wine makes 6 bottles of Martini style vermouth. It can be fortified by adding 1 measure of vodka or brandy to each 750ml bottle. If you prefer the vermouth to be a little sweeter or smoother, then add Brewers Glycerine to taste.

Wine 5: Allow the wine to ferment to a specific gravity of 1.005 then syphon it from the sediment and add finings. Leave it in a cool place for 5 days to rough clear. Then syphon from the sediment into 500ml pressurised bottles beer bottles. Add 2 Brew Fizz Carbonation drops per bottle. Secure and leave in a warm place around 24C (75F) for 5 days. Then store in a cool place for 2-3 months to clear and condition. Chill in a fridge for 24 hrs before opening bottles and pouring carefully (avoid pouring out the sediment at the bottom of the bottle). This creates a sparkling Cava style white wine.

This is a great way to start experimenting with different additions to completely change the character of wines. Once you have got the hang of it there are a number of ways that you can adapt wine kits. Consider adding additional ingredients to enhance the flavour and complexity of your wine.

Oak: Add oak chunks or chips, during fermentation or ageing to impart oak-derived flavours such as vanilla, spice, and toast. For white wines oak additions work well with Chardonnay kits and for red wines Cabernet Sauvignon, Merlot, and Malbec, commonly found in Bordeaux-style blends, benefit greatly from the oak ageing process. The tannins in these grape varietals integrate beautifully with the flavours imparted by the oak, resulting in complex and age-worthy wines.

Fruit: Incorporate fresh or frozen fruit puree, juice, or zest to introduce new flavours and aromas to your wines. Popular options include berries, citrus fruits, and stone fruits. Always ensure that purees and juices are free from preservatives which could inhibit fermentation. Organic products are the best choice.

Some wine kits are available which are fruit based. SG Wines sell a range of Country Wines, which make 1-gallon (5 litres) of 10% ABV wine. The range includes Apricot, Elderflower, Peach, Strawberry, Bilberry, Black Cherry, and Cherry flavours. They make a good base for blending with other wines as well as offering a convenient way to build up a stock of country fruit wines.

Wine Expert produce a 5-gallon (22.5 litres) Island Mist range, which makes a lighter 6% fruit wine. These kits produce fresh and fruity wines in just 4 weeks! It is possible to increase the ABV by adding more sugar, or they can be used as a basis for blending with other wines. A delicious, refreshing alternative to wine and coolers, Winexpert Island Mist is a fun and fruity variation with the perfect balance of fresh, crisp, and distinct wines bursting with full fruit flavour. The range includes Peach & Apricot, Strawberry, Raspberry & Peach Sangria, Green Apple, Black Cherry, and Blood Orange Sangria. These wines make an excellent base for cocktails and mixers or can used to an add extra dimension of interest to your wine collection.

Botanicals: Experiment with herbs, spices, and botanicals such as cinnamon, cloves, ginger, and herbs de Provence to add depth and complexity to your wine. They can also be used to make a vermouth style wine, which is a great base for mixer drinks.

Honey: If you are adding sugar to your recipe or kit then you might consider substituting part of the sugar with honey. This will impart a subtle sweetness and floral character to the wine. Different honeys will provide different characteristics. Lighter honeys, such as orange blossom or clover, have a milder flavour and are ideal to use. Lighter honey will not overpower other subtle flavours provided by the grape or other ingredients. For a heavy fruit based

Adjusting Sweetness Levels: Wine kits typically include a predetermined amount of sugar to achieve a specific sweetness level. It is possible to adjust the sweetness of your wine to fine tune it to your personal preference. To increase the sweetness, add additional sugar or sweeteners such as honey or agave syrup. Organic light agave syrup is made from the Mexican salmeana agave plant. It is super sweet, mild, runny and delicious. With its lower glycaemic index, it makes an excellent replacement for white sugar. For vegans it can also be used instead of honey.

If you add extra sugar to the must before fermentation begins, then the likelihood is that this will be consumed by the yeast and a higher ABV wine will result. To achieve extra sweetness without increasing the alcohol content then the sugar must be added at the end of the fermentation process. This could encourage a post-fermentation, however, so it is important to pasteurise the wine to prevent this. Adding potassium sorbate should minimise the risk of post-fermentation but there will still be a slight risk. Pasteurisation is the best option. Alternatively, you could use wine sweetener or brewers glycerine to sweeten your wine. These are non-fermentable by yeast.

Modifying Acidity and Tannins: Acidity and tannins play important roles in shaping the structure and mouthfeel of wine. To adjust acidity: add tartaric acid, malic acid, or citric acid to increase acidity, or blend with lower-acid wines to decrease acidity. Adding grape tannin powder or oak chips will enhance tannin levels and mouthfeel in your wine.

Experimenting with Yeast Strains: Explore different yeast strains to influence the fermentation process and flavour profile of your wine. Each yeast strain offers unique characteristics, including fermentation speed, temperature tolerance, and flavour expression. Although wine kits will always be supplied with a yeast, you may wish to experiment with different strains to discover the ones that best complement your desired wine style.

Blending Wines: Blending wines from different batches or kits will allow you to create custom blends with unique flavour profiles and characteristics. Blending is considered in more depth in a later section as it is a subtle process. Experiment with different blending ratios to achieve the desired balance of flavours, aromas, and structure. You do not have to blend on a 50:50 basis. Blending is a great way to enhance your wine making and as your palette becomes more discerning, and your skills improve, you will be able to fine-tune the process to maximise the quality of your winemaking. The most important thing is to keep detailed records. Always maintain detailed records of your winemaking experiments, including ingredients, quantities, techniques, and tasting notes.

By adapting wine kits and experimenting with different ingredients, techniques, and adjustments, you can unlock a world of creativity and customisation. Whether you're aiming for bold and robust reds, crisp and aromatic whites, or fruity and refreshing rosés, the possibilities for customization are endless. Enjoy the journey of exploration and discovery as you craft your own signature wines at home.

Chapter 4. The Process for Making Basic Craft Wines.

Craft (country) winemaking follows a slightly different process than kit wines, but these wines are still easy to make and can provide a lot of fun. It is possible to blend country wines with kit wines to provide interesting hybrid flavours. Often fruit is freely available, or on offer cheaply at supermarkets when it is reaching its sell by date. Craft wines are very cost-effective and require very little extra equipment.

Begin by selecting the correct amount of fruit, flowers, or vegetables, for the quantity you are going to make. Keep in mind your desired sweetness and alcohol content. If you are experimenting with a new recipe then it may be prudent to begin by making a one-gallon batch. However, craft wines can take time to mature and reach their best, so when you are happy with the recipe you may wish to make larger quantities. As suggested earlier, most of the equipment for making wine is configured to either 5 litres (1 gallon) or 22.5 litres (5 gallons). Therefore, the recipes in this book are formulated to these batch sizes.

Recipes either recommend adding boiling water or cold water to fruits and other ingredients in a bucket. The advantage of using boiling water is that it will kill off any wild yeast or bacteria that may reside on the surface of fruits and other ingredients. However, high temperatures can compromise the delicate flavours of ingredients. Therefore, many winemakers prefer a cold infusion method. This involves Stirring the ingredients and sugar into water at a temperature not exceeding 40C/104F until the sugar is fully dissolved. This creates what is known as the "must." When adopting the cold infusion method, the way to kill off any unwanted wild yeast or bacteria is by adding a crushed Campden tablet to the must in the bucket. Then leave covered for 24 hours, before stirring vigorously and then adding the yeast.

Yeast cannot survive at higher temperatures, so it is important that the temperature of the must is suitable for yeast inoculation. This is typically in the range of 18-24°C (65-75°F). Extreme temperature fluctuations should be avoided during fermentation, as they can stress the yeast. A heating pad is a useful accessory to maintain a good constant temperature, particularly when ambient temperatures are colder.

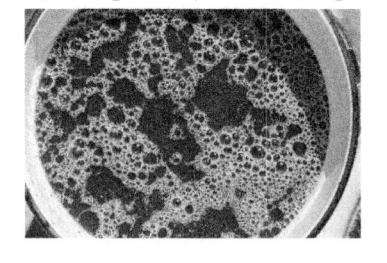

It is important to introduce oxygen into the must at the same time as adding the yeast by vigorously stirring for at least 2 minutes. Yeast requires oxygen during the early stages of fermentation for healthy cell growth. Oxygen is also needed during the first few days of primary fermenting craft wines to help extract the flavours. This is done by covering the bucket with a cloth and allowing fermentation to take place aerobically (with air) for five days. Minimal alcohol will be produced during this stage, but maximum flavour extraction will be achieved. After five days the fruit, flowers, or vegetables should be strained out and the must transferred to a secondary fermenter fitted with an airlock. Once the secondary fermentation begins, oxygen exposure should be minimised so try to avoid removing the lid from your fermenter and ensure the airlock always has water in it. The yeast will need an initial supply of oxygen to support the whole fermentation process and achieve a good level of attenuation. Attenuation is the degree to which yeast ferments the sugar in the must. A 50% attenuation means that 50% of the sugars have been converted into alcohol and CO2 by yeast. 100% attenuation means that all the sugars have been consumed by yeast. Adding Pure Brew with the yeast will ensure higher levels of attenuation.

Always follow the instructions provided with your chosen yeast strain to pitch it properly. Healthy yeast is essential for a successful fermentation process. The sachet instructions will provide the ideal temperature for a successful fermentation. Most yeasts can be added directly to the must, but you can make a yeast starter if you prefer. This will ensure the yeast hits the ground running and is also recommended for re-starts if your fermentation stops prematurely. To make a yeast starter, sanitise a small glass and half-fill with the must. Then add 1 teaspoon of sugar and a squeeze of a lemon. Add the yeast and stir well. Then cover with a cloth and leave in a warm place (24C/75F) until a head starts to form and fermentation is visible.

This should take 40-60 minutes. Then stir well and add to the bulk of the must. Stir the must vigorously with a sanitised brewing paddle for 2 minutes.

Make sure you have left sufficient space in the fermentation vessel for the initial foaming that occurs during fermentation. At the start of fermentation there will be vigorous activity, but this should die down after a few days. For kit wines, attach an airlock to allow gases to escape while preventing contaminants from entering the fermenter. If you are making craft wines, then the lid of the fermenter should be left partly open for the first few days (whilst the yeast is fermenting the pulp). This allows air into the mix to enable an aerobic fermentation, which will maximise the fruit flavour extraction.

After five days strain off the fruit and return the must to the sanitised fermenter, fitted with an airlock containing water. Then complete the anaerobic fermentation to convert the remaining sugar into alcohol (this is known as the secondary fermentation period). Be patient, fermentation can take anywhere from ten days to several weeks, depending on various factors. Monitor the airlock activity, and refrain from opening the vessel unnecessarily. Patience is a virtue in wine making as some craft wines will take considerably longer to ferment out than kit wines do. The wait will certainly be worthwhile.

Once fermentation appears to have stopped, transfer the wine to a second fermentation vessel, leaving sediment behind. This process, known as racking, helps clarify the wine. The end of fermentation is indicated by bubbles stopping emerging from the airlock. It is worth taking a hydrometer reading at this stage. If the wine has completely fermented the hydrometer should read 0.996.

Your wine should now be cleared, and the yeast killed off to prevent further post-fermentation (unless you are making a sparkling wine). Add a crushed Campden tablet and a dose of Potassium Sorbate to kill any remaining yeast and then add wine finings to the must. Keep in a cool place (13C/55 F or below) for 7 days for the wine to rough clear. It can then be re-racked from any further sediment and to achieve a professional clarity you should finally pass it through a Vinbrite Filter. Filtering will remove any minute traces of dead yeast and other colloidal suspended particles, which could cause off-tastes. It will also ensure that your wine looks the same as a commercial equivalent. Finally, syphon your wine into sanitised bottles and fit a cork. To give the wine a professional appearance, attach a label and a plastic shrink seal. These are available from your specialist home brew shop. Then allow the wine to age and mature to enhance the final flavour. Remember, fine wines benefit from patience. Ageing in the bottle for several months or even years will result in a smoother and more refined product.

Making Wine from Grapes:

Growing your own Vines:

Growing wines from grapes can be rewarding especially if the grapes are picked from your own vines. Many winemakers' plant and cultivate their own vines to provide their own sustainable source of grapes.

There are a growing number of UK businesses that are successfully producing commercial wines. Some of the notable UK winemakers include:

Nyetimber: Nyetimber is one of England's most renowned sparkling wine producers, located in West Sussex. They specialize in traditional method sparkling wines made from classic Champagne grape varieties such as Chardonnay, Pinot Noir, and Pinot Meunier.

Ridgeview Wine Estate: Ridgeview is another prominent English sparkling wine producer, located in Sussex. They are known for their high-quality traditional method sparkling wines, which have received numerous awards and accolades.

Chapel Down: Chapel Down is one of the largest wine producers in England, with vineyards in Kent, Sussex, and Essex. They produce a wide range of still and sparkling wines, including traditional method sparkling wines, still whites, reds, and rosés.

Bolney Wine Estate: Bolney Wine Estate is a family-owned winery located in West Sussex. They specialize in English wines made from classic grape varieties such as Pinot Noir, Chardonnay, and Bacchus, as well as lesser-known varieties like Kerner and Schönburger.

Hush Heath Estate: Hush Heath Estate is situated in Kent and is known for its still and sparkling wines, including the award-winning Balfour Brut Rosé. They also produce cider and apple wines from their orchards.

Camel Valley Vineyard: Camel Valley Vineyard is located in Cornwall and is one of the leading producers of English sparkling wines. Their wines have received numerous awards and accolades, including several gold medals at the International Wine Challenge.

Denbies Wine Estate: Denbies Wine Estate is one of the largest wine producers in the UK, located in Surrey. They have a wide range of wines, including still and sparkling wines, made from a variety of grape varieties grown on their estate.

Halfpenny Green Vineyard: Established in 1983, The vineyard is situated in the picturesque countryside of South Staffordshire, near the village of Bobbington. The region benefits from a temperate climate and well-drained soils, which are conducive to grape growing. Halfpenny Green Vineyard spans over 30 acres of vineyards, planted with a variety of grape varieties suitable for the English climate. These include classic varieties such as Chardonnay, Pinot Noir, and Seyval Blanc, as well as lesser-known varieties like Regent and Solaris. They produce a range of still and sparkling wines, including white, rosé, red, and sparkling wines. Their wines are crafted using traditional winemaking methods and are known for their quality, consistency, and distinctive English character.

These are just a few examples of UK winemakers who are making significant contributions to the country's wine industry. The UK's wine scene is dynamic and evolving, with many other talented winemakers and emerging wine regions gaining recognition both domestically and internationally.

Why not try your hand at creating your own small-scale vineyard at home by planting your own vines. In the UK, where the climate can be cool and unpredictable, selecting grape varieties suited to the conditions is essential for successful home cultivation. Some grape varieties that are known to grow well in the UK:

Bacchus: Bacchus is a white grape variety that thrives in cooler climates and is well-suited to the UK's conditions. It produces aromatic wines with flavours of citrus, elderflower, and gooseberry, similar to Sauvignon Blanc.

Ortega: Ortega is another white grape variety that performs well in the UK's cooler climate. It produces aromatic wines with flavours of peach, pear, and floral notes, making it suitable for still and sparkling wines.

Pinot Noir: Pinot Noir is a versatile red grape variety that can tolerate cooler climates. It is used to produce both still and sparkling wines, with flavours of red berries, earthy notes, and a silky texture.

Rondo: Rondo is a red grape variety bred for its disease resistance and suitability to cooler climates. It produces wines with dark fruit flavours, firm tannins, and good acidity, making it an excellent choice for red wines in the UK.

Regent: Regent is another red grape variety that performs well in cooler climates. It produces wines with flavours of blackberries, cherries, and spice, and it is known for its disease resistance and reliability in the UK.

Chardonnay: Chardonnay is a white grape variety that can adapt to a wide range of climates, including cooler regions. It produces wines with flavours ranging from crisp green apple to creamy vanilla, depending on the winemaking style.

Siegerrebe: Siegerrebe is a white grape variety known for its intense aromatics and floral characteristics. It is well-suited to cooler climates and is used to produce aromatic white wines with pronounced lychee, rose petal, and spice flavours.

Black Hamburg: Also known as Black Muscat or Muscat Hamburg. Black Hamburg is a dark-skinned grape variety that belongs to the Muscat family. It is renowned for its rich, aromatic flavours and is often used to produce sweet and fortified wines, as well as table grapes and dessert wines. The grapes have a deep purple to black colour when fully ripe and are medium sized with thick skins. They grow in loose clusters. The hallmark of Black Hamburg grapes is their intense and aromatic flavour profile. They are known for their pronounced muscat aroma, which includes floral notes of rose petals and orange blossom, as well as fruity aromas of ripe berries, musk, and spices. The flavour is sweet and luscious, with a distinctive muscat character that lingers on the palate.

These are just a few examples of grape varieties that can thrive in the UK's climate and are suitable for home cultivation. When selecting grape vines for your home vineyard, consider factors such as local climate conditions, soil type, and available space, and choose varieties that are well-suited to your specific growing conditions. Additionally, consult with local nurseries for advice on grape varieties that are known to perform well in your area.

Growing and cultivating grapevines in the UK requires careful attention to the climate, soil conditions, and vine care practices to ensure successful growth and fruit production. Try to choose a site for your home vineyard that receives plenty of sunlight and has good air circulation to minimize the risk of fungal diseases. South-facing slopes are ideal for maximising sun exposure and heat accumulation, which can help ripen grapes in cooler climates. Avoid low-lying areas that are prone to frost pockets and poor drainage.

Test the soil to assess its pH, drainage, and nutrient levels. Grapevines thrive in well-drained soils with a pH between 6.0 and 7.0. Sandy loam or loamy soils are preferred, but grapevines can also grow in clay or limestone soils with proper amendments. Improve soil fertility and structure by adding organic matter, such as compost or well-rotted manure before planting.

Choose grape varieties that are well-suited to the UK's climate and growing conditions. Consider factors such as disease resistance, cold hardiness, and ripening time when selecting grape varieties for your garden. Consult with local nurseries for recommendations on grape varieties that perform well in your area.

Plant grapevines in early spring or late autumn when the soil is workable, and temperatures are mild. Dig planting holes large enough to accommodate the vine's root system and amend the soil with organic matter if needed. Space grapevines according to the variety's requirements, typically 6-10 feet apart in rows with 6-8 feet between rows.

Train grapevines to a support system, such as trellises or wires, to encourage upward growth and proper vine structure. Prune grapevines annually during the dormant season (late winter to early spring) to remove dead or diseased wood, improve airflow, and promote fruit production. Follow pruning guidelines specific to your grape variety and training system.

Provide regular irrigation to newly planted grapevines to establish root systems, and water established vines during dry periods to ensure adequate moisture levels. Avoid overwatering, as soggy soil can lead to root rot and fungal diseases. Use drip irrigation or soaker hoses, if possible, to deliver water directly to the base of the vines and minimize water waste.

Monitor soil fertility and nutrient levels regularly and fertilise grapevines as needed to maintain healthy growth and fruit production. Apply a balanced fertiliser in early spring before bud break and again in late spring or early summer if additional nutrients are required.

Implement integrated pest management (IPM) practices to control pests and diseases in your vineyard. Monitor vines regularly for signs of pest damage or disease symptoms, and take appropriate action, such as pruning affected parts, applying organic or synthetic pesticides where necessary.

Harvest grapes when they reach optimal ripeness, typically in late summer or early autumn. Monitor grape maturity by tasting the berries and checking sugar levels (measured as °Brix) with a refractometer. Harvest grapes by hand and handle them gently to avoid bruising or damage.

After harvesting, process grapes promptly to prevent spoilage and maintain fruit quality. Crush grapes to extract the juice, then ferment the juice into wine using one of the recipes listed in this book. Store harvested grapes in a cool, humid environment to prolong shelf life and prevent dehydration.

By following these steps and best practices for grapevine cultivation, you can successfully grow and cultivate grapevines in the UK and produce high-quality wines from your own grapes.

Making Wine from your own Grapes:

Unlike fruit and vegetable wines, it is difficult to be prescriptive when recommending a grape wine recipe. Grapes will vary in sugar content, depending on the variety selected and the weather/harvest conditions. Furthermore, the colour of red wines will be extracted from the grape skins and there can be some variation between years. It is important to use a hydrometer to establish the precise sugar level of your grapes, and the use of a wine press will make the process more effective.

As a general rule, you will need around 5-8 Kg (12 – 18lb) of grapes to make 5 litres (one-gallon) of wine. If you are making red wine then you will need to keep the grape skins and ferment on the pulp for 5 days in a covered bucket, to extract the full colour and flavour. For white wine it is possible to press the juice and ferment it directly under airlock. If your grapes have a low sugar content, or you do not have sufficient grapes, you can add grape concentrate to boost flavour, body, and alcohol. It is also acceptable to add extra sugar to bring up the alcohol content, although as far as possible you should try to extract the required sugar from the natural grapes.

The starting gravity of grape wine (also known as the original gravity), refers to the density of the grape juice or must before fermentation begins. This measurement is typically taken using a hydrometer or refractometer and is expressed as a specific gravity (SG) reading or in degrees Brix (°Bx), which indicates the sugar content of the juice. In general, the starting gravity of grape wine will range from approximately 1.070 to 1.100 SG (or 17 to 25 °Bx) for dry wines, with higher readings indicating higher sugar content and potential alcohol levels. For sweet or dessert wines, the starting gravity may be higher, often exceeding 1.100 SG (or 25 °Bx), to produce wines with higher residual sugar levels and sweeter flavour profiles.

The acid content of your grapes can also vary between years, so it is useful to add an acid testing kit to your list of winemaking supplies. This will allow you to make minor adjustments to achieve the correct final acidity. The correct acidity for wine depends on several factors, including the type and style of wine being produced, the grape variety used, and personal preferences. Acidity plays a crucial role in wine, contributing to its balance, structure, and overall flavour profile.

Total acidity (TA) refers to the overall level of acidity in wine, typically measured in grams per litre (g/L) of tartaric acid or its equivalent. The total acidity of wine can vary widely depending on factors such as grape variety, climate, and winemaking techniques. pH is a measure of the acidity or alkalinity of wine on a scale from 0 to 14, with lower values indicating higher acidity and higher values indicating lower acidity. Most wines have a pH level between 3.0 and 4.0, with white wines having higher acidity (lower pH) than red wines. Different wine styles may have different acidity levels to achieve the desired flavour profile.

White wines typically have higher acidity levels (lower pH) compared to red wines. This higher acidity contributes to the crispness, freshness, and vibrancy of white wines.

The pH of white wines typically falls within the range of 3.0 to 3.5, with certain grape varieties or styles potentially falling slightly outside this range. Varieties such as Sauvignon Blanc, Riesling, and Chenin Blanc are known for their high acidity levels and often have pH values on the lower end of the spectrum to counterbalance their fruity or floral flavours.

Red wines generally have lower acidity levels (higher pH) compared to white wines. This lower acidity contributes to the smoother, softer mouthfeel of red wines. The pH of red wines typically falls within the range of 3.5 to 4.0, with some exceptions. Varieties such as Cabernet Sauvignon, Merlot, and Syrah tend to have slightly higher pH values, reflecting their softer acidity and richer, more robust flavour profiles.

The ideal acidity level for wine is often described in terms of balance, where acidity is one of several components (including sweetness, tannin, and alcohol) that contribute to a harmonious overall impression. Balanced acidity can enhance the wine's freshness, brightness, and ageing potential, while excessive acidity can lead to a sharp or sour taste.

Acidity levels in wine can also vary depending on the geographical region and local climate. Cooler climate regions tend to produce wines with higher acidity levels due to slower ripening and retention of natural acidity in the grapes. In warmer climates, grapes may lose acidity more rapidly during ripening, resulting in wines with lower acidity levels.

Winemakers can adjust acidity levels in wine through various winemaking techniques, such as blending different grape varieties, adjusting fermentation temperatures, or using malolactic fermentation to soften acidity. There is no single "correct" acidity level for wine, as it is a matter of personal taste and stylistic preference. However, well-balanced acidity is considered desirable in wine, contributing to its complexity, longevity, and overall enjoyment.

To increase the acidity of wine, you can add acid blend. The amount of acid blend to add depends on the starting pH of the wine and the target pH you want to achieve. Typically, you would measure the pH of the wine using a pH meter or pH test strips and then calculate the amount of acid blend needed based on the desired increase in acidity.

The process begins by first measuring the pH of the wine, and determining the target pH you want to achieve. A calculate the difference between the current pH and the target pH.

Use a wine acid blend calculation can then be made to determine the amount of acid blend needed to achieve the desired increase in acidity.

The specific formula or calculator you use may vary, but typically this would be:

Amount of acid blend to add (in teaspoons) = (Target pH - Current pH) X (1 gallon of wine) X (acid factor)

The acid factor represents the strength of the acid blend and may vary depending on the brand or type of acid blend you're using. A common acid factor is around 0.1 to 0.15 teaspoons per gallon per pH unit.

Therefore, for example, let's say you have 1 gallon of wine with a current pH of 3.5, and you want to increase the pH to 3.4. Using an acid factor of 0.1 teaspoons per gallon per pH unit:

Amount of acid blend to add = (3.4 - 3.5) X 1 X 0.1

= -0.1 X 0.1

= -0.01 teaspoons

In this case, you would need to add 0.01 teaspoons of acid blend to increase the pH of 1 gallon of wine from 3.5 to 3.4.

It is important to proceed with caution when adjusting acidity, as adding too much acid can negatively impact the flavour and balance of the wine. It is always recommended to make small adjustments and taste the wine frequently to ensure the desired balance is achieved.

From this information it is clear that no recipe can be totally prescriptive regarding the amount of sugar and acid to add to achieve consistent results. The best way to make grape wine is to collect the necessary quantity of grapes and wash them to remove any dirt. Then press the grapes through a wine press to extract the juice. When sufficient juice has been extracted (according to the volume of wine you are making), take a hydrometer reading. If the reading is lower than the required starting gravity, then add more grape juice if volume allows. Otherwise, slowly add an invert sugar solution (made by dissolving 1kg of sugar in 1 litre of water, together with 1 teaspoon of acid blend) and keep stirring to thoroughly mix. Take hydrometer readings until the required OG is achieved. Grape concentrate can be used instead of invert sugar (or in combination with it) to boost body and flavour in the wine.

Your recipe will provide other ingredients to add to achieve a healthy fermentation. Most grapes will contain sufficient acid to produce a balanced wine but by testing the must with an acid test kit, you will be able to make fine adjustments by adding acid blend or an acid reducer if required.

You can make white wine from red or green grapes as long as the skins are discarded. As there is no need to ferment on the skins, the must (grape juice plus added sugar or grape concentrate) can be fermented directly in a fermenter fitted with an airlock. However, if you wish to make red wine it will be necessary to pour the grape juice into a sanitised bucket and then add the skins. Then following the recipe, loosely cover the bucket and ferment aerobically on the pulp for 5 days. This will extract the colour from the grape skins and ensure a red wine is achieved. After 5 days strain the must from the pulp and ferment anaerobically under airlock to finish the process.

Extended Maceration:

Extended maceration involves leaving the grape skins in contact with the fermenting wine for an extended period after fermentation is complete. This technique is commonly used with red wines to extract additional colour, flavour, and tannins. Here's how to master extended maceration:

Monitor Tannin Extraction: Taste the wine regularly during extended maceration to monitor tannin levels. Over-extraction can result in harsh, astringent wines, so it's important to find the right balance.

Temperature Control: Maintain stable temperatures during extended maceration to ensure consistent extraction and fermentation kinetics.

Punch Downs and Pump Overs: Continue performing punch downs or pump overs during extended maceration to keep the skins in contact with the fermenting wine and promote colour and flavour extraction.

Punch downs, also known as pigeage (from the French language), involve manually pushing down the floating grape skins and pulp that rise to the top of the fermentation back into the fermenting wine. Winemakers typically use a tool called a punch down tool, which can vary in design but generally consists of a long handle with a flat or concave disc at the end. The tool is used to gently push the grape solids down into the liquid, ensuring that they remain in contact with the fermenting wine. Punch downs are typically performed multiple times per day, depending on the stage of fermentation. Early in fermentation, punch downs may be more frequent to ensure good extraction, while later in fermentation, they may be performed less frequently.

Pump overs, also known as remontage (again, from the French language), involve pumping wine from the bottom of the fermentation vessel and spraying it over the top of the floating grape skins. A pump is used to circulate the fermenting wine from the bottom of the vessel through a hose or pipe equipped with a nozzle or spray head, which disperses the wine evenly over the cap of grape solids. Pump overs are typically performed once or twice daily according to the stage of fermentation. Like punch downs, their frequency may vary throughout the fermentation process.

Pump overs promote gentle mixing and agitation of the fermenting wine and grape solids, ensuring even extraction of colour, flavour, and tannins. They also help prevent the formation of a dense cap of grape solids, which can inhibit fermentation and extraction. The purpose of punch downs is to ensure thorough contact between the grape solids and the fermenting wine, promoting extraction of colour, flavour, and tannins from the skins and seeds. This helps develop the wine's structure, complexity, and mouthfeel.

Performing pump overs requires more equipment so most home winemakers following an extending maceration process will just use a long-handled paddle to push down or pull up the grape skins.

The prizewinning wines section in this book provides a selection of grape recipes which are easy to follow and produce delicious grape wines.

Chapter 5. Making Mead:

Mead is an alcoholic beverage made by fermenting honey with water, and often with additional flavourings such as fruits, spices, grains, or hops. It is one of the oldest known alcoholic beverages, with a history that dates back thousands of years and spans cultures around the world. Mead can vary considerably in flavour, sweetness, and alcohol content depending on the ingredients used and the recipe being followed. It is easy to extend your winemaking skills and delve into the world of mead. The techniques are very similar to those required for winemaking.

Mead exhibits a wide range of styles, each offering distinct characteristics based on variations in honey types, yeast strains, and additional ingredients. Traditional mead, for instance, emphasises the pure essence of honey, while melomels incorporate fruits, metheglins introduce spices, and Cyser blends honey with apple juice or cider.

As a versatile beverage, mead can range from still to sparkling, sweet to dry, and light to highly alcoholic. It embodies a connection to historical and mythological narratives, often being associated with celebrations and rituals in various cultures. In modern times, mead has experienced a resurgence, attracting both traditionalists and experimentalists who appreciate its depth of flavour, cultural significance, and the creative possibilities it offers to those who embark on the journey of mead making.

Choosing the right honey is a crucial step in crafting a prizewinning mead. Experimenting with different honey varieties allows you to explore a wide range of flavours, from delicate and floral to robust and earthy. As you embark on your mead making journey, consider the characteristics of each honey type and how they harmonise with your desired style and flavour profile. With the right honey in hand, you're well on your way to creating meads that captivate and inspire.

There are various ways of introducing honey into mead. Traditionally the honey is dissolved in water at around 38°C (100°F) then yeast is added to start fermentation. It is important not to pour boiling water over honey to dissolve it, since this will destroy some of the finer flavours.

The choice of yeast is an important decision in mead making, as it directly influences the flavour, aroma, and character of the final product. In days gone by wild strains of yeast were used but these were unreliable and produced off-flavours and low alcohol yields. Later, mead makers progressed to using bakers' yeasts and then general-purpose wine yeasts, but these also produced lower ABV's and less clean flavours. Contemporary mead makers are fortunate in that specialist home brew shops carry a variety of technical yeast strains that are suitable for different mead styles. These strains provide better attenuation and healthier fermentations. They effectively contribute to the final quality by adding subtle flavours. Your specialist home brew shop will provide guidance on the most appropriate yeasts for your mead and help you to understand their unique characteristics. Note that fermentation ties for mead may be longer than for other wines and it is important to add a good yeast nutrient at the start of the process.

There are a number of sub categories of mead. These include Traditional Mead (also known as Show Mead), Sack Mead (a stronger sweeter style), Melomel (fruit infused with the honey), Metheglin (spiced mead), Sparkling Mead, Pyment (grapes infused with the honey), and Cyser (apple-based mead).

If you are new to mead making, then it is recommended that you start with one of the recipes in this book to make a traditional mead. Once you have achieved success then you can progress to one of the other styles. Traditional mead keeps things simple but bear in mind that by following the same recipe you can still achieve a wide range of flavours by adjusting the honey varieties or the yeast strains. Made with just honey, water, and yeast, traditional mead is a pure and straightforward representation of the craft. Dry, semi-sweet, or sweet traditional meads offer a spectrum of sweetness levels to cater to various preferences. It is generally accepted that the maximum ABV for a traditional mead should not exceed 11%.

Adding fruits and spices to mead to make melomels and metheglins opens a whole world of opportunities for experimentation. The range of flavours, colours, and aromas that can be achieved add a whole new dimension of interest for mead makers. Part of the science of mead making is learning when to add other ingredients into the fermentation to get the best results.

You can purchase pre-packed mead infusions to add extra creativity to your mead making. Manufacturers such as Harris Homecraft produce a range of infusions supplied ready to use with tea/spice bags and full instructions. These include carefully selected blends of spices which have been thoroughly researched. The range is supplied with recipes/instructions and available through homebrew shops.

The range includes:

Chocolate Cinnamon Mead Infusion: Includes cacao nibs, cassia bark.

Chocolate Orange Mead Infusion: Includes cacao nibs, bitter orange peel.

Chocolate Vanilla Mead Infusion: Includes cacao nibs, vanilla pods.

Metheglin Spiced Mead Infusion: Includes lemon peel, bitter orange peel, coriander seeds, ginger, all spice.

Winter Spice Blend Mead Infusion: Includes cassia bark, cloves, all spice, nutmeg.

Exotic Spice Blend Mead Infusion: Includes cardamom, star anise, ginger nibs.

Mediterranean Citrus Blend Mead Infusion: Includes orange peel, lemon zest, coriander.

Pyments are meads made with the addition of grapes or grape juices. Alternatively, they may be grape-based wine kits made or sweetened with honey, or a mead blended with grape-based wine after fermentation. Technically, mead with grapes is a form of melomel but it has earned itself its own category over the years. It is quite easy to make a pyment by adapting a wine kit. Simply add honey instead of sugar when making the kit. Alternatively (for a kit that does not require extra sugar to be added) add extra honey at the fermentation stage to increase the ABV and give a delicious honey flavour to your wine. If you do not wish to increase the alcohol level, then you could back sweeten the wine with honey.

If you wish to delve deeper into the fascinating world of mead making, the book "The Art of Mead Making: A Comprehensive Guide" covers everything you need to know and offers some excellent recipes across a range of styles.

Chapter 6. Making Sparkling Wines:

The popularity of sparkling wines has grown significantly over the years, driven by various factors that have contributed to their appeal among consumers. Sparkling wines are often associated with celebrations and special occasions, such as weddings, Christmas, New Year's Eve, Diwali, and anniversaries. The effervescence and festive nature of sparkling wines make them a favourite choice for toasting and commemorating milestones.

Sparkling wines are versatile and can be enjoyed in a variety of settings and occasions. They pair well with a wide range of foods, from appetisers and seafood to main courses and desserts, making them suitable for diverse dining experiences.

The effervescence of sparkling wines provides a refreshing and light drinking experience, making them especially appealing during warmer months or as aperitifs before meals. The crisp acidity and lively bubbles invigorate the palate and stimulate the senses. They are sold in a range of styles and sweetness levels, catering to different preferences and tastes. From bone-dry Brut to sweet Demi-Sec, there is a sparkling wine style to suit every palate, occasion, and culinary pairing.

Sparkling wines are produced in various wine regions around the world, including Champagne in France, Prosecco in Italy, Cava in Spain, and sparkling wines in regions such as California, Australia, and New Zealand. This global diversity offers consumers a wide selection of sparkling wines to choose from, each with its unique characteristics and terroir. They are becoming more accessible and affordable, with a growing number of producers offering high-quality sparkling wines at reasonable price points. Dynamic pricing policies are often adopted by retailers, so a brand of champagne may be sold at different prices to appeal to consumers at certain calendar touchpoints, such as Christmas. Sparkling wines, such as Prosecco, form the base of many popular cocktails, which has further increased their popularity.

It is quite easy to make your own sparkling wine at a fraction of the price of a commercial bottle. There are, however, a few things to be aware of before setting off on an experiment into the world of bubbles. Firstly, if you intend to generate the sparkle naturally, it is important to avoid the use of sulphites and preservatives such a s potassium sorbate, at the end of the fermentation process. Secondly, you need to think about how you will store your sparkling wines. It is important that any bottles used are capable of holding carbonated drinks. Otherwise, you can experience exploding bottles. Bottle closures need to be considered too. You will need to use champagne corks and cages to prevent corks from popping. Some grape styles are more suitable for sparkling wines so give some consideration to selection and blending to get the right acid balance.

The basic winemaking process up to the end of fermentation will be the same as for standard wines. The method will differ once fermentation is complete. You will need to consider how you wish to carbonate the wine. There are three basic methods that can be followed.

1. *The traditional process* (*méthode champenoise*). This process involves a secondary fermentation that creates the bubbles (carbonation) in the wine. It is a traditional method for making sparkling wine, which is known in France as the méthode champenoise or méthode traditionnelle.

Start by making a base wine, typically a dry white wine with high acidity. The base wine can be made from grape varieties such as Chardonnay, Pinot Noir, and Sauvignon Blanc, or a blend of these varieties.

If you are using your own grapes, harvest them at optimal ripeness and process them into juice. Ferment the juice into a still wine, ensuring that it is dry (i.e., all sugars have been fermented into alcohol) and has good acidity.

Blending is a very successful process for making sparkling wines. You can experiment and blend base wines from different grape varieties or wine kit suppliers to achieve the desired flavour profile and consistency.

The traditional method adopted in France involves the addition of a 'Liqueur de Tirage'. This is a mixture of wine, sugar, and yeast that is added to the base wine just before bottling to initiate the secondary fermentation process, which creates the bubbles (carbonation) in the wine.

Fill clean champagne style bottles with the base wine and add a precise amount of liqueur de tirage to each bottle. Seal the bottles with temporary caps or closures to contain the pressure from carbonation.

Store the bottles horizontally in a cool, dark room, allowing the secondary fermentation to take place. During secondary fermentation, the added yeast consumes the added sugar, producing alcohol and carbon dioxide, which becomes trapped in the wine, creating bubbles.

The secondary fermentation typically lasts several weeks to several months, depending on factors such as temperature and desired level of effervescence.

After secondary fermentation, the wine is left to age on the lees (spent yeast cells) for an extended period. This ageing process, known as autolysis, contributes to the complexity and character of the sparkling wine, imparting flavours such as brioche, toast, and nuttiness.

To consolidate the lees in the neck of the bottle for removal, the bottles are gradually rotated and tilted in a process called riddling or remuage. Traditionally, this was done manually by turning and tilting the bottles, but modern methods use mechanical riddling machines.

Once the lees have been consolidated near the bottle neck, the bottles are chilled and the necks are frozen in a solution, forming a plug of frozen wine and lees.

The temporary caps are removed, and the pressure from the carbonation pushes out the frozen plug, expelling the lees. This process is called disgorging.

After disgorging, a small amount of wine and sugar solution, known as the dosage, is added to each bottle to adjust sweetness levels and balance the acidity of the wine. The amount of sugar in the dosage determines the sweetness level of the final sparkling wine.

The bottles are corked using champagne corks and wire cages. These are available from home winemaking shops. The sparkling wine is then aged for a period of time, allowing the wine to integrate and develop further in flavour and complexity. The length of ageing can vary depending on the style of sparkling wine being produced.

2. Natural Carbonation through a secondary fermentation. This is a simpler method to achieve carbonation through a secondary fermentation. It does, however, create a small sediment in the bottles so care has to be taken when pouring.

To follow this secondary fermentation route, once clear, syphon the wine from any sediment into bottles that are designed to hold fizzy drinks. Your homebrew shop can supply either champagne style bottles with corks/cages or alternatively PET style beer bottles (which are a cheaper option if you are not gifting the wine). Leave a 2cm space at the top of the bottle and add 2 brew fizz carbonation drops. Secure the bottles, shake them, then store in a warm place (24C/75F) for 7-10 days. Then move the bottles to a cool room to age them for a minimum of 3-6 months. Bottles should be carefully placed upright in a fridge to chill for 24 hours before drinking. Open the bottles carefully and gently pour the contents into glasses or a decanter in one process. This will avoid pouring out any fine sediment at the bottom of the bottle, which will inevitably form because of the carbonation process. This method is ideal if you wish to make a Cava style wine.

Making your own version of Cava:

It is possible to make your own version of Cava using the natural carbonation method.

Cava is a Spanish sparkling wine that is produced primarily in the Catalonia region, although it is also made in other parts of Spain. It is made using the traditional method (similar to Champagne), where secondary fermentation occurs in the bottle, resulting in fine bubbles and complex flavours.

Cava is typically made from a blend of indigenous Spanish grape varieties grown in Catalonia, including Macabeo, Xarel.lo, and Parellada. Other grape varieties such as Chardonnay and Pinot Grigio may also be used, although to a lesser extent. Chardonnay and Pinot Grigio are the best wine kit styles to use if you are trying to copy the Cava style. You may wish to experiment with a blend of these two styles.

Cava is known for its crisp acidity, lively bubbles, and vibrant fruit flavours. It often exhibits notes of green apple, citrus, pear, and stone fruits, with hints of toasted bread, nuts, and floral aromas. The ageing process on lees adds complexity and richness to the wine, contributing to its distinctive character.

Cava is classified into several categories based on ageing requirements:

Cava: The standard category for Cava, which has undergone a minimum of nine months of aging on lees.

Cava Reserva: Cava that has been aged for a minimum of 15 months on lees.

Cava Gran Reserva: The highest category for Cava, which has been aged for a minimum of 30 months on lees. These wines tend to be more complex and expressive, with greater depth of flavour and aging potential.

Cava is best served chilled, typically between 6-8°C (42-46°F), in flute or tulip-shaped glasses to preserve its effervescence and aromas. It is a versatile wine that pairs well with a variety of foods, including seafood, poultry, tapas, charcuterie, and light pasta dishes. Its acidity and bubbles make it a refreshing accompaniment to a wide range of cuisines and occasions.

Cava is one of the most popular sparkling wines in the world and is widely exported to markets around the globe. It offers excellent value for its quality and is often seen as an affordable alternative to Champagne. In recent years, there has been a growing interest in premium and aged Cavas, particularly Cava Gran Reserva, as consumers seek out wines with greater complexity, character, and ageing potential.

3. Forced Carbonation. This process requires a little more equipment and access to a source of CO2 gas. If you make beer, then you may already have this equipment. This method allows you to achieve a commercial clarity as you can still sulphite the wine and filter it at the end of fermentation. Following the fining stage, filter your wine through a Vinbrite Wine Filter to achieve a professional clarity. Then syphon the wine into a 5-litre mini-keg, or corny keg (available in 9, 12, and 19 litres sizes) and fit a regulator connected to a CO2 cylinder. Force-carbonate the wine to a pressure of around 25-30 psi. Leave under pressure for 7-10 days. Allow the wine to bulk age in the keg for 3-6 months in a cool room. Then chill down the keg and return the pressure to 25psi for 2 days before drinking to allow the wine to absorb the gas.

Alternatively, a 5-litre party keg, fitted with a top dispensing tap/gas injector can be used. This is a simpler option that uses a small 16g CO2 gas bulb. There is some scope to adjust the gas flow but not to the same degree as with a mini keg.

A useful calculator can be found at https://www.hopsteiner.com/uk/psi-calculator/. The carbonation level of sparkling wines must reach a level greater than 2 volumes of CO2 to be classed as 'sparkling wine'. As a guide, champagne normally contains 4 volumes of CO2. The lower you can reduce the temperature; the more effective force-carbonation will be.

It is possible to experiment and turn any matured wine into a sparkling wine using the force-carbonation technique. Simply pour the wine as quickly and smoothly as possible into a pressurised keg. Then purge any air from kegs immediately the wine is transferred into them. This is achieved by adding CO2 and then releasing the purge valve for a second or two. The first burst of gas out will be air and only CO2 should then remain over the wine, preventing any subsequent oxygen or bacterial spoilage which could otherwise occur from the air contact.

Making your own version of Prosecco:

By adopting the forced carbonation method, it is quite easy to make your own tribute to Prosecco.

Prosecco is a popular sparkling wine that originates from the Veneto region of Italy, specifically from the areas around the towns of Conegliano and Valdobbiadene. It is made primarily from the Glera grape variety, although small amounts of other grape varieties such as Verdiso, Bianchetta Trevigiana, Perera, and Glera Lunga may also be used. Prosecco is known for its fresh and fruity flavours, delicate bubbles, and approachable style, making it a favourite among wine lovers worldwide.

Prosecco is typically made using the forced carbonation method. They refer to it as the Charmat method (or the tank method), in which the secondary fermentation, responsible for creating the bubbles, takes place in large, pressurised stainless-steel tanks rather than individual bottles. This method allows for a more cost-effective and efficient production process, resulting in a fresher and fruitier style of sparkling wine compared to traditional method sparkling wines like Champagne.

Prosecco is known for its vibrant and fruit-forward flavours, which often include notes of green apple, pear, citrus, white peach, and floral aromas such as acacia and wisteria. It tends to be lighter in body and less yeasty than traditional method sparkling wines, with a crisp acidity and a clean, refreshing finish. The best way of achieving this finish is by choosing a wine kit as a base, which matches these characteristics. Whilst it is feasible to use grapes, it may be more difficult to match these precisely with the characteristics of Prosecco.

You should also consider your final level of sweetness. Commercial Prosecco is classified into several categories based on sweetness levels:

Prosecco DOC (Denominazione di Origine Controllata): This is the most common designation for Prosecco and includes a range of sweetness levels from Brut (dry) to Extra Dry (slightly sweet) and Dry (semi-sweet).

Prosecco Superiore DOCG (Denominazione di Origine Controllata e Garantita): This designation applies to Prosecco wines produced in the premium growing areas of Conegliano-Valdobbiadene and Asolo. These wines are typically higher in quality and may have more nuanced flavours and aromas.

Cartizze: Cartizze is a prestigious sub-zone within the Prosecco Superiore DOCG area known for producing some of the finest and most sought-after Prosecco wines. Wines from Cartizze are often labelled as such and are considered to be among the highest quality expressions of Prosecco.

Prosecco is best served chilled, typically between 6-8°C (42-46°F), in tulip-shaped glasses to preserve its delicate aromas and effervescence.

It is a versatile wine that can be enjoyed on its own as an apéritif or paired with a variety of dishes, including seafood, salads, light pasta dishes, appetisers, and mild cheeses. Its bright acidity and fruitiness make it an excellent accompaniment to a wide range of cuisines.

Prosecco has experienced a surge in popularity in recent years, driven by its accessibility, affordability, and consumer-friendly style. It is widely available and is often favoured for casual gatherings, celebrations, and everyday enjoyment.

The global demand for Prosecco continues to grow, with exports from Italy reaching record levels and producers exploring new markets and opportunities to meet the increasing demand for this beloved sparkling wine. Overall, Prosecco is cherished for its lively and approachable character. It's refreshing flavours, effervescence, and affordability have earned it a permanent place in the hearts of modern wine enthusiasts.

Commercial Prosecco is increasingly being served in bars from carbonated kegs. However, to protect the brand identity the wine is only allowed to be called Prosecco if it is supplied in a bottle. The keg version of the wine is known as Frizzante.

In the recipe section, there are some delicious recipes for making sparkling wines, together with variations using flowers and fruits. These make delightful summer drinks and are also excellent as a base for mixers and cocktails.

Chapter 7. Making Cider:

Cider holds a significant place in British drinking culture and is enjoying a resurgence in popularity. In recent years, there has been a noticeable increase in cider consumption across the UK, driven by changing consumer preferences, the availability of craft and artisanal ciders, and innovative cider styles. There is also an increase in cider's popularity in the USA, where non-fermented (non-alcoholic) apple juice is referred to as cider, and the alcoholic version is known as hard cider. From the crisp English ciders to the sweeter American versions, and not forgetting the traditional Spanish 'sidra', each region has its unique take on this age-old beverage.

Cider has been produced in the UK for centuries, with a long history of cidermaking in regions such as the West Country (Devon, Somerset, and Herefordshire). Cidermaking has deep roots in rural communities, where orchards abound, and cider festivals and events are held to celebrate the harvest and showcase local cider producers. British cider has gained international recognition and is exported to countries around the world, boosting the UK's reputation as a cider-producing nation.

Besides being a delightful drink cider has some potential health benefits too. Cider contains vitamins and minerals, predominantly potassium. It's also a source of antioxidants, thanks to the apples. Research has shown that cider, like wine, contains polyphenolic compounds that can be beneficial for heart health. But remember, moderation is key!

The rise of the craft cider movement has brought attention to small-scale cider producers and their traditional methods of cidermaking, attracting consumers seeking authentic and artisanal beverages. This attention has brought it onto the radar of home winemakers and brewers, since it is quite easy to make cider using standard brewing equipment. Similarly to wine, cider can be made from kits (available from home brew shops) and there is a wide range of styles and fruit infusions available. Alternatively, it can be made from apples or apple juice. A wide range of cider styles, from traditional still and sparkling ciders to flavoured and fruit-infused varieties can be made. This diversity appeals to a broad spectrum of consumers with varying taste preferences. Cider kit producers are continually innovating and experimenting with new ingredients, techniques, and packaging formats to differentiate their products and appeal to modern consumers.

Making cider from kits is a convenient and straightforward way for beginners to start their cidermaking journey and for experienced cidermakers to produce consistent results with minimal effort. Cider kits typically contain all the necessary ingredients and instructions for making cider at home, including apple juice concentrate, yeast, and additives.

The process of making these kits is the same as for making a beer or wine. The juice is poured into a sanitised 22.5 litre (5-gallons) sanitised fermenter. Some kits may require additional sugar, which is dissolved into the juice. Then then water is added to make the solution up to 22.5 litres. Some hot water may be used to reach a final temperature around 22C (72F). Then stir in the sachet of yeast supplied with the kit. At this stage it is worth adding a sachet or dose of Pure Brew, which will condition the water and add a nutrient feed.

Fit a lid and airlock to the fermenter and leave in a warm place (22C/72F) until fermentation is complete. This is indicated by airlock activity ceasing and a final gravity below 1.008.

At this point you have choices to make. Your cider can be cloudy or clear, and scrumpy flat or sparkling. If you want a cloudy style, then do not use any finings. For clear ciders add a dose of Cider Clear or Cider Brite finings to the fermenter and leave in a cool place for a few days to clear.

For still ciders simply bottle or keg the cider and leave it for 2-3 weeks to mature before drinking. For sparkling ciders, syphon the cider into pressurised beer bottles and add 1-2 brew fizz carbonation drops per bottle (according to the amount of carbonation you prefer). Secure the caps and store the bottles in a warm place (24C/74F) for 5 days to carbonate. Then leave them in a cool place for 2 -3 weeks to condition and clear. It is recommended that the bottles are stored in a fridge for 2 days before drinking. Pour carefully as there will be a little sediment in the bottom of each bottle as a result of the secondary fermentation (conditioning process).

To make cider from apple juice it is important to select juice that is free from preservatives which could inhibit fermentation. Alternatively, you may prefer to use a press and extract juice from your own apples. To achieve this, cut apples into small pieces, which will help in juice extraction. Unlike wine, you need to extract the juice from the pulp when making cider. As a rough guide 9 kg (20 lbs) of apples will provide 1 gallon (4.5litres) of juice. A blend of different types of apples will give the best results and if possible, throw in a few crab-apples. If you have access to an apple press, add the apple segments into the press bag and press out the juice into a fermenter.

If you do not have a press or a fruit blender available, then crush the apples in a bucket using either a potato masher or a hefty wooden post. Then squeeze the juice through a muslin or nylon bag.

If you are seeking a scrumpy style, then put the crushed pulp and juice together into a fermenting bucket and cover with a cloth or a loose-fitting lid. Then add a crushed Campden tablet to kill off any wild yeast. After 24 hours stir the apples and add the yeast. Ferment in the bucket under the cloth for 2-3 days then strain through a muslin or nylon bag into a second fermenter.

If you are using pressed juice, then simply put the juice directly into the fermenter and fit an airlock and bung. Add a crushed Campden tablet (to kill off bacteria and wild yeast) and leave for 24 hours. Then stir well and add a sachet off Cider Yeast and a dose of Pectinaze. Then for either method, continue to ferment in a warm place (22C/72F) until bubbles stop emerging from the airlock. A hydrometer reading of below 1.008 will indicate the cider has finished fermenting. It can then be bottled or kegged following the same process as described above for cider kits.

One common issue you might encounter is cloudy cider. This is only an issue if you prefer a clear cider, and it can be caused by pectin in the apples. While it doesn't necessarily affect the taste, you can clear it up by adding Pectinaze at the start of your process.

Another typical problem is unusual smells. As cider ferments, it can sometimes emit a sulphur or rotten egg-like smell. This often happens when yeast is stressed due to a lack of nutrients or a rapid fermentation process. You can combat this issue by using Pure Brew or a yeast nutrient at the start of fermentation. If the smell emerges midway through, try gently stirring the cider to release the trapped gas.

Lastly, if your cider tastes too sweet or too dry, remember that this can be adjusted. If it's too sweet, additional yeast or time can help finish the fermentation process. If it's too dry, adding unfermented juice or a sweetener that won't ferment can help balance the flavours.

There are two recipes in the prizewinning recipes section of this book to make delicious ciders from apples. It is perfectly acceptable to swap the apples for pears. By definition you will then be making a perry rather than a cider.

Chapter 8. Blending Wines:

Blending wines is an art form that allows winemakers to create unique and delicious wines by combining different wines, grape varieties, or fruits. From the world-renowned Bordeaux blends to the nuanced Tempranillos' of Spain, blending plays a vital role in shaping the character and quality of wines.

Blending involves the careful selection and mixing of wines to achieve a desired style, balance, and complexity. It allows winemakers to enhance aromas, flavours, structure, and overall quality by synergising the unique characteristics of individual components.

Different grape varieties contribute distinct flavours, aromas, acidity, tannins, and mouthfeel to a wine. Understanding the characteristics of each grape variety is essential for creating balanced blends.

From a commercial perspective, wines from different vineyards or regions can offer diverse expressions due to variations in climate, soil, and viticultural practices. Blending wines from multiple vineyards or terroirs can add depth and complexity to the final blend. Blending wines from multiple vintages, known as "multi-vintage" or "non-vintage" blending, allows commercial winemakers to achieve consistency in style and quality, even in challenging growing seasons.

Experimentation is key to finding the perfect blend. Commercial winemakers conduct numerous tasting trials, adjusting blending ratios and components until the desired balance and character are achieved. They create small-scale blends in the cellar, tasting and evaluating each blend before scaling up to larger volumes. Tasting individual wine components (such as different grape varieties or vineyard lots) allows them to understand their unique characteristics and how they contribute to the final blend. Some wineries use computer software to analyse and simulate blending options, providing insights into potential blends and their projected characteristics.

Achieving balance between acidity, tannins, sweetness, and alcohol is essential for creating a harmonious blend that is neither too tart nor too heavy.

Blending different components should aim to add layers of flavour, aroma, and texture, enhancing the overall complexity and depth of the wine.

Maintaining consistency in style and quality across bottlings is crucial. Blending ensures continuity and reliability in the wine's profile. It should strive to create a seamless integration of components, where no single element dominates but instead works together in harmony to create a unified expression.

Bordeaux is renowned for its classic red blends, typically incorporating Cabernet Sauvignon, Merlot, Cabernet Franc, Petit Verdot, and Malbec. These blends vary in composition depending on the region within Bordeaux and the winemaker's style.

The Rhône Valley in France produces a diverse range of blends, from the Syrah-dominated wines of the Northern Rhône to the Grenache-based blends of the Southern Rhône (such as Châteauneuf-du-Pape).

Champagne Cuvées are crafted from blends of Chardonnay, Pinot Noir, and Pinot Meunier grapes, each contributing to the wine's structure, aroma, and flavour. The art of blending plays a critical role in achieving the signature elegance and complexity of Champagne.

You can experiment with blending wines at home using commercial wines as well as your home-made wines. Start with small quantities, even as small as a single wine glass and keep detailed notes to track blending ratios and preferences. This is a great way to gain experience. Remember that blending wines is both a science and an art, requiring technical expertise, sensory acuity, and creative intuition. Whether crafting a Bordeaux-style red blend, a Rose wine from a blend of white and red wines, or a Rhône-inspired GSM, mastering the art of blending opens endless possibilities for creating exceptional wines that delight the palate and captivate the senses.

New wine styles have developed through experimentation and careful blending processes. One success story is GSM. GSM, short for Grenache,

Syrah, and Mourvèdre, is a wine style originating from the Rhône Valley in France. It has since gained popularity in other wine regions around the world, particularly in Australia and the United States. In Australia, GSM are produced primarily in the McLaren Vale and Barossa Valley regions. In the United States, they are commonly made in California, particularly in regions such as Paso Robles and the Central Coast, where the Mediterranean climate is conducive to growing these grape varieties.

The blend typically combines these three grape varieties to create wines that are rich, full-bodied, and complex, with a wide array of flavours and aromas. Grenache is known for its ripe red fruit flavours, low tannins, and high alcohol content, Grenache contributes richness, sweetness, and warmth to GSM blends. Syrah (Shiraz) adds depth, structure, and complexity to the blend with its dark fruit flavours, peppery spice, and firm tannins. It contributes depth and intensity. Mourvèdre (Monastrell) contributes earthy, gamey notes, as well as dark fruit flavours and firm tannins. It adds structure, depth, and ageability to GSM blends.

GSM wine is gaining popularity in the UK and is now available in a wine kit, which produces results to match the commercial equivalent. Wine Expert offer GSM styles in their classic range. The grape blend in the kit includes red fruit notes (ripe cherry, raspberry, and strawberry) from Grenache; dark fruit (blackberry, plum, and blueberry) flavours from Syrah; and earthy, spicy undertones (leather, tobacco, cinnamon), and gamey notes from Mourvèdre. The combination of these elements in the kit creates a layered and complex wine with a balance of fruit, spice, and earthy nuances.

In France, Pinot Noir-Chardonnay Blends are very successful. Burgundy's renowned Pinot Noir and Chardonnay wines often showcase single varietal expressions. However, some producers create exceptional blends by combining these two grape varieties. These blends offer the best of both worlds, with Pinot Noir's elegance and Chardonnay's richness and complexity.

Rhone Valley Blends are also popular choices amongst wine connoisseurs. Rhône Valley wines, particularly those from the Southern Rhône, feature blends such as Châteauneuf-du-Pape (Grenache, Syrah, Mourvèdre, and others) and Côtes du Rhône (Grenache, Syrah, Mourvèdre). These blends showcase rich fruit, spice, and earthy complexity, with wines demonstrating exceptional balance.

Rioja Gran Reserva wines from Spain typically blend Tempranillo with small proportions of Garnacha, Graciano, and Mazuelo. These blends undergo extended ageing in oak barrels, resulting in wines with complex aromas, mature fruit flavours, and polished tannins.

Blending Wines made from Kits:

If you are producing homemade wines from kits and are building your supplies, some suggestions for selecting and blending kits would include:

Sauvignon Blanc and Chardonnay: Blending Sauvignon Blanc and Chardonnay can result in a delightful wine that combines the distinctive characteristics of both grape varieties. The Dark Rock Sauvignon Blanc kit produces a wine with a bright acidity, citrusy flavours, and herbaceous notes. It offers refreshing acidity, with aromas of grapefruit, lime, green apple, and grass. The SG Chardonnay kit is known for its versatility and ability to ferment in temperature conditions which fluctuate. It produces an unoaked wine with rich and creamy flavours, with notes of tropical fruit, and vanilla.

The blending ratio will depend on personal preference and the desired style of the final wine. Taste each wine separately to understand its individual characteristics. Take note of the acidity, fruit flavours, aroma, and mouthfeel of both the Sauvignon Blanc and Chardonnay. This will help you determine how to blend them effectively.

Then start by blending 30% Sauvignon Blanc and 70% Chardonnay in a wine glass and adjust the ratio according to taste. Mix the Sauvignon Blanc and Chardonnay together in the glass and stir gently to ensure thorough blending. Taste the blend periodically as you mix to assess the flavour profile and adjust as needed. Use a plastic graduated syringe to achieve accurate measures, and experiment with different blending ratios to achieve the desired balance of acidity, fruitiness, and texture. When you are happy with the ratios then scale up the quantities for the final batch.

The resulting blend of your Sauvignon Blanc and Chardonnay should offer a harmonious combination of bright acidity, citrusy notes, and tropical fruit flavours from the Sauvignon Blanc, complemented by the richness, body, and creamy texture of the Chardonnay.

Depending on the final ratio, you can create a wine that is crisp and refreshing, with zesty citrus flavours and a hint of minerality, or a wine that is fuller-bodied, with ripe tropical fruit flavours and a creamy mouthfeel.

The wine will benefit from short to medium-term ageing in the bottle to allow the flavours to integrate and develop complexity.

Pinot Grigio and Riesling: Blending Pinot Grigio with Riesling can create a delightful white wine that combines the crisp acidity and delicate flavours of Pinot Grigio with the aromatic intensity and fruity sweetness of Riesling. For this blend make an On the House Riesling Kit. This produces a white wine with an aromatic intensity, vibrant acidity, flavours of citrus, stone fruit, and honey. It is a smooth medium white wine. The second wine is an SG Wines Platinum Pinot Grigio kit. This kit produces a wine with a light body, crisp acidity, and subtle flavours of citrus, green apple, and pear. It typically produces dry wine with a clean, refreshing finish.

Once each kit is completed and filtered, taste each wine separately to understand its individual characteristics. Take note of the acidity, fruit flavours, aroma, and mouthfeel of both the Pinot Grigio and Riesling. This will help you determine how to blend them effectively. The blending ratio of Pinot Grigio and Riesling will depend on personal preference, the characteristics of each wine, and the desired style of the final blend. A common ratio is around 70-80% Pinot Grigio and 20-30% Riesling, but this will vary based on your taste preference.

Start by blending small amounts in a glass and experiment with different blending ratios to achieve the desired balance of acidity, sweetness, and flavour intensity.

The ideal blend of should provide a combination of crisp acidity, delicate fruit flavours, and aromatic intensity. The Pinot Grigio provides a clean, refreshing backbone, while the Riesling adds floral and fruity notes, as well as a hint of sweetness. Depending on your final blending ratio, you can create a wine that is dry and refreshing, with vibrant citrus and green apple flavours (with a higher Pinot Grigio content), or one that is slightly less dry, with hints of peach, apricot, and honey (with a higher Riesling content).

This blend is typically best enjoyed young and fresh to preserve its vibrant acidity and fruit flavours. However, it may benefit from short-term ageing for 3-6 months in the bottle to allow the flavours to integrate and develop complexity.

Cabernet Sauvignon and Merlot: Blending Cabernet Sauvignon and Merlot is a classic combination that is widely practiced in winemaking, particularly in Bordeaux-style blends. The Wine Expert Cabernet Sauvignon kit produces a wine with bold flavours, firm tannins, and ageing potential. It offers dark fruit flavours such as blackcurrant, blackberry, and plum. The Dark Rock Merlot kit produces a wine with a soft, approachable character and smooth texture. It features flavours of ripe red and black fruits such as cherry, plum, and raspberry, with hints of tobacco, and chocolate.

For this blend Make a Wine Expert Reserve Cabernet Sauvignon and a Dark Rock Merlot kit. Once the wines have been cleared and filtered blend on the basis of 70% Cabernet Sauvignon to 30% Merlot. The Cabernet Sauvignon will provide softness and character, which will be complimented by the tobacco notes, fruitiness, and body of the Merlot.

First, taste each wine separately to understand its individual characteristics. Take note of the tannins, acidity, fruit flavours, aroma, and mouthfeel of both the Cabernet Sauvignon and Merlot. This will help you determine how to blend them effectively. Blend a small batch in a wine glass and tweak the ratios if necessary to achieve the desired flavour profile. The resulting blend of Cabernet Sauvignon and Merlot should offer bold fruit flavours, firm tannins, and smooth texture. The Cabernet Sauvignon provides structure, depth, and ageing potential, while the Merlot contributes richness, and softness. Your goal is to create a wine that is full-bodied, with ripe dark fruit flavours, integrated tannins, and a long, satisfying finish.

This blend will benefit from ageing in bulk with the addition of oak chunks. This will provide a roundness and allow the flavours to integrate and develop complexity. It has the potential to age gracefully for up to a year, softening tannins and gaining complexity with time.

Rioja and Tempranillo: Blending Rioja wine with Tempranillo will result in a wine with a unique character and flavour profile. Tempranillo is the primary grape variety used in Rioja wines but blending it with other grapes or different styles of Rioja can create a wine with enhanced complexity and depth. Rioja is a wine region in Spain known for producing high-quality red wines primarily from the Tempranillo grape. Rioja is Spain in a glass, it owes its name to one of the seven rivers that meander their way through the area's mountainous north, where the vineyard-lined valley is home to a variety of grapes. Rioja wines can vary in style from young and fruity (Joven), to oak barrel aged (Crianza, Reserva, and Gran Reserva), each offering different levels of complexity, tannins, and ageing potential. Tempranillo is the dominant grape variety in Rioja wines, known for its deep colour, bold fruit flavours, and firm tannins. The Dark Rock Tempranillo kit produces a wine with aromas and flavours of dark berries, plum, cherry, tobacco, and spices, with a characteristic earthy undertone. Beaverdale Rojo Tinto is a dry wine full of black fruit flavours with hints of vanilla, spice and oak. It has a blend of Tempranillo and Garnache grapes. The Garnache grapes give colour and power to the wine.

Make both kits and once completed and filtered taste each wine to appreciate the individual qualities. Then blend in the same way as described above. A blend of 70% Rioja and 30% Tempranillo will provide a harmonious combination of ripe fruit flavours, structured tannins, and complex aromas. The Rojo Tinto wine will contribute oak-derived flavours such as vanilla, spice, and toast, while the Tempranillo adds depth, richness, and intensity.

This ratio will create a wine that is youthful and fruit-forward. For a style that is more mature, with layered flavours and a long, lingering finish, use an 80% Rioja: 20% Tempranillo blend and mature in bulk on oak chunks for 6-12 months.

Malbec and Shiraz: Malbec, known for its deep colour and rich, fruity flavours, can be blended with various other wines to enhance its characteristics or create more complex blends. It works well with Merlot, Cabernet Sauvignon, and Shiraz. This blend focuses on Shiraz, also known as Syrah, which is the oldest vine/grape type. Shiraz contributes peppery spice, dark berry flavours, and a hint of smokiness to a blend. Blending Shiraz with Malbec will result in a bold, full-bodied wine with layers of flavour and a long, satisfying finish.

You should try to choose high-quality Shiraz and Malbec wine kits for blending. Look for wines that showcase the typical characteristics of each grape variety, such as Shiraz's peppery spice and dark berry flavours, and Malbec's deep colour and rich fruitiness. Wine Expert's Reserve range produce excellent wines, which compare to commercial equivalents of around £15. This is a really good blend to produce in March/April in preparation for Christmas. Make one Wine Expert Reserve Malbec and one Wine Expert Reserve Shiraz. Once they have finished fermenting, stabilise and clear them, then pass them through a Vinbrite Filter to achieve a rich commercial clarity.

Taste each wine individually to assess its aroma, flavour, acidity, tannin structure, and overall balance. Take notes on the characteristics of each wine and consider how they might complement or enhance one another when blended.

Start by blending small quantities of the Shiraz and Malbec wines in a wine glass using different ratios to see how they interact. Begin with equal parts of each wine and gradually adjust the proportions until you achieve your preferred flavour profile.

Keep in mind that blending Shiraz and Malbec can produce a wide range of flavour combinations, from bold and spicy to smooth and fruit-forward. Experimentation is key to finding the blend that best suits your taste preferences.

Taste the blended wine as you go, adjusting the proportions if necessary to achieve the desired balance of flavours.

After blending, allow the wine to rest for a short period to allow the flavours to meld together. This can be done by resealing the container and letting it sit at room temperature for several hours or overnight. Taste the blended wine again after resting to see if any further adjustments are needed. If necessary, fine-tune the blend by adding small quantities of either Shiraz or Malbec to adjust the flavour profile. Pay attention to how each addition affects the overall balance of the wine. Make a note of the proportions used and when you are happy with the final ratios scale up the quantities to blend depending on the number of bottles you want to make.

You do not need to blend the whole batch. For variation, keep some bottles as pure Malbec, some as pure Shiraz, and some as a blend. That way you will build up a variety of bottles in your wine collection. These wines will benefit from a longer maturation time to fully age them. Ideally, they should be matured for 9-12 months before drinking, to reach their best.

Blending Wines made from Craft Country Wines:

Blending craft country wines can be a rewarding way to create unique and flavourful drinks. Craft wines, also known as country wines or non-grape wines, are made from fruits other than grapes. These can include wines made from elderberries, dandelions, rhubarb, or even vegetables like pumpkin or beetroot. Country wines can contribute unique flavours and textures to a blend, adding complexity and depth.

Fruit wines made from berries (such as elderberry, raspberry, blackberry, or strawberry), stone fruits (such as peach or plum), or other fruits (such as apple or pear) can offer vibrant flavours and aromas that can complement or enhance other wines in a blend. These wines can add acidity, sweetness, or fruitiness to the final blend. They can be blended successfully with kit wines but start with a ratio of 80% kit wine to 20% fruit wine, to avoid masking the subtle flavours from the grapes.

When blending two fruit wines taste each one individually and make a note of the strength of their flavours, colours, and aromas. Rank them on a scale of 1-10. Try to achieve a good balance in the final ratio where one fruit flavour does not overpower the other. Start with a 70:30 ratio where the 70% is contributed by the wine with the lowest ranking. Use a plastic syringe to record accurate measurements and start by blending small quantities in a wine glass. For white and rose wines it is useful to chill the blend in a glass when you feel you have the correct ratio. A chilled wine may present a different taste experience. The blending process requires patience. Once you are certain that the balance of flavours, aroma, acidity, and tannin is correct, then scale up the quantities to blend the rest of your wine.

When blending wines made from flowers (such as elderflowers, dandelions, rose petals etc) be aware of the contribution they can make and the subtlety of flavours and aromas. Some flowers, such as rose petals, are quite delicate but can add a refreshing and delicate aroma to blush wine blends. Others such as elderflowers, can provide a powerful punch so should be used with care. An elderflower wine is very useful to keep in stock as it blends well with other white wines to produce a distinctive flavour and aroma, that is reminiscent of German Rhine style wines. It is very effective when blended with Riesling, Gewurztraminer, and Liebfraumilch wines. Start with a 10% ratio of elderflower wine and increase the amount according to your preference.

Wines made from vegetables and cereals (such as carrot, rice, wheat, barley, parsnip) can provide body and mouthfeel to blends. They are also useful when making fortified wines to add robustness and strength. However, their flavour can easily overpower more subtle wines so be careful with ratios and make sure there is a match between the flavours, aromas, acidity, and tannin content of each wine. Use the 1-10 scale and consider the balance. Blend small amounts and be prepared to abandon the experiment if the blend does not work well.

Mead can be a versatile component in wine blending. Depending on the type of honey used and any additional flavourings (such as fruits or spices), mead can offer sweetness, floral notes, or herbal aromas that can complement other wines in a blend.

Wines infused with herbs, spices, or botanicals can add complexity and aromatic depth to a blend. Herbal wines, such as those made with lavender, rosemary, or chamomile, can provide floral notes and subtle herbal nuances. Spiced wines, such as mulled wine or spiced apple wine, can offer warming spices like cinnamon, cloves, or nutmeg. It is possible to buy mulled wine infusions which can be added to red wine to produce a delicious Christmas drink. There is a fantastic recipe for producing mulled wine in the recipe section of this book.

Fortified wines, such as port-style wines or sherry-style wines, can add richness, sweetness, and complexity to a blend. Fortification with distilled spirits like brandy or neutral spirits can increase alcohol content and enhance the wine's ageing potential. These wines can be used to add depth and structure to a blend.

Blending red and white wines together can result in unique and innovative blends that offer a balance of fruitiness, acidity, and tannins. For example, blending a fruity red wine with a crisp white wine can create a refreshing and aromatic rosé-style blend. Experimenting with different blending ratios can yield exciting results. Start with 70% white wine to 30% red wine and increase the red to achieve a fuller, deeper flavour and colour. If necessary, add some brewer's glycerine if you prefer a medium-sweet rosé style.

Aged wines, whether homemade or commercially produced, can bring complexity and maturity to a blend. Wines that have been aged in oak barrels or bottles for several years can develop nuanced flavours, smooth tannins, and integrated aromas that can enhance the overall character of a blend. Don't be afraid to blend your home-made wine with a commercial bottle. This is a great way to experiment. Keep the commercial bottle and conduct a psychological experiment. Pour half of the final blend into the commercial bottle and half into a home-made wine bottle. Then pour your friends a drink from each and ask them to do a taste test. Nine times out of ten they will say they prefer the wine from the commercial bottle, even though it is exactly the same wine. That demonstrates the power of perception and branding!

Occasionally you might make a wine which is too sweet for the style or your preference. This may have been due to the fermentation stopping prematurely. If this occurs, then you should still stabilise and clear the wine as normal. Then it can be blended with a drier wine to eliminate the sweetness. The correct ratio will depend on the amount of sugar in the wine and the finish you are seeking. Start by mixing small, calculated quantities in a wine glass until you reach your preferred taste. Then scale up the quantities to blend the rest of the batch. This process can also be used to smoothen or sweeten a wine which you feel is too dry for your palate. It is an alternative to adding wine sweetener or brewers' glycerine.

In conclusion, blending is a useful process for rescuing wines that do not meet your expectation, or to fine tune flavours to bring out the best characteristics in two or more styles. It is also good fun and can add an extra dimension to your winemaking. As you build up your knowledge of different wine styles and develop your palate, blending will become an art form. When blending homemade wines, it is essential to taste each component individually and experiment with different ratios to achieve the desired flavour profile and balance. Keeping detailed notes throughout the blending process is vital as it can help you replicate successful blends in the future and refine your blending techniques over time. Sods law states that your best blend ever will be the one you forgot to record!

Chapter 9. Ageing and Maturing Wine:

Ageing and maturing wine is a crucial step in the winemaking process that allows the flavours to meld, develop complexity, and ensures a smoother, more refined drink. Ultimately, patience is the key. Craft wines benefit from extended ageing and will improve with time. Some wines, especially fruits with high tannin contents content (or complex ingredients), or those with a higher alcohol, may take twelve months or more to reach their peak. The benefit of having a scheduled production process will mean that you are not itching to try a young wine because of a shortage of stock. It is accepted that it will take a while for new winemakers to reach that point, so it is a good idea to make early batches of styles, such as kit wines, that have shorter maturation periods.

A key consideration is how to store your wine once it is stabilised and filtered. The choices are basically to bottle age or barrel age it. Both methods have their merits. Barrel ageing allows the wine to mature in bulk, and there is some evidence to suggest that bulk ageing is more effective. It does have the added advantage of enabling the wine to come into contact with oak if desired.

Barrel ageing involves transferring your wine to a suitable ageing vessel, such as plastic or glass carboys, stainless steel tanks or oak barrels. Oak barrels are an excellent choice as they will add vanillin, tannin, and flavour to the wine, in much the same way that they do to malt whiskies. If you cannot acquire an oak barrel, then the addition of oak chunks to the carboy will provide a similar (if less enhanced) contribution.

Ensure that the vessel is properly sanitised to prevent contamination and that it can be sealed effectively. Where possible fit a pressure blow off valve, airlock, or a safety cork to release any unexpected pressure build up. It is important to minimise exposure to oxygen during ageing, as this can lead to oxidation and off-flavours.

Store your ageing wine in a cool, stable environment. Ideally the temperature should be as close to 13C (55F) as possible during the maturation period. Fluctuations in temperature can affect the ageing process. It is important to avoid extreme heat or cold, as it can have a negative impact on the flavours. Therefore, storing wine away in your house loft is not a good idea as the loft will be very cold in winter and very hot during the height of summer.

It is good practice to avoid a large air space above the barrelled wine to prevent oxidation. After filling barrels with wine sprinkle half a crushed Campden tablet over the surface before sealing the container. If you are using a stainless-steel pressure keg, purge the air space with CO_2 to create a pure environment. Try to minimise the number of times the barrel/carboy is opened during maturation as this will introduce oxygen in. That said, it will be necessary to taste the wine periodically to decide when to end bulk ageing and bottle the wine.

The alternative to barrel ageing is to bottle your wine directly after clearing and allow it to mature in its final bottle. The benefits of bottle maturing are that it may be easier to store and there is a lower risk of oxidation or spoilage through bacterial airborne contact. It is easier to sample your wine at various stages to decide the optimum maturation period, without exposing the rest of the batch to air. However, the ageing process may not be so effective as it is for barrel ageing, and it is not possible to add oak chunks to bottles. Furthermore, if any post-fermentation occurs this may mean bottles have to be emptied back into a fermenter to enable the subsequent activity to ferment out. Nevertheless, the simplicity and straightforward process of bottle ageing makes it the preferred choice of many winemakers. When bottling, label your bottles with the batch details and ageing dates. Keep detailed records of the ingredients, fermentation process, and any adjustments made during ageing. This information can be valuable for future batches.

Some winemakers prefer to store their wine in a wine box for convenience. Wine boxes have advantages in that the wine is faster to transfer from the fermenter and you can pour off any volume to suit your needs. As wine is dispensed from a wine box, the inner bag shrinks around the wine preventing any air contamination. Wine boxes are available in a range of sizes from 5-20 litres. It is recommended that wine stored in a wine box is consumed within 6 months.

It is important to regularly monitor your wine during ageing to determine the optimum maturation time. This should be around 3-12 months depending on factors such as the alcohol content. Some basic kit wines may be ready to drink after a few weeks. They are best consumed early as they will not benefit from long-term ageing.

Taste samples periodically to track the changes in flavour, aroma, and overall character. This will help you determine the optimal ageing period. At the start the wine may taste harsh, or astringent, but through ageing the taste can change out of all recognition and provide you with a final product which will impress you, your family, and your friends.

Remember that each wine is unique, and the optimal ageing time can vary based on the recipe and personal preferences. Experimentation and careful monitoring will help determine the ideal maturation period for your specific wine. Specific recipes will provide guidance on likely maturation times for their style.

Finally, it is time to savour the fruits of your labour. Pour a glass, appreciate the aromas, and enjoy the unique taste of your homemade wine.

Chapter 10. Bottling and labelling your Wine:

Bottling and labelling your homemade wine is the final step in the winemaking process, marking the culmination of your efforts and preparing your wine for enjoyment and sharing. Appearance of the wine is important and showcasing your finished product in the correct bottle, with a label and shrink top closure can make it indistinguishable from a commercial wine. Wine bottles are available from home brew shops in 70cl size and in a clear or green finish. A green finish will prevent colour erosion in red wines, but the final choice of bottle is down to your own preference. The choice of bottle colour amongst commercial wine producers is influenced by cultural or regional preferences, with certain wine-producing regions favouring specific colours based on tradition or market expectations.

Clear glass bottles allow the wine's colour and clarity to be fully visible, making them ideal for showcasing pale-coloured wines such as whites, rosés, and some lighter reds. However, clear bottles offer less protection against light exposure, which can lead to premature ageing or degradation of the wine's flavours and aromas.

Green glass bottles provide greater protection against light exposure and are often used for wines that require longer ageing, such as premium white wines, full-bodied reds, and fortified wines. Green bottles are also favoured for sparkling wines, as they help preserve the wine's freshness and carbonation. However, it is important that sparkling wines are bottled in champagne style bottles which are capable of holding the pressure.

Speeding up the Bottling Process:

It is important to sanitise bottles before use to prevent wine spoilage. However, the process of sanitising 30 bottles for a five-gallon batch can be time consuming and off putting for many winemakers. However, it can be made easier and faster by using a bottle washer and bottle drainer.

A bottle washer makes sterilising bottles a doddle. Simply add a No Rinse sanitising solution to the base of the washer, place the wine bottle neck over the centre stem and push down a few times. This sprays the sanitiser onto all surfaces of the bottle. Just a few quick pumps will sanitise all the inner parts of the bottles.

The bottle washer is usually used in combination with a bottle drainer, which helps to speed up the process. Simply store your sanitised bottles on the tree, and the liquid drains away into the collecting base. Any liquid in the bottle will drain out and fall in the base, which has a recessed well to stop any spills onto work surfaces. The layers stack on each other, so you can choose the number of layers you need, according to the amount of wine being bottled.

Bottle Closures:

Traditional bottles require a cork to be fitted to secure them. Three styles of corks are available to home winemakers:

Plastic topped corks can be easily removed and replaced if some wine is left in the bottle. Bottles secured with these corks should be stored upright rather than in a wine rack to avoid any leakage over a prolonged period of time. There can be some latitude in the size of bottle necks so make sure that there is a match between the size of the cork and your bottle.

Tapered corks look like standard wine corks. However, they are easier to fit and do not need to be applied using a corking tool. They are removed with a cork screw. They often do not have a wax coating on the outside, so may need to be pre-soaked for 20 minutes in warm water. before use. This makes the cork more supple and allows it to be inserted further into the bottleneck. When using tapered corks it is recommended that wine bottles are stored upright and not laid down in a wine rack as the seal will not be as secure as straight corks. They are not recommended for use on screw-top bottles.

Straight corks are the most secure fit but need to be applied using a corking tool. When storing wine over a few months or more, ideally bottles should be laid down in a wine rack. This keeps the cork moist and stops it drying out, keeping the wine inside away from the air. Only straight corks should be used if you intend to lay the wine down, as all of the cork is pressed against the bottleneck making a good seal. Straight corks usually have a natural wax coating on the outside, making them easy to insert in the bottles. There is no soaking required with these corks, they can be inserted into the bottles directly using a corking tool.

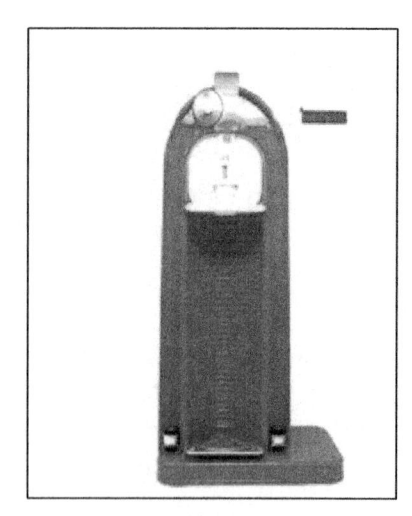

Two popular Corking Tools for fitting straight corks: a Two Handled Corker and Bench Style Corker

Once corked, a shrink seal can be secured over the top to give the wine a professional appearance. These are available in a variety of colours from home winemaking shops. They are shrunk onto the bottle using the steam from a kettle. Shrink seals are a great way of finishing off your wine bottles appearance.

Finally, add a label to the bottle to identify the batch. Create or select labels that reflect the personality and style of your wine, incorporating elements such as the wine's name, grape variety, vintage, and any relevant graphics or imagery. Wine bottle labels can be purchased from home winemaking stores or you may choose to use label designing software to produce your own. https://www.winelabelizer.com provides a useful tool for designing wine labels. Alternatively, a range of easy-removal labels are available from www.darkrockbrewing.co.uk

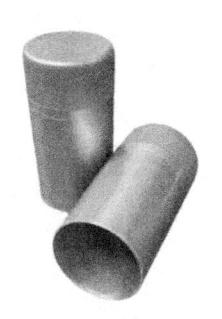

It is possible to reuse commercial screw-top wine bottles. They can be secured with a Novatwist screw cap and seal, which are available in a variety of colours. Carefully remove the original metal or plastic seal and push/screw the Novatwist onto the bottle to secure. Once fitted the bottle can be used again later using the same closure.

When bottling, it is important to ensure that all equipment, including bottles, corks or caps, siphoning tools, and bottling equipment, is thoroughly cleaned and sanitised prior to use.

If the wine has sediment or haze it will not look appealing so make sure it has been fined and filtered to clarify it before bottling, to ensure a crystal clear and visually appealing final product.

Also make sure your wine has been stabilised by adding sulphites or other preservatives to inhibit microbial growth and oxidation, ensuring it remains stable during storage and ageing.

Transfer the wine from the fermentation vessel to clean bottles using a syphon tube, automatic syphon or racking cane, being careful to minimise exposure to oxygen and sediment. Fill each bottle with wine, leaving an appropriate amount of headspace (typically ½ to 1 inch) at the top to allow for expansion and contraction during storage.

If you are planning to mature your wine for more than 3-6 months, then fit straight corks and store bottles horizontally to keep the cork moist and prevent it from drying out (which could lead to air leakage and oxidation over time). Try to store your wine in a cool, dark, and stable environment, such as a cellar or wine fridge, to allow ageing and preserve freshness and flavour. Avoid areas where there are likely to be wide temperature fluctuations, such as loft spaces.

Chapter 11. Advanced Winemaking Techniques and Equipment:

Once you have mastered the basics of winemaking and have some successes under your belt, there are some areas that can be examined in greater depth to improve the quality and consistency of your wines. Other items of equipment are also available that will elevate your enjoyment of the hobby. These will be explored further in this section.

Acid Balance:

pH is a measure of the acidity or basicity of a solution. In winemaking, pH levels influence microbial stability, colour stability, and taste perception. Titratable Acidity (TA): TA refers to the total concentration of acids in the wine, primarily tartaric, malic, and sometimes citric acids. It is measured in grams per litre (g/L) of tartaric acid equivalent.

Ensuring the right balance of acid at the start of fermentation is the first step to success. Most wines fall around a pH reading of 3 or 4. For white wines, a desirable reading is a pH of approximately 3.2, while the best pH for red wines is around 3.6. The ideal pH reading for cider is between 3.2 – 3.6. A weaker acid content of pH 4.0 or above can lead to flavour problems and make the juice more prone to bacterial infection.

If your juice has too much acid, you will need to reduce it with Acid Reducer so that you achieve a healthy fermentation and produce a better tasting drink. Acid Reducer is a fine powder of Calcium Carbonate (Precipitated Chalk) that is added to the Wine or Cider, at a starting rate of 7g per 5 litres (1gallon). This will reduce the acidity by around 1.5 ppt (part per thousand). When added, it will release CO_2 (carbon dioxide) as a gas as it neutralises the acid and it may also foam up, so ensure there is sufficient head space in the container before adding. Sometimes this process can also produce sediment as the acid is neutralised so if added to a finished Wine or Cider, leave it in a cold place for one week to allow any acid crystals to fall out as sediment.

If your wine or cider lacks acid, then you can increase the acid content by adding either Acid Blend or Lactic Acid. Lactic acid is a by-product of fermentation and is always present in trace amounts in any wine, or cider. Using lactic acid to increase wine acidity is a technique frequently employed by winemakers to adjust the pH and overall acidity levels of a wine. Lactic acid, often associated with the creamy taste found in dairy products, can be added to wine to increase its acidity without significantly altering its flavour profile.

Before adjusting acidity, perform a comprehensive analysis of the wine's pH and TA using a wine testing kit or by sending samples to a laboratory. This will provide crucial information for determining the extent of acid adjustment required.

Determine the desired pH and TA levels based on the wine style and varietal characteristics. Guidelines for ideal pH and TA levels vary depending on the wine type (e.g., white, red, rosé) and regional preferences.

Lactic acid solutions typically come in various strengths (e.g., 60% lactic acid). Calculate the volume of lactic acid solution needed to achieve the desired acidity adjustment based on the wine volume and target acidity levels. It is advisable to make incremental additions of lactic acid, testing the wine's pH and TA after each addition to avoid over-acidification.

After each acid addition, thoroughly mix the wine to ensure uniform distribution of the added lactic acid. Allow the wine to rest for a period of time (e.g., a few days to a week) to allow the added acid to integrate fully and for any sediment to settle. Conduct sensory evaluations to assess the impact of the acid adjustments on the wine's flavour profile. Consider factors such as taste balance, mouthfeel, and overall harmony. If necessary, make further adjustments to achieve the desired balance between acidity, fruitiness, and other flavour components.

It is a good idea to keep detailed records of the acid adjustment process, including the quantities of lactic acid added, the resulting pH and TA levels, and sensory observations. This documentation will be valuable for future reference and replication.

Exercise caution and precision when adding lactic acid to avoid over-acidification, which can lead to unbalanced or tart-tasting wines. Use a pH meter or pH test strips to measure the initial pH of the wine. Determine the target pH based on the wine style and varietal characteristics. Aim for a pH level that is appropriate for the specific type of wine you are making.

Pectin Reduction:

Pectin needs to be factored into craft winemaking since it can cause clearing problems. Pectin is a complex group of carbohydrates bonded together with sugars. These are present in most cell walls and are particularly abundant in the non-woody parts of plants. In human digestion, pectin binds to cholesterol in the gastrointestinal tract and slows glucose absorption by trapping carbohydrates. The main use for pectin is as a gelling agent, thickening agent and also a stabiliser in food. It gives the jelly-like consistency to jams or marmalades, which would otherwise be sweet juices.

All fruits and vegetables used in winemaking will contain some pectin. Ingredients such as pears, apples, damsons, guavas, quince, plums, gooseberries, oranges, and other citrus fruits contain large amounts of pectin. Conversely, soft fruits, such as cherries, grapes, and strawberries, contain only small amounts of pectin.

The pectin in the fruit will try to set the haze, making it cloudy, with a waxy haze. Traditional finings will not work if pectin is present since the pectin will surround the haze particles. Finings work by attaching to the haze particles, making them heavier and therefore fall down quicker. If the finings cannot attach to the particles, they will not work. By adding Pectinaze, the pectin will be destroyed so the wine or cider will be able to clear.

Pectinaze is a highly concentrated form of liquid Pectic Enzyme. It is supplied in an easy-to-use 15ml plastic bottle. The dose rate for wines and ciders is 10 drops per 5 litres (1 gallon). Each bottle contains enough enzyme to treat 20 gallons of wine or cider. It does not matter if you add too much, you cannot overdose on this enzyme, in fact, the more you use the faster it works. Pectinaze will remove both soluble and insoluble pectin as well as arabanes. Araban (Arabinoxylan) is a type of hemicellulase (xylanase) found in some plant cell walls & can cause cloudiness in juices.

Starch Reduction:

Starch is a type of carbohydrate. Its molecules are made up of large numbers of carbon, hydrogen, and oxygen atoms. Starch is a white solid at room temperature and does not dissolve in cold water. Most plants, including rice, potatoes, and wheat, store their energy as starch. This explains why these foods – and anything made from wheat flour – are high in starch.

Starch has many uses. Your body digests starch to make glucose, which is a vital energy source for every cell. Food companies use starch to thicken processed foods, and to make sweeteners. However, the starch in the ingredients used in winemaking can make your wine cloudy. Finings work by attaching to the haze particles, making them heavier and therefore fall down quicker. If the finings cannot attach to the particles, they will not work. By adding Amylase, the starch will be destroyed so the wine will be able to clear.

All fruits and vegetables used in winemaking will contain some starch. Ingredients such as bananas, potato, parsnip, rice, and wheat contain large amounts of starch, while unripe apples contain as much as 15% starch. Always try to use ripe fruit whenever possible. When making a wine from vegetables, always add Amylaze to the wine.

Amylaze is a highly concentrated form of liquid fungal alpha-amylase. It is supplied in an easy to use 15ml plastic bottle. The dose rate is 10 drops per 5 litres (1 gallon). It does not matter if you add too much, you cannot overdose on this enzyme, in fact, the more you use the faster it works. Each bottle contains enough enzyme to treat 20 gallons.

Pectin Test Kits:

Pectin test kits allow home winemakers to test all wines for presence of pectin, which is a major cause of cloudy wines. These kits also contain a treatment to eliminate any problems that are identified by the test. Each kit contains replaceable reagent, treatment solution, and a pipette and sample test tube to ensure accurate measurements are achieved.

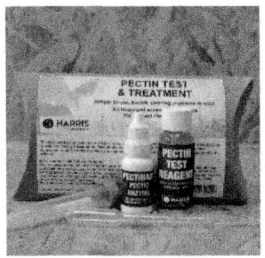

To test for pectin, add 1ml of wine to the test tube using the pipette. Then add 3ml of Pectin Test Reagent. Secure the test tube cap and shake for a few seconds. Leave for 30 minutes then view the solution against a light source. The presence of white sediment (sometimes white string like strands) or a white cloud in the solution indicates the presence of pectin. If untreated the wine may be difficult to clear. To treat the problem, add 10 drops of Pectinaze per gallon of wine (more may be added if necessary). For professional clarities, always filter your wine after treatment, through a Vinbrite Filter before bottling/storing.

Starch Test Kits:

Starch test kits allow home winemakers to test all craft country wines for the presence of Starch which is a major cause of cloudy wines. These kits also contain a treatment to eliminate any problems that are identified by the test. Each kit contains replaceable reagent, treatment solution, and a pipette and sample test tube to ensure accurate measurements are achieved.

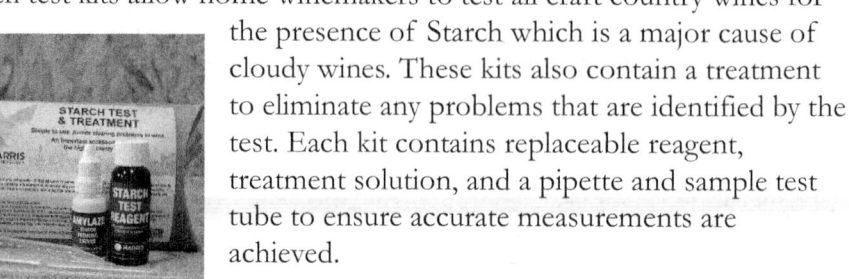

To test a wine for starch, add 2ml of Starch Test Reagent to the test tube, using the pipette. Then add 6ml of wine or must. Secure the test tube cap and shake for a few seconds. If the solution remains an amber or brown colour, then starch is not present. If the colour changes to a deep red or blue/black, then starch is present, and the resulting drink may not be clear.

To treat the problem, add 10 drops of Amylaze (more may be added if necessary) per gallon of wine. For professional clarities, always filter your wine afterwards through a Vinbrite Filter before bottling/storing.

Winemakers Test Kit

A complete Winemakers Test Kit is a useful addition to your equipment and is simple to use. It performs the most important wine analysis. A Winemakers Test Kit is a recommended accessory for improving winemaking skills and ensuring best quality results. These kits typically include:

Wine pH Test Strips
Sulphite Test Strips
Pectin Test Reagent
Starch Test Reagent
10ml Test Tube
3ml Pipette
Full easy to follow instructions.

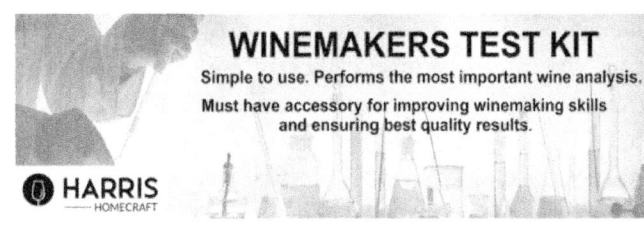

Wine Filtration- Why it is necessary:

Bouquet and taste are important, but the appearance of a wine is normally its first attraction. Take a glass of water from the tap, hold it up to the light and observe the brilliance. We take this for granted. Wines can also shine like this, providing you follow a few simple rules.

Newcomers to winemaking are more likely to obtain reasonable clarities when they use the "quickie" wine kits, with instructions by numbers, and those made from the wide range of grape concentrate. The old school of craft winemakers often refer to "making wines like their Grandparents did", but this is not to be recommended. In many cases, they relied upon wild yeast for fermenting, had never heard of tannin, nutrient or enzymes and probably paid little attention to hygiene. Craft country wines, using so many different ingredients (which vary in themselves from year to year), are the areas where the worst clearing problems occur. This is especially so when older recipes are being followed.

Following a tried and tested fining and filtering regime is the way to get consistently clear wines. Filtering ensures that there will be no foreign matter or dead yeast particles to produce off-flavours and the wine is healthier to proceed with maturation. Most commercial filters rely on the use of disposable and replaceable filter pads. By using a wine filter, it is possible to filter hazy wines, with true colour and commercial clarities, within the same day – which is very impressive. However, hazes consist of millions of microscopic particles that are too light to settle. A large proportion of these normally pass through or clog the finest filtering materials, and this is the reason why filtering alone may not be effective. Commercial winemakers do not use filtration as a shortcut to avoid fining. They use it as a finishing process to achieve professional brilliance.

Providing there has been a well-balanced must and steady fermentation, many wines can clear reasonably well without assistance. If you have been able to maintain these conditions and the wine clears on its own, it may then be acceptable or be filtered directly to brilliance without fining. As identified earlier, there are three main causes of hazy wines. These are the presence of protein (which is present in all living matter), starch, and pectin.

Hazes can, therefore, be formed from all fruit and vegetables used in winemaking. Haze particles are very small, some are jelly-like and are only slightly heavier than water. This means that they will be very slow to settle. Another unfortunate tendency with haze particles is their ability to attract a glue-like layer onto the surface of a filter pad. This soon cuts down the wine flow through the filter to a trickle and the clarity of the wine may be affected.

With simple forethought, it is easy to obtain brilliant wines almost every time. The filter pad inside a wine filter cannot work miracles! Passing a thick wine through any kind of filter will not produce a good result. It will clog the filter and even stop the flow. This may seem an odd statement to make, but because filter pads are sensitive, they perform much better when used for polishing a reasonably clear wine. The key to achieving professional brilliance is to follow a similar routine to that of commercial winemakers.

Always add Pectinaze or a similar pectic enzyme, preferably at the time of adding the yeast or during fermentation. For a wine that remains cloudy after fermentation, repeat the dose and leave in a warm place for 3-4 days. For craft fruit wines that have a high pectin content, double the dose of Pectinaze.

Adding Pectinaze or pectic enzyme will improve wine quality, especially the final colour. Subsequently, using wine finings will prepare the wine for filtering. The finings will combine with the minute haze particles, making them larger and allowing them to fall as a sediment in the jar, resulting in a much clearer wine. After syphoning from the sediment, the filter will then polish the wine to produce a true colour with professional brilliance.

Some winemakers avoid using finings because they consider the balance of the wine may be disturbed. There is no evidence that adding enzymes and finings will alter the wine chemistry. The photograph on the right shows the difference between a wine which has been cleared only with finings (the glass on the left), and the same wine after it has been passed through a Vinbrite Filter (the glass on the right). The filtered wine is indistinguishable from a commercial wine and is much more appealing to the drinker.

The Vinbrite Filter is gravity-based filter suitable for filtering up to five-gallon batches of wine. With this filter, there is a choice of three types of filter pads.

Prime Pads are a pre-treatment filter pad to remove by removing larger solids and colloidal particles that may block finer filter pads.

Crystalbrite Pads are thin pads that offer fast filtering flow rates.

Filtabrite Pads are thick pads. Although slower in operation, they can achieve the highest possible wine clarity.

The Vinbrite Filter is the bestselling filter in the world. It is extremely cost-effective to run, simple to operate, and produces excellent and consistent results.

Advanced Hydrometers and Refractometers:

Although the standard glass hydrometer is used by the vast majority of winemakers, there are now advanced digital hydrometers available that do not require wine samples to be removed from the bulk. Digital hydrometers are innovative tools that have simplified the process of monitoring the fermentation progress and determining the alcohol content in home winemaking. These devices offer several advantages over traditional glass hydrometers, including greater flexibility, convenience, and the ability to track fermentation parameters digitally.

Digital Hydrometers:

Digital hydrometers utilise electronic sensors to measure the specific gravity (density) of the fermenting wine. This measurement is then used to calculate the alcohol content and monitor fermentation progress. Most are equipped with wireless connectivity features, allowing them to transmit real-time fermentation data to a smartphone, tablet, or computer via Bluetooth or Wi-Fi. The fermentation data, including specific gravity readings, temperature, and alcohol content, are typically displayed on a digital screen or within a dedicated mobile app.

Digital hydrometers often provide more accurate and precise measurements compared to traditional glass hydrometers, reducing the margin of error in determining alcohol content and fermentation progress. They streamline the process of monitoring fermentation by eliminating the need for manual readings and calculations. The wireless connectivity feature allows winemakers to track fermentation data remotely and receive real-time alerts. With digital hydrometers, winemakers can monitor fermentation progress more efficiently, freeing up time for other winemaking tasks. Unlike glass hydrometers, which can break easily, digital hydrometers are durable and reusable, making them a long-term investment for home winemakers.

It is important to calibrate a digital hydrometer before use to ensure accurate measurements. Follow the manufacturer's instructions for calibration carefully. Then it is simply a matter of placing the digital hydrometer in a fermenting wine and allowing it to take measurements at regular intervals. The specific gravity readings and fermentation progress can then be monitored using the digital display or mobile app. Winemakers can analyse the fermentation data, including specific gravity trends and temperature fluctuations, to make informed decisions about the fermentation process, such as when to rack the wine or when fermentation is complete.

Digital hydrometers have a higher upfront cost compared to traditional glass hydrometers, but they offer added functionality and convenience. Before making a purchase ensure that the digital hydrometer you choose is compatible with your winemaking setup and devices (e.g., smartphone, tablet). They should be regularly cleaned and maintained according to the manufacturer's instructions to ensure accurate measurements and longevity.

Digital hydrometers have become valuable tools for home winemakers, offering greater precision, convenience, and efficiency in monitoring fermentation and determining alcohol content. With their advanced features and wireless connectivity, digital hydrometers have become indispensable gadgets for those seeking to elevate their winemaking practices.

Refractometers:

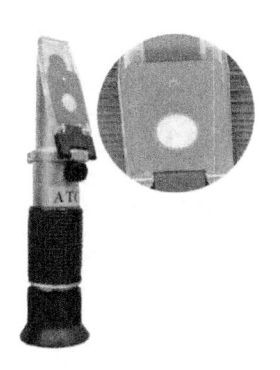

Refractometers are useful tools used in home winemaking for measuring the sugar content of grape juice or wine must. They differ from hydrometers in that they work on the principle of light refraction through a liquid sample. This process allows winemakers to determine the sugar concentration, which is crucial for monitoring grape ripeness and assessing fermentation progress. It is, therefore, a valuable tool when making wine from fresh grapes. It can also be used for general home winemaking too.

Refractometers measure the refractive index of a liquid sample, which is the degree to which light is bent as it passes through the sample. This bending of light is influenced by the concentration of dissolved solids, primarily sugars, in the liquid.

Refractometers are calibrated to measure the refractive index in units such as Brix, which is a measurement of the sugar content in the sample. Brix readings are commonly used to estimate potential alcohol content in wine. Good refractometers will provide dual scales with the Brix scale on one side and Specific Gravity on the other.

To use a refractometer, a small sample of grape juice or wine is placed on the refractometer's prism surface. The refractometer is then held up to a light source, and the user looks through the eyepiece to observe the line where light and shadow meet. The position of this line on the Brix scale indicates the sugar concentration of the sample. Better refractometers have a built in LED light source which makes them easier to read in any light conditions.

Traditional handheld refractometers are compact devices, manually operated and only require a small sample size. They are portable and easy to use, making them suitable for home winemakers. The added advantage is that no wine is wasted as only a small sample is needed to obtain an accurate reading. Digital refractometers are also available which offer digital readouts of Brix readings, providing greater accuracy and precision compared to traditional handheld models. Some digital refractometers also offer temperature compensation features to adjust for temperature variations in the sample. These devices are more expensive than manual versions.

Refractometers can be used to monitor the sugar levels (Brix) in grapes. This helps winemakers determine the optimal time for harvesting, based on desired sugar ripeness levels for the intended wine style. They are also used during fermentation to track the progress of sugar conversion into alcohol. By taking periodic Brix or SG readings, winemakers can estimate the alcohol content of the fermenting wine and determine when fermentation is complete.

When using a refractometer, ensure that the sample is free from air bubbles or debris, as these can affect the accuracy of the reading. If using a digital refractometer, take note of any temperature compensation features and follow the manufacturer's instructions for calibration and use. Regularly calibrate the refractometer using distilled water or a calibration solution to maintain accuracy.

While refractometers provide a quick and convenient way to estimate sugar content, they may not be as accurate towards the end of fermentation when alcohol has been produced. Therefore, a hydrometer is often needed as well. Refractometers are designed to measure sugar content and are not suitable for determining other parameters such as acidity or pH.

Refractometers are, therefore, valuable tools for home winemakers, providing rapid and convenient measurements of sugar content during winemaking and fermentation. By incorporating a refractometer into your winemaking toolkit, you can make informed decisions to produce wines of consistent quality and style.

Dispensing Wine from Kegs:

There are an increasing number of home winemakers and brewers that are building their own bars at home. Some of these are quite elaborate and dispense beer through commercial taps, also known as faucets (faucet derives from fausset, a mediaeval French word for a bung in a barrel). They are usually connected to a Corny Leg, either with a length of beer line and John Guest connectors, or by a tap fitted directly to the keg. This set up is then connected to a pub style CO2 gas canister through a gas regulator. As discussed earlier, this set up can be used to make sparkling wine too. In winemaking, the process of carbonation, or the introduction of carbon dioxide bubbles into the wine, associated with sparkling wines such as Champagne, Prosecco, and sparkling wines, can be made using forced carbonation techniques.

It is, however, possible to use this equipment configuration to dispense still wines too. This avoids the need to bottle your wine and ensures that perfectly conditioned wine is available on demand through a bar tap. However, it is not possible to dispense wine using CO2 gas since this will carbonate the wine. For dispensing still wine it is necessary to use a 70:30 mix of CO2 and Nitrogen (N2). Note, however, that this mix requires a different regulator, as a CO2 regulator will not work.

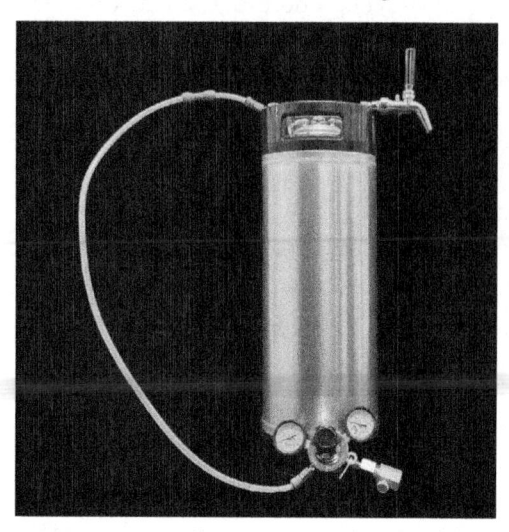

Using a 70:30 gas mix of nitrogen (N2) and carbon dioxide (CO2) is not likely to make wine sparkle if the pressure is kept low. The 70:30 gas mix (often referred to as Guinness gas), is primarily used in the beer industry for dispensing certain beer styles, particularly stouts and porters. It is used to achieve a creamy texture, smooth mouthfeel, and reduced carbonation level in the beer, which are desirable characteristics for these styles. The purpose of using a 70:30 gas mix for wine is primarily to dispense wine from a corny keg in a manner that minimises oxidation and preserves the wine's freshness and flavour.

The higher proportion of nitrogen (N2) in the gas mix compared to carbon dioxide (CO2) results in smaller bubbles and less carbonation in the wine, which is desirable since carbonation needs to be avoided in still wines. Still wines are typically fermented to dryness, meaning that the yeast has consumed all of the available sugars, resulting in a still (non-sparkling) wine. A 70:30 gas mix will add a layer of gas over the wine, which will preserve it. The automatic addition of more gas through the regulator as wine is dispensed will ensure that there is never any air in the keg, and so avoids air spoilage issues. A low pressure is needed, which will avoid carbonation but will be just enough to pour the beer through the system. This will provide wine on demand and ensure that the wine stays in fresh condition for a long time. Using a 70:30 gas mix (70% nitrogen and 30%

carbon dioxide) to dispense wine from a corny keg is, therefore, a viable option, especially if you are aiming to preserve the wine's quality and characteristics while ensuring efficient dispensing.

To employ this system, first ensure that your corny keg is clean and sanitised before filling it with wine. Use a no rinse solution such as Suresan to sanitise the keg thoroughly. Suresan will not affect the stainless steel. Make sure that the draw tube is also sanitised. Then carefully syphon your wine into the keg avoiding air contact as far as possible. Then lock down the keg lid.

Connect a gas line from a from a regulator fitted to the 70:30 gas cylinder, to the gas inlet post on the corny keg. A ball lock 'gas in' disconnect fitting is used to make the connection. Connectors and gas are available from good home brew shops.

Apply some gas and make sure the connections are secure and leak-free. Purge the release valve on the corny keg 2 -3 times for 3 seconds to release any air from inside the keg. This will ensure the wine is preserved as it will be covered by the CO_2/N_2 gas mix.

To dispense wine from the corny keg, fit a tap/faucet to the beer outlet post on the corny keg. Taps are available which fit directly onto the keg, or you may prefer to use some beer line to connect to a commercial style bar faucet. If this is the case, use a 'beer out' disconnect fitting to connect the line to the keg's outlet post.

Adjust the gas pressure as needed to achieve the desired flow rate and dispensing pressure. The optimal pressure will depend on factors such as the length and diameter of the dispensing line and the temperature of the wine. Try to keep the pressure as low as possible to avoid carbonating your wine.

The benefit of using a 70:30 Gas Mix is preservation of freshness. The use of nitrogen helps prevent oxidation and maintains the wine's freshness over time, particularly if the wine is stored in the keg for an extended period. The 70:30 gas mix allows for precise control over the dispensing pressure and flow rate, ensuring that the wine is dispensed smoothly without excessive agitation or foaming. The lower proportion of carbon dioxide in the gas mix helps minimise carbonation in the wine, which is beneficial for certain wine styles that are not intended to be sparkling.

Try to maintain appropriate temperature control for the wine style, throughout the dispensing process to prevent temperature-related issues such as foaming or off-flavours. It is also important to regularly clean and sanitise all equipment used in the dispensing process to prevent contamination and maintain the wine's quality. This includes the faucet, disconnect fittings, and pipe line.

By using a 70:30 gas mix to dispense wine from a corny keg, you can effectively preserve the wine's quality while ensuring efficient dispensing and serving. Experiment with different gas pressures and dispensing techniques to find the optimal setup for your specific wine and dispensing setup.

Chapter 12. Troubleshooting Common Issues:

Winemaking is a rewarding pursuit, but like any craft, it comes with its challenges. In this section, we will explore common pitfalls and complications that winemakers encounter and equip you with the knowledge to sidestep these issues. From sanitation hiccups to fermentation surprises, the troubleshooting process will guide you to ensure your winemaking endeavours are as smooth as possible. Winemakers often ask for advice and solutions to these problems:

Sanitation Issues.

One of the most frequent culprits of winemaking mishaps is inadequate sanitation. Infections from unwanted bacteria or wild yeast can lead to off-flavours and spoil your batch. The solution is simple but crucial: maintain a rigorous sanitisation routine. Clean and sanitise all equipment thoroughly before each use and be especially attentive to anything that comes into contact with the wine post-fermentation.

Stuck Fermentation - Fermentation has finished but the final gravity (FG) is higher than expected.

A stuck fermentation can be disheartening, but understanding the causes is the first step towards a remedy. Factors such as improper yeast health, nutrient deficiencies, or suboptimal temperature control can contribute to fermentation stalls. Start by ensuring a healthy yeast pitch, providing adequate nutrients, and maintaining a consistent fermentation temperature within the yeast's preferred range.

Each wine will have a target Final Gravity which you should get close to. If the gravity has remained stable over 3 days at the end of fermentation, then the wine has effectively finished its fermentation. The more grape concentrate that is provided in a kit wine, the higher the FG will be. Some stronger red wines may not ferment below 1.005 so do not worry. If you think that there is still residual sugar in the wine, then allow more time for fermentation to complete. If you experience a stuck fermentation, then the yeast may have been killed prematurely. This may be due to a spike in the temperature, or if the alcohol content is high towards the end of fermentation. Yeasts will have varying degrees of alcohol tolerance. To rectify the problem, make a fresh yeast starter by adding one-third of the Wine Must to a glass. Then add two-thirds water at 24C (75F). Stir in a teaspoonful of sugar and a small squirt of lemon juice (to add a touch of acid). Then whisk a sachet of high alcohol tolerant Restart Yeast (such as Harris Restart Yeast) for 30 seconds and cover with a cloth. Leave in a warm place for around an hour until a head forms and there are visible signs that the fermentation has started. Then pour the starter into the bulk of wine and stir vigorously. Leave in a warm place (24C) for fermentation to continue. This technique should kick-start most stuck fermentations. If the fermentation is close to completion and a starter will not work, then a second option is to add yeast stopper, clear and filter the wine, then blend it with a drier wine. This will reduce the final sweetness.

Off-putting Odours.

Unpleasant aromas, often described as sulphur-like or rotten egg odours, can arise during fermentation. This issue is typically attributed to stressed yeast. Proper yeast rehydration, nutrient supplementation, and vigilant temperature control can mitigate these unwelcome scents. Effective aeration at the start of fermentation will ensure necessary oxygen levels and help dissipate volatile compounds.

Wine can be short of nitrogen, so it is important to add a good quality nutrient to the must at the same time as adding the yeast. Diammonium Phosphate is a popular nutrient, but its effectiveness is limited to 9%ABV. Therefore, if adding Diammonium Phosphate, a blended nutrient mix with Ammonium Sulphite is recommended.

Water is a major ingredient of wine and the quality of water used can make a big difference to the final taste and aroma. Where possible use bottled/spring water rather than tap water which may contain unwanted chlorine and chloramine. Adding Pure Brew with the yeast will prevent off-tastes and smells from excess chlorine and chloramine in tap water. It also contains a highly effective nutrient mix which will ensure a healthy fermentation.

Cloudy Wine.

Most wines will clear to a certain degree on their own if left in a cool place for a period. Some, however, will be stubborn and remain cloudy. Usually this is due to proteins that remain in suspension and the solution is to add good quality wine finings and then filter your wine. Another reason may be the presence of pectin. Some fruits have a high pectin which can prevent the clearing process from taking place. The existence of pectin can prevent finings from working properly. Finings work by electrolytic attraction, encouraging protein particles to clump together (a process called flocculation) and once heavy enough, to fall out as a sediment. However, pectin can prevent the electrolytes from combining. A good way of explaining the issue is to consider frogspawn. Imagine the black dot of a tadpole is a protein particle. The jelly that surrounds it is pectin and that prevents finings from getting through. The best way of breaking down pectin is by adding pectinaze at the start of fermentation with the fruit. The existence of residual pectin at the end can be identified by using a pectin testing reagent available from specialist home brew shops. If a test identifies the existence of pectin in your wine, then simply add more pectinaze and return the wine to a warm place for a few days. It may be necessary to then add more finings and filter the wine to achieve a final brilliant clarity.

Unwanted Sediment.

Excessive sediment in your wine can be a disappointment, especially if you were aiming for a crystal-clear finished product. To minimise sediment, practice careful racking at the end of the fermentation process. Allow the wine to stand in a cool place for a few days at the end of the fermentation to rough clear. Clarifying agents such as, Chitosan, Kieselsol, or Isinglass can be added to assist in settling yeast, protein, and other particles, producing a cleaner and more visually appealing wine. Carefully syphon the wine from any sediment as soon as possible as it is detrimental to allow it to lie on the sediment for too long. Filtering a rough cleared wine is highly recommended to enhance its appearance and quality.

Filtering will not impact on the final taste in any way other than removing any suspended colloidal particles (which could impair the final taste). A filtered wine will always have a brighter, more commercial appearance.

Post-fermentation haze or sediment.

A completely clear wine may subsequently develop a haze or a dusting of sediment. This may be caused by post-fermentation. When your wine is cleared all dead yeast particles and other debris will have been removed. However, live yeast cells will still be present, and these will contribute to the ageing process. If there is any remaining sugar in the wine, or it has been back sweetened, then these live yeast cells have the perfect environment in which to re-ferment. This may make the wine taste slightly sparkling and/or throw out a sediment. To prevent post-fermentation your wine should be stabilised or pasteurised after fermentation and removing the initial sediment. To stabilise, add a crushed Campden tablet and a dose of Potassium Sorbate. This creates an environment which stops yeast activity and is around 95% effective in preventing re-fermentation. If you do not wish to add chemicals or want to reach 100% effectiveness, then the solution is to pasteurise your wine. This involves heating the wine in a suitable pan (pre-sanitised) and there is a direct relationship between the temperature and time taken to achieve results. The temperature also must be balanced against the potential breakdown of subtle flavours and aromas at higher temperatures. To maintain quality, it is not recommended to pasteurise at temperatures above 70C (158F). The recommended temperature range is 60C (140F) for 25 minutes up to 66C (151F) for 5 minutes. 60C is unlikely to have any detrimental effects on the final quality of the wine and so is the preferred pasteurisation temperature.

Wine tastes sour or vinegary.

Your Wine or Must may have become contaminated. This could be as a result of ineffective sanitisation or poor temperature control. Avoid lifting the lid frequently during/after the fermentation process as this could introduce a microbial airborne bacterium into the wine such as acetic bacteria. Unfortunately, contaminated wine needs to be discarded and all equipment deep cleaned/sterilised with Steri-Cleen or similar before use. This problem is a rare occurrence.

Wine has a slight off-flavour.

The most common cause of an off flavour is due to the wine not being syphoned off the sediment promptly at the end of fermentation. Other causes can be ineffective sanitisation of equipment immediately prior to use.

Ropiness.

This is an extremely rare problem. The wine looks silky and shiny and has a thick appearance. When poured it looks oily. The cause is a bacterium of the lactic acid group. The problem can be treated by adding 2 crushed Campden tablets per gallon and stirring them into the wine vigorously. Leave for one week then syphon the wine from the sediment that will have formed. The wine will not be harmed or the flavour impaired.

There is a strange white skin or flecks of white on the top of the wine.

This will have been caused by airborne bacteria (probably caused by wine being left too long in the fermenter after fermentation has ended and the bucket lid being removed frequently) or through poor sanitisation. Discard the wine and deep clean/sterilise all equipment with Steri-Cleen before using again.

Malolactic fermentation (MLF).

MLF (Malolactic fermentation) can take place once alcoholic fermentation has finished and is another reason why a clear wine may throw out a slight haze or dusting of sediment. It is carried out by lactic acid bacteria, which convert the tart malic acid into lactic acids. MLF softens acidity, creates a creamy, buttery flavour in the wine, and produces carbon dioxide. It is sometimes encouraged by winemakers to help in the maturing process by raising the wine temperature and avoiding adding sulphites after the fermentation. It can be avoided by storage at cool temperatures or filtering (which removes the lactic acid bacteria). If MLF is experienced simply leave the process to complete, then re-filter your wine.

Overly Sweet or Dry Wines.

Achieving the desired sweetness level in wine can be tricky. If your wine turns out too sweet, you may have added too much sugar or halted fermentation. Conversely, if it's too dry, the yeast might have consumed all available sugars.

It is easier to correct an overly dry wine than one that is too sweet. If your wine is too dry, then it can be sweetened with a sugar or honey solution. Dissolve 250g of sugar or light honey in a little water and add the solution to the bulk of your wine in small quantities. Stir to thoroughly mix and undertake a taste test. Repeat the process until the preferred level of sweetness is achieved. The process should be undertaken in small stages as you can add more sweetness, if necessary, but if you add too much it is not possible to reduce it afterwards. It is important to consider stabilising or pasteurising a sweetened wine to avoid post-fermentation. Alternatively, you could add a commercial wine sweetener to back sweeten as this is a saccharine based unfermentable solution. Brewers' glycerine can also be used to smoothen your wine and add a sweet roundness to the final taste. Glycerine is less aggressive than Wine Sweetener.

If your wine has stopped prematurely (e.g. a reading of 1040 to 1025 would indicate this) and has not been stabilised it may be possible to re-ferment it by adding a restart yeast (such as Harris Restart) and returning the wine to a warm place in a fermenter fitted with an airlock. Prepare a yeast starter to give the wine the best opportunity to restart. Alternatively, you may have added too much sugar or fruit, and the yeast cannot ferment it all. Yeasts will have specific alcohol tolerances and once they are reached the yeast will become exhausted. Many yeasts cannot survive above 14% ABV and any further unfermented sugar will remain as sweetness. In such cases it is not possible to remove the sugar. The only option is to clear and stabilise the wine and subsequently blend it with a drier wine.

Fermentation not progressing.

Sometimes CO_2 will escape around the side of your fermentation bucket rather than through the fitted airlock (make sure the airlock has water in it). Signs of fermentation are a foam on the surface of the wine in the early stages and CO_2 being given off. Also falling hydrometer readings over 2 days should indicate sugar is being converted. If fermentation is not occurring it could be that the Must was too hot when the yeast was introduced, which has killed it. Alternatively check that the ambient temperature of the room and fermenter is not outside the tolerance of the yeast. If necessary, add a fresh sachet of Restart Yeast.

Oxygen Intrusion.

Oxygen is a friend at the start of winemaking but becomes a foe once fermentation is underway. Excessive exposure to oxygen towards the end or post-fermentation can lead to oxidation, resulting in off-flavours and diminished aromas. The signs of oxidation in wine are a darkened brownish colour change and a flat taste. Oxidation happens when a wines' exposure to air triggers a series of chemical reactions that convert ethanol (what we commonly refer to as alcohol) into acetaldehyde. This concentrates colour and creates aromas and flavours that are generally considered to be grassy or nutty. To avoid oxidation, ensure airlocks have water in them during fermentation and minimise unnecessary transfers or agitation. When racking or bottling, take precautions to limit oxygen contact. An oxidised wine may be revived by adding a little vitamin C powder to it.

Fizzy wine and popped corks.

This problem can occur if fermentation continues after bottling, due to residual sugars or incomplete stabilisation. Avoid this explosive situation by ensuring fermentation is complete, and stabilising or pasteurising your wine.

Wine can be bulk aged, or bottle aged. Bulk ageing the wine in a sealed container may promote better maturation and will also minimise inconvenience if post-fermentation occurs. However, it ties up space and containers. Therefore, many winemakers prefer to bottle their wine as soon as it is finalised and to label and store it in wine racks. This is fine but do keep an eye out for signs of post-fermentation. If it occurs, then the wine should be returned to a fermenter and placed in a warm room to complete any residual fermentation. Then it should be re-filtered once you are sure that the fermentation has completed.

High or low Acidity Levels.

Low acidity can be a problem especially in wines with higher alcohol contents. The aim is to balance the wines alcohol with acidity and residual sweetness. If you are making a higher alcohol wine, then it is important to properly balance it, so it is drinkable. As a rule, the higher the residual ABV and sweetness the higher the final total acid should be. You can purchase an acid test kit from good home brew shops which can help you to achieve correct acid levels. Acid levels in a full-bodied red wine could be as high as 0.85% or 8.5 grams per litre while a dry white wine could be as low as 0.6% or 6 grams per litre. Sweetness and acid are a subjective taste thing. It is important that you are happy with the final taste so sample the wine and adjust acid with acid blend if necessary.

Some craft wines have very low acid levels because the fruit, flowers, or vegetables have low acid levels. Older recipes will recommend adding either citric, malic, or tartaric acid at the start. Acid blend is more commonly used these days since it offers a more balanced acid profile to wines. Low final acidity can be corrected by adding acid blend after the wine has rough cleared.

High acid levels may occur if too much acid is added at the start, or where fruits with high acid contents are used. In the event that your wine is too acidic, the problem can be resolved by adding acid reducer (precipitated chalk) which is available from home brew shops.

Fusels.

Fusels, also known as fusel alcohols, are higher alcohols that can contribute harsh and undesirable flavours to wine. These compounds often result from stressed yeast or excessive fermentation temperatures. Managing and preventing fusel production is important for producing a smooth and enjoyable wine. Some common issues related to fusels in wine include:

- *High Fermentation Temperatures.* Yeast can produce more fusels at elevated temperatures. It is important to control fermentation temperatures within the optimal range for your chosen yeast strain and to avoid temperature spikes. During months with higher ambient temperatures try to ferment your wine in a cooler room.

- *Inadequate Yeast Nutrition.* Insufficient nutrients for the yeast can lead to stress, producing more fusels. Ensure that you provide the yeast with proper nutrients, including nitrogen, vitamins, zinc, and minerals. Use Pure Brew or good commercially available yeast nutrients and follow recommended dosage guidelines.
- *Under pitching or Overpitching Yeast.* Too few yeast cells (under pitching) or an excessive number of cells (over pitching) can stress the yeast and contribute to fusel production. Try to pitch the appropriate amount of yeast based on your batch size and initial gravity. Follow yeast pitching rate recommendations provided by the yeast manufacturer.
- *Aeration Issues.* Inadequate aeration during the early stages of fermentation can stress yeast and promote fusel production. It is important to oxygenate the must before pitching yeast. Use a sanitised stirring paddle or long handled spoon and stir vigorously for 2 minutes when adding yeast and Pure Brew. Some winemakers use an aeration stone to ensure proper oxygen levels at the beginning of fermentation.
- *Proper Sugar-to-Water Ratio.* Using an excessive amount of sugar can lead to a higher gravity must, stressing the yeast and promoting fusel production. Always calculate and use the appropriate sugar-to-water ratio based on the recipe you are following. This ensures a balanced environment for fermentation.
- *Extended Fermentation Periods.* Prolonged fermentation periods can contribute to fusel production. Monitor fermentation closely and rack the wine into a secondary fermenter once fermentation is complete. Leaving the wine on the yeast lees for an extended period may contribute to off-flavours.
- *Ageing and Dilution.* Fusels can mellow over time, but if the wine still has harsh flavours, ageing alone may not be sufficient. Diluting the wine with additional water or blending it with a wine that has lower fusel alcohol content can help to balance the flavours and minimise the problem.
- *Choosing appropriate Yeast Strains.* Certain yeast strains are more prone to producing fusels. Choose yeast strains that are known for producing clean and well-balanced wines. Research the characteristics of different yeast strains and select one that suits your desired flavour profile. Feedback on wine forums has

suggested that D-47 yeast tends to contribute to higher fusels, especially when fermented above 23C (73F).

By addressing these factors, you can minimise the risk of fusel production and enhance the overall quality of your wine. Regular monitoring, proper yeast management, and maintaining optimal fermentation conditions are key to avoiding fusel-related issues in winemaking.

Pellicle Formation.

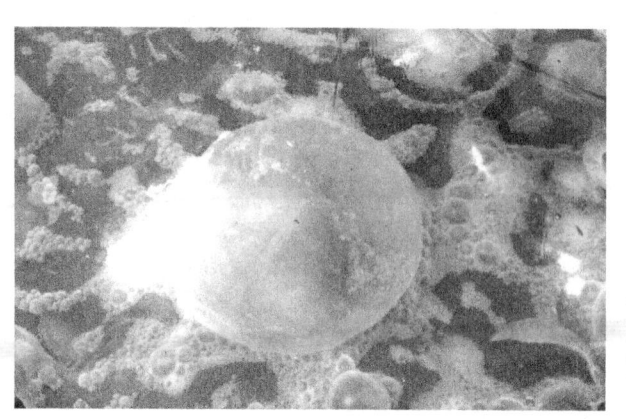

If your wine develops a skin on the surface or mould-like bubbles this can be concerning. The cause of this appearance could be the formation of a pellicle. A pellicle is a polysaccharide biofilm that forms on the surface of a fermentation. It is formed by some types of yeast and bacteria when oxygen is present. The appearance may be white, off-white, or clear, and it generally has a powdery, waxy, or slimy appearance, often with bubbles or wrinkles. Pellicles are sought after by sherry producers and often yeasts have a sherry flor to promote a pellicle. They are also promoted in the production of sour beers.

A pellicle is a result of the complex interplay between microorganisms present in the wine, primarily wild yeast strains and bacteria. As the fermentation progresses, these microorganisms engage, creating a protective layer on the surface of the liquid. This layer acts as a shield, preventing the intrusion of harmful bacteria while allowing beneficial microorganisms to thrive.

The vast majority of commercial wine and ale yeasts will not develop pellicles and so visible signs of pellicles are an indication of contamination in your wine by wild microbes. A pellicle is created by brettanomyces (a form of wild yeast) and various lactic acid bacteria (lactobacillus and pediococcus) which act an oxygen barrier. Usual causes are taking the fermenter lid off too many times particularly towards the end of fermentation or having too much head space above the must. Fresh fruits may carry over wild yeasts/bacteria which is why it is important to either add sulphite to them or pour boiling water over at the start of the process.

Simply stirring the must or syphoning the wine off a pellicle will not resolve the problem. It will return. Usually, pellicles take a few weeks to fully form. If the film has a hairy or fuzzy appearance, then this may be mould rather than a pellicle. It is possible to still drink wine that has experienced a pellicle biofilm in it. It will taste different (and possibly sour), though so the decision is a personal choice. Experienced winemakers often embrace the pellicle as a natural part of the brewing process. While it may look different from batch to batch, its presence is a reminder of the living ecosystem within the fermenting vessel. Some winemakers intentionally expose their wine to wild yeast and bacteria to encourage the development of unique and complex flavours, turning the pellicle into an aspect of their craft.

To prevent a reoccurrence of the pellicle (or mould formation), all equipment that has been in contact with the wine should be deep cleaned by soaking it in a strong solution of a powerful steriliser such as Steri-Cleen.

Chapter 13. Serving Wine:

Serving wine involves a few steps to ensure you and your guests can fully enjoy the experience. Wine is traditionally served in a glass. The shape of the glass allows you to appreciate the aroma and flavours of the wine. White wine glasses have smaller openings, allowing the aromas of your wine to be concentrated if you swirl it around. Red wine glasses have wider openings, allowing them to release the full flavours.

Serving temperature is a key consideration. The serving temperature for wine varies depending on the type of wine, as different wines are best enjoyed at different temperatures:

Light-bodied reds (e.g., Pinot Noir): Serve slightly chilled, around 55-60°F (13-15°C). Lighter reds benefit from a slight chill to enhance their freshness and acidity.

Medium-bodied reds (e.g., Merlot, Sangiovese): Serve at cellar temperature, around 60-65°F (15-18°C). This allows the wine's aromas and flavours to fully express themselves without being overly warm.

Full-bodied reds (e.g., Cabernet Sauvignon, Shiraz/Syrah): Serve at room temperature or slightly below, around 60-65°F (15-18°C). Room temperature may be too warm for these wines, so a slight chill can help balance their robust flavours and tannins.

Light-bodied whites (e.g., Sauvignon Blanc, Pinot Grigio): Serve well chilled, around 45-50°F (7-10°C). Chilling enhances the wine's crispness and acidity, making it refreshing and enjoyable.

Medium-bodied whites (e.g., Chardonnay, Chenin Blanc): Serve chilled, around 50-55°F (10-13°C). Slightly warmer than light-bodied whites, this temperature allows for the wine's aromas and flavours to develop fully without being too cold.

Full-bodied whites (e.g., oaked Chardonnay, Viognier): Serve lightly chilled, around 55-60°F (13-15°C). Light chilling preserves the wine's texture and richness without muting its flavours.

Rosé Wines: Serve well chilled, around 45-55°F (7-13°C). Chilling enhances the wine's freshness and acidity, making it crisp and refreshing.

Sparkling Wine: Serve well chilled, around 40-45°F (4-7°C). Chilling preserves the wine's effervescence and crispness, making it lively and refreshing.

Fortified Wine (e.g., Port, Sherry): Serve at room temperature or slightly below, around 60-65°F (15-18°C). Fortified wines are often enjoyed as digestifs and serving them slightly warmer allows their complex flavours and aromas to shine.

If you have an aged or complex wine, consider decanting it. Pouring it into a decanter allows the wine to breathe, enhancing its flavours and aromas. Allow ten minutes for the wine to breathe before serving. Then pour it gently into your glass, avoiding excessive splashing. Hold the glass at the base to prevent warming the wine with your hands.

Take a moment to observe the colour and clarity of the wine. Note any aromas that you can detect. Swirl it around to see if it has legs. The term "legs" in the context of wine, refers to the rivulets that form and slowly run down the inside of the glass after you swirl the liquid. The appearance of legs is influenced by factors such as alcohol content, viscosity, and sweetness. Here's how you can identify and interpret legs in wine:

•	Swirl the Glass: Swirl the wine gently in the glass to coat the sides. This action helps create the legs by thinning the liquid and allowing it to adhere to the glass.

•	Observe the Rivulets: After swirling, look at the inside of the glass. You should see thin rivulets or streaks forming on the surface of the glass. These are the legs.

•	Thickness and Speed: Legs can vary in thickness and speed. Thicker legs may indicate a higher alcohol content or greater viscosity. The speed at which the legs move down the glass can also provide insights into the wines' body and alcohol content.

- Alcohol Content: In general, the presence of pronounced legs might suggest a higher alcohol content. The legs are formed due to the evaporation of alcohol, and a higher alcohol content often results in more visible and slower-moving legs.

- Viscosity and Sugar Content: The viscosity of wine, influenced by factors like sugar content and the presence of additives, can affect the appearance of legs. Sweeter wines may exhibit thicker and slower legs due to the higher sugar content.

Ensure that the glass is clean and free from any residues, as contaminants on the glass can affect the formation of legs. It is worth noting that while legs can provide some insights into the characteristics of wine, they are not the sole indicators of quality or taste. The aroma, flavour, and mouthfeel are equally important factors in assessing a wine.

Following a visual inspection, smell the wine to identify subtle aromas and contributions from additions such as fruits and flowers. There should be no chemical or off-smells detected, or an overpowering smell of alcohol (this may indicate the wine needs longer to mature).

Finally, take small sips to savour the flavours. Allow the wine to roll around your palate to fully appreciate its complexity. Try to take in some air as you sip the wine. Note the first foretastes and any aftertastes that linger after you have swallowed the wine.

If you have opened a bottle of wine and have some left, reseal it tightly and store it in a cool, dark place. The quality will degrade if exposed to air, and light. Temperature fluctuations can also affect the quality.

Chapter 14. Making Spirit Based Drinks and Liqueurs:

Many winemakers extend their hobby to making their own liqueurs and spirit-based drinks at home. This is a sector of the market which has seen significant growth since the covid pandemic. There is a superb range of equipment and hundreds of spirit/liqueur flavours available from home winemaking shops to support this sector. It can be a fun and rewarding endeavour, allowing you to experiment with different flavours, ingredients, and techniques to create unique and delicious drinks. You can craft homemade liqueurs, spirits, infusions, and cocktails which are as good as their commercial equivalents, at a fraction of the price.

Liqueurs are sweetened spirits flavoured with fruits, herbs, spices, nuts, or botanicals. Making liqueurs at home involves infusing flavourings into a base spirit and sweetening the mixture to taste. The process starts with a base spirit. Choose a base spirit such as vodka, rum, brandy, or whiskey, depending on the desired flavour profile. Choose a value priced spirit, such as a supermarkets own brand to keep the cost down.

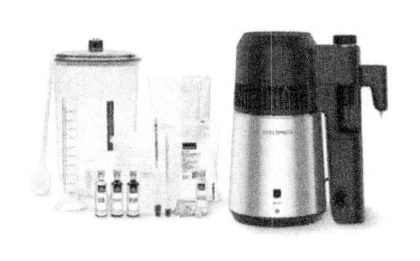

Equipment is available from home brew shops to make your own base spirit (subject to legal restrictions in specific countries). Still Spirits are a New Zealand based manufacturer that supply automatic distilling machines to produce high quality base spirit. The Air Still, Air Still Pro, and T500 Turbo Still are easy to use machines that can produce base alcohol. Home distilling equipment allows enthusiasts to produce distilled spirits such as whiskey, vodka, gin, rum, and brandy in their own homes. However, it is essential to emphasise that distilling alcohol at home may be subject to legal restrictions and regulations in many countries. It is recommended that you research and understand the legal implications and requirements before engaging in home distillation. The typical equipment used in home distilling includes the standard equipment used to ferment wine (fermenter, airlock, hydrometer, filter, etc) plus a 'Still'.

The still is the primary piece of equipment used in distillation, responsible for separating alcohol from the fermented liquid. There are two main types of stills used in home distilling. Pot stills (such as the Air Still Pro) consist of a large pot or boiler where the fermented liquid (mash or wash) is heated, vaporised, and then condensed into alcohol. They are relatively simple in design and are suitable for producing spirits with rich and flavourful characteristics, such as vodka, whiskey, and rum. Reflux stills (such as the T500 Turbo Still) feature a column or column packed with material (such as copper ferrules or ceramic beads) that allows for multiple distillation stages within the same unit. They are more efficient than pot stills and are commonly used for producing high-proof, neutral spirits such as vodka and gin.

To make your own spirit you first need to make a 'spirit wash'. This requires a sachet of high ABV yeast, a sachet of carbon, and a sachet of spirit finings. Still Spirits provide these together in their Pure Turbo Pack.

Sanitise all equipment and a 25 litres fermenter before use. Then dissolve 7kg of brewing sugar (or 6kg of household sugar) into 21 litres of water. Add some hot water to reach a final temperature of 30-40C. Then stir in the yeast and sachet of carbon, which will turn the liquid black. The carbon removes any unwanted flavours and aromas, keeping the wash as pure as possible. Fit a lid and airlock, then ferment in a warm place (24C/75F). Fermentation will have completed when airlock activity ceases and the final specific gravity is around 0.996.

Once fermentation has finished, add a sachet of spirit finings and leave in a cool place to clear for 24 hours. The black carbon will fall as a sediment, but the wash will not look perfectly clear. It will look a similar colour to wallpaper paste.

At this point the wash should be filtered through a Vinbrite Filter fitted with a Prime Pad. This will remove any suspended colloidal particles which could carry over into the still. Although the filtered wash will not look completely clear, all solid particles and dead yeast will have been removed. This will improve the quality of the final base spirit. The aim is to achieve a completely neutral taste so there is no interference with flavours that are subsequently added. The filtered wash is then poured into a still which will convert it into base spirit.

An Air Still holds 4 litres of wash at a time, and there will be enough wash for 6 fills of the still. Add the wash up to the full line in the pot chamber. Then add ceramic boil enhancers and 1 cap of Distillers Conditioner (which are both supplied with the Air Still). Then simply put the top of the still on, plug it in, switch on and put the collector jug under the still nozzle. It will take 1 hour approximately to reach the required temperature, then you will see distilled alcohol dripping from the spout. It will take about 1 hour 30 minutes to collect 800ml of spirit, then the machine should be turned off. Check with a spirit hydrometer to determine the final ABV. It is usual to achieve an ABV of around 55-60% ABV. The T500 Turbo Still and Air Still Pro machines can generate base spirit at around 90% ABV. This spirit can then be diluted with water to achieve the required ABV (normally 40% ABV for spirits).

The Air Still Pro offers a range of extra benefits, including increased capacity, improved efficiency, advanced control options, enhanced safety features, versatility, quality construction, and ease of use. These features make it an excellent choice for home distillers looking to take their distillation hobby to the next level.

A reflux still such as Still Spirits T500 Turbo Still operates in a different way to the Air Still. It is capable of producing high-proof, neutral spirits suitable for a variety of applications, including vodka, gin, and flavoured liqueurs. Typically, it will produce neutral base spirit of around 90%ABV, so is very efficient. The T500 Turbo Still is larger and more substantial than the Air Still due to its inclusion of a fractionating column. It is designed for home use but will require a little more space and setup compared to the Air Still. It's reflux distillation process allows for precise control over the purity and alcohol content of the final product. The T500 connects to a water supply (usually via a supplied connector that attaches to a kitchen mixer tap) and water trickles through the column to maintain the correct temperature. The T500 will process a complete 22.5 litres (5 gallons) wash in one pass so it is more convenient and more time efficient to use.

The table below shows the dilution quantities to achieve specific ABV levels. Alternatively, a plug-in dilution calculator is available at www.darkrockbrewing.co.uk/calculators.

Spirit %	To make 1 litre @ 40% abv		To make 1.2 Litres @ 40% abv	
	Spirit	Water	Spirit	Water
61	660 ml	340 ml	790 ml	410 ml
60	670 ml	330 ml	800 ml	400 ml
59	680 ml	320 ml	810 ml	390 ml
58	690 ml	310 ml	830 ml	370 ml
57	700 ml	300 ml	840 ml	360 ml
56	715 ml	285 ml	860 ml	340 ml
55	730 ml	270 ml	870 ml	330 ml
54	740 ml	260 ml	890 ml	310 ml
53	755 ml	245 ml	910 ml	290 ml
52	770 ml	230 ml	925 ml	275 ml
51	785 ml	215 ml	940 ml	260 ml
50	800 ml	200 ml	960 ml	240 ml
49	820 ml	180 ml	980 ml	220 ml
48	830 ml	170 ml	1000 ml	200 ml
47	850 ml	150 ml	1020 ml	180 ml
46	870 ml	130 ml	1040 ml	160 ml
45	890 ml	110 ml	1070 ml	130 ml
44	910 ml	90 ml	1090 ml	110 ml

Whichever still is used, the final base spirit should then be passed through the carbon filter block supplied with the still. Soak the carbon cartridge in hot water for several minutes to activate it then pass the diluted spirit through the carbon cartridge fitted into its plastic chamber. Carbon filtering is a very slow process as the longer the spirit is in contact with the carbon, the more effective the process will be. It will take about 8 hours to filter 1.2 litres (best to leave it overnight). Once filtered you should have a quantity of around 6.6 litres of base spirit which will form the basis of all liqueurs and spirit. The cost will be approximately £2.15 per litre which is significantly cheaper than commercial spirit.

The use of Base Spirit is also a common method for producing commercial spirits. For example, most gins are made by adding botanicals to base spirit, which are then re-distilled to extract the flavour of juniper berries and other additions.

Once you have either made, or purchased a base spirit, the final stage is to add a flavour to replicate your favourite spirit or liqueur. A wide range of spirit and liqueur flavours are available from home brew shops, which are simply added to the base spirit in a bottle. They are ready for drinking immediately after mixing, but some will benefit from a few days maturation if you can be patient.

As an alternative to liquid flavours, you may wish to buy a botanical pack which can be added to an accessory botanical basket fitted into the still. The base spirit can be distilled through the botanicals to achieve the final flavour. This process, known as the infusion method, emulates the way in which most commercial gins are produced. A second infusion method is sometimes referred to as the 'bathtub method'. This is a throwback to prohibition days in the United States when gin was produced undercover in bath tubs. The method involves steeping selected botanicals in a base spirit in a sealed container (such as a Kilner Jar) for a period of time and then filtering through a filter paper to remove solids. The amount of time the botanicals are infused in the base spirit forms the basis of the spirit making art. Some botanicals are quite powerful and only need to be infused for a few hours. Others may need a few days. Fruits, herbs, spices, or coffee beans can all be effectively used to infuse into the spirit. Sugar, simple syrup, honey, or agave nectar can then be used as required to sweeten the liqueur to taste. Still Spirits produce thickening and sweetening base packs to add to their flavours, to make schnapps and cream-based liqueurs.

It is possible to pass home-made wines through a still, to produce spirits. This can be useful if you have a wine which, once completed, does not meet your expectations. Simply pour the wine into the still (to the fill line) and distil it. Grape based wines make delicious brandies and if infused for a week in oak chunks, the colour and flavour will be further enhanced. By distilling an apple-based wine you can make a wonderful calvados. This means you will never have to worry about discarding an unsuccessful wine experiment.

The Art of Mixology - Making Cocktails and Mixers:

Making your own cocktails and mixers at home can be a rewarding and fun experience, allowing you to customise flavours, experiment with ingredients, and impress your friends and family with unique and delicious drinks. You will need to acquire some basic equipment. This includes:

Cocktail Shaker: For shaking ingredients together with ice to chill and mix them.

Mixing Glass: Alternatively, for stirring ingredients with ice.

Muddler: For muddling herbs, fruits, or sugar to release their flavours.

Jigger: For measuring precise amounts of ingredients.

Bar Spoon: A long spiral stemmed spoon for stirring cocktails and reaching the bottom of tall glasses.

Strainer: For straining out ice and other solid ingredients from cocktails.

Citrus Juicer: For freshly squeezed citrus juices.

Fine Mesh Strainer: For straining out small particles or seeds from juices.

Ice Cubes or Ice Moulds: For chilling cocktails.

Basic cocktail ingredients which you should keep to hand in your bar include:

Base Spirits: Such as vodka, gin, rum, whiskey, tequila, and brandy.

Liqueurs: Flavoured liqueurs such as triple sec, vermouth, amaretto, or flavoured syrups.

Citrus: Freshly squeezed lemon, lime, and orange juice.

Sweeteners: Simple syrup (equal parts sugar and water dissolved), honey syrup, agave nectar, or flavoured syrups. Simple syrup can be purchased commercially or easily made at home by combining equal parts sugar and water in a saucepan. Heat until the sugar dissolves, then cool before using.

Fruit Purees: Blend fresh or frozen fruits with water or simple syrup in a food blender to make fruit purees for cocktails.

Syrups and Cordials: Keep a stock of syrups such as grenadine Experiment with making your own flavoured syrups, cordials, or liqueurs using herbs, spices, fruits, or flowers. Citrus syrup can be made by mixing simple syrup with citrus zest or juice for flavoured syrups.

Bitters: Aromatic or flavoured bitters add depth and complexity to cocktails.

Sodas and Mixers: Tonic water, soda water, ginger beer, cola, or other flavoured sodas.

Fresh Botanicals and Infusions: Herbs (mint, basil), fruits (berries, citrus, juniper berries), vegetables (cucumber), and spices (ginger, cinnamon). These can also be used to decorate glasses.

It is a good idea to start with classic cocktail recipes like the Martini, Mojito, Margarita, Old Fashioned, or Manhattan. Once you are comfortable with these basic recipes, experiment with variations by substituting ingredients or adding new flavours. Wherever possible, use fresh, seasonal ingredients to create cocktails that highlight the flavours of the season. This will be more cost effective too. You can tailor cocktails to your personal taste preferences by adjusting sweetness, acidity, or strength. Remember to garnish cocktails with fresh herbs, citrus twists, or fruit skewers for visual appeal and added flavour. The most popular cocktails include:

Margarita: A classic cocktail made with tequila, lime juice, triple sec (orange liqueur), and often served with a salt rim. It's refreshing citrus flavour and versatility have made it a favourite choice for many cocktail enthusiasts.

Martini: A timeless cocktail traditionally made with gin and dry vermouth, garnished with an olive or lemon twist. Variations include the vodka martini (made with vodka instead of gin) and the dirty martini (with added olive brine).

Mojito: A refreshing Cuban cocktail made with white rum, fresh lime juice, mint leaves, sugar, and soda water. Its combination of sweetness, citrus, and mint flavours makes it a popular choice, especially during the summer months.

Old Fashioned: A classic cocktail consisting of whiskey (usually bourbon or rye), sugar, bitters, and a twist of citrus peel. This is a timeless favourite known for its simplicity and depth of flavour.

Cosmopolitan: A stylish and vibrant cocktail made with vodka, triple sec, cranberry juice, and fresh lime juice. Its pink hue and tart-sweet flavour have made it a popular choice in cocktail bars and social gatherings.

Daiquiri: A simple yet elegant cocktail made with rum, lime juice, and simple syrup. It's refreshing citrus flavour and balanced sweetness have contributed to its popularity, with variations including the strawberry daiquiri and the frozen daiquiri.

Negroni: A classic Italian cocktail made with equal parts gin, sweet vermouth, and Campari, garnished with an orange twist. Its bold and bitter flavour profile has gained a dedicated following among cocktail enthusiasts worldwide.

Piña Colada: A tropical cocktail originating from Puerto Rico, made with rum, coconut cream, and pineapple juice, often served blended with ice. Its creamy texture and tropical flavours evoke visions of sunny beaches and leisurely vacations.

Painkiller: The Painkiller Cocktail is a delightful, tropical drink that transports you to the sunny shores of the Caribbean with its blend of navy rum, pineapple juice, coconut cream, and orange juice. Originally created in the British Virgin Islands, it is favoured for its creamy texture and refreshing flavours. This cocktail is an interesting alternative to the Piña Colada.

Porn Star Martini: A modern and stylish cocktail known for its vibrant flavours and striking presentation. Created in the early 2000s by bartender Douglas Ankrah, this cocktail has gained popularity worldwide for its combination of fruity sweetness, tartness, and aromatic vanilla notes. It is made with vanilla vodka, passion fruit liqueur, lime juice, and prosecco.

Café Espresso Martini: A sophisticated and indulgent cocktail that combines the rich flavours of coffee with the boldness of vodka and the sweetness of coffee liqueur.

Vesper: The Vesper Cocktail is a classic drink made famous by Ian Fleming's James Bond novel, Casino Royale. It is a sophisticated and 'highly potent' cocktail that blends gin, vodka, and Lillet Blanc, resulting in a crisp and aromatic drink. Naturally it should be made 'shaken not stirred'.

The terms "cocktails" and "mixers" are often used interchangeably, but they refer to distinct components. Cocktails are mixed drinks composed of two or more ingredients, typically including a base spirit (such as vodka, gin, rum, whiskey, or tequila) combined with other ingredients like juices, syrups, liqueurs, bitters, or sodas. The base spirit provides the primary alcoholic component. However, some cocktails may contain low or no alcohol, known as mocktails or non-alcoholic cocktails, which still offer complex flavours and textures without the intoxicating effects. Mixers are non-alcoholic beverages or ingredients used to dilute, flavour, or enhance the taste of alcoholic drinks, including cocktails. They may be added in smaller or larger quantities compared to the base spirit and play a supporting role in the overall flavour profile of the drink.

Mixers serve various purposes, such as adding sweetness (simple syrup, grenadine), acidity (citrus juice), carbonation (soda water, tonic water), bitterness (bitters), or flavour (fruit juices, flavoured syrups) to the drink. Cocktails often incorporate mixers as essential components to achieve the desired flavour, balance, and texture. Mixers provide the foundation for many classic and contemporary cocktails, serving as vehicles for showcasing the flavours of the base spirit and other ingredients.

While mixers can be enjoyed on their own as standalone beverages, cocktails combine mixers with alcohol and other ingredients to create complex drinking experiences. The art of cocktail-making involves selecting and balancing the right mixers and ingredients to achieve harmony and excellence in flavour and presentation.

Presentation is everything with cocktails and mixers. Try to use appropriate glassware for each cocktail, such as a martini glass, highball glass, or rocks glass. Also, use large, clear ice cubes or spheres where possible for better chilling and presentation. To really get into the cocktail scene you should try to practice proper shaking, stirring, and straining techniques for well-balanced cocktails, and decorate cocktails with appropriate garnishes to enhance the aroma and appearance.

By experimenting with different ingredients and techniques, you can create your own signature cocktails and mixers that reflect your taste and creativity. Have fun exploring new flavours and combinations, and don't be afraid to try new things!

Developing Mixology Skills:

Mixology is more than just the act of mixing drinks; it is an art form that requires creativity, passion, and attention to detail. It is also a science, which involves the careful balance of flavours, textures, and aromas to create refreshing, inviting cocktails. Mastering mixology skills is essential for creating visually stunning cocktails. Mixology is an opportunity for artistic expression. Play with colours, textures, and shapes to design cocktails that are as visually striking as they are delicious.

The key to achieving balance in a cocktail is to carefully consider the interplay of sweet, sour, bitter, and salty flavours. Each ingredient should complement and enhance the others, rather than overpowering them. Mixology requires careful consideration of these four primary taste elements: sweet, sour, bitter, and salty. Achieving the perfect balance of these flavours is key to crafting a memorable drink. It is, therefore, important to understand the basic flavour profiles of different spirits, liqueurs, fruits, herbs, and spices. Each ingredient brings its own unique characteristics to a cocktail, and understanding how they interact is fundamental to creating harmonious blends.

Spirits such as vodka, gin, rum, whisky, and tequila form the backbone of most cocktails. Each type of spirit has its own distinct flavour profile, ranging from the clean and neutral taste of vodka to the complex and rich flavours of aged whiskey.

Liqueurs add sweetness, depth, and complexity to cocktails. From the herbal notes of Chartreuse to the citrusy zing of Cointreau, there are a wide variety of liqueurs to explore and experiment with

Fresh fruits, juices, and syrups provide natural sweetness and acidity to cocktails. Citrus fruits like lemon, lime, and orange are particularly popular in mixology due to their bright flavours and ability to balance other ingredients.

Aromatics add depth and complexity to cocktails, engaging the senses and enhancing the overall drinking experience. Utilise fresh herbs, spices, and aromatic garnishes to elevate the aromatics of your cocktails. From the peppery kick of basil to the earthy warmth of cinnamon, experimenting with herbs and spices can take your cocktails to the next level.

Sweetness can come from a variety of sources, including sugar, fruit juices, and liqueurs. Balancing sweetness is essential to prevent a cocktail from becoming cloying or overpowering.

Sourness adds acidity and brightness to cocktails, helping to cut through sweetness and balance flavours. Citrus juices are the most common source of sourness in cocktails, but vinegars and shrubs can also be used to add acidity.

Bitterness adds depth and complexity to cocktails, balancing sweetness and enhancing other flavours. Bitter ingredients such as bitters, Amari, and Vermouth can be used sparingly to add complexity without overwhelming the palate.

Saltiness can enhance other flavours and balance sweetness and acidity. A pinch of salt can elevate the flavours of a cocktail and create a more rounded and cohesive drinking experience.

Once you have mastered the basics of flavour profiles and balancing, it's time to delve into the art of mixing. Texture plays a role in the enjoyment of a cocktail, so experiment with different techniques, such as shaking, stirring, and layering, to create cocktails with luxurious mouthfeel and satisfying texture.

There are several techniques that bartenders use to ensure that each cocktail is perfectly blended and chilled.

Stirring is the preferred technique for cocktails that contain only spirits or clear ingredients, such as martinis and negronis. Stirring gently chills the drink without diluting it too much and helps to maintain clarity and texture.

Shaking is a technique used for cocktails that contain fruit juices, syrups, or creamy ingredients, such as daiquiris and margaritas. Shaking aerates the drink, creating a frothy texture and chilling it quickly.

Muddling involves gently crushing fresh herbs, fruits, or spices in the bottom of a glass to release their flavours and aromas. Muddling is commonly used in cocktails like mojitos and old fashioneds to add depth and complexity.

Layering is a technique used to create visually stunning cocktails with distinct layers of colour and flavour, such as the tequila sunrise. By carefully pouring ingredients over the back of a spoon, bartenders can create beautiful, layered drinks such as the pousse-café.

The presentation of a cocktail is just as important as its flavour. A well-garnished cocktail not only looks more appealing but can also enhance the drinking experience by engaging the senses. The choice of glassware can greatly impact the presentation of a cocktail. Select glassware that complements the style and personality of the drink. Choosing the right glassware for your cocktail can help to showcase its colours, aromas, and textures. From classic martini glasses to tall highball glasses, there is a wide variety of glassware to choose from to suit every type of cocktail.

Garnishes add visual appeal and aromatic complexity to cocktails. From citrus twists and fruit wedges to fresh herbs and edible flowers, there are endless possibilities when it comes to garnishing cocktails. Experiment with different garnishes to find the perfect finishing touch for your drinks. Garnishes can also add aromatic complexity to a cocktail.

Mastering mixology skills is a journey of exploration and experimentation. By understanding flavour profiles, balancing ingredients, mastering mixing techniques, and paying attention to presentation, you can elevate your cocktails from simple drinks to works of art. At the heart of mixology lies creativity and innovation. The best mixologists are constantly pushing the boundaries of flavour and technique, experimenting with new ingredients and methods to create original and exciting cocktails.

Mixology is a playground for flavour exploration. Experiment with different spirits, liqueurs, fruits, herbs, and spices to discover unique flavour combinations. Drawing inspiration from the seasons can lead to inventive and fresh cocktails. Where possible, utilise seasonal fruits, herbs, and spices to create drinks that capture the essence of each season.

Armed with a selection of your home-made wines, spirits, and liqueurs, you have all of the necessary ingredients to make mixers and cocktails at a fraction of the price of commercial equivalents. Some selected recipes are outlined under the recipe section of this book.

Chapter 15. Sustainability and Biodiversity in Winemaking:

By definition, sustainable winemaking is a method of producing wine that is environmentally friendly, socially responsible, and economically viable. It involves implementing practices that minimise the negative impact of winemaking on the environment while also preserving the quality and taste of the wine. Making your own wine certainly aligns with this ethos and it is easy to demonstrate how it contributes to a more sustainable lifestyle. Apart from being cost effective (which is probably the strongest argument for making your own wines), there is no better way to ensure that the wine you drink is healthy for both you and the environment, than making it yourself. Making homemade wine allows you control the process, from sourcing ingredients to ensuring what goes into each bottle. You can be confident that the ingredients and supplies you are using are eco-friendly and do not contain any unknown chemicals or preservatives.

Home winemaking is not just a hobby; it's a craft that connects individuals to the land, the seasons, and the biodiversity that thrives within the countryside and vineyards. As the world grapples with the challenges of climate change and environmental degradation, there's a growing interest in craft, and sustainable practices, even at the smallest scales of production. Winemaking from countryside ingredients highlights the cycle of growth and focuses on the seasonality of fruits, flowers, and vegetables. Picking your own ingredients is a great way to involve children in the process and educate them about nature and the countryside. How many of us remember fondly accompanying our parents and grandparents to pick elderberries, plums, and apples to make wines and cider. In today's fast paced lifestyles and reliance on social media, craft winemaking is a way to unwind and involve the whole family in an interesting and fulfilling hobby, whilst at the same time getting outdoors and enjoying some fresh air. By planting fruit trees, and berry bushes in your garden, you can contribute to the environment and provide a sustainable source of ingredients for wine making. The intersection of biodiversity and sustainability can easily be explored in the context of home winemaking and in your own garden.

The countryside and gardens are vibrant ecosystems teeming with biodiversity. Fruit trees and bushes host a multitude of plant and animal species that contribute to their health and resilience. This is true in vineyards too. From cover crops that prevent erosion and fix nitrogen in the soil to insects that act as natural predators against pests, biodiversity plays a crucial role in maintaining vineyard balance.

When engaging with home winemaking, it is easy to recognise the importance of preserving and enhancing biodiversity. By nurturing a diverse array of plant life and creating habitats for beneficial insects and animals, home winemakers can contribute to the overall health of their local ecosystems. Flowering shrubs encourage bees, whose populations are declining, and are essential to our own existence.

Sustainability in home winemaking involves minimising environmental impact while maximising the quality of the final product. This encompasses various practices aimed at conserving resources, reducing waste, and fostering ecological balance. Try to source products from local shops or from online stores that choose re-cycled packaging in preference to bespoke branded outer boxes. After all it doesn't matter what it looks like when you receive your parcel, as it will quickly be thrown away.

Before making wine, you should always clean your equipment. However some cleaners contain harsh chemicals, that are neither safe for your skin nor the environment. To be environmentally friendly choose a sanitiser that contains no damaging chemicals and prioritises oxygen. No Rinse Sanitisers, such as Suresan are an effective cleaning solution that require no rinsing and are safe for sanitising aluminium, stainless steel, and other metals and plastics.

From composting fruit pulp, minimising waste, and maximising recycling efforts, you can make a small but integral contribution through sustainable winemaking practices. This extends to trying wherever possible to buy from retailers who use recycled packaging materials.

Recycling bottles and equipment can also make a small but positive impact on the environment. Whether you have left over commercial wine bottles or bottles from your last batch of homemade wine, you can re-use wine bottles many times. Re-using wine bottles reduces the waste produced when you are making wine. It is also a cost-effective solution for anyone on a budget.

Maintaining hedgerows, planting native vegetation, and creating wildlife habitats within gardens, promotes biodiversity and supports the health of local ecosystems.

On a commercial level, the biodiversity present in vineyards influences not only environmental sustainability but also the quality and character of the wine produced. Diverse ecosystems contribute to soil fertility, which in turn affects grapevine health and grape quality. Furthermore, the presence of beneficial insects and microorganisms can help regulate pest populations and enhance soil biodiversity, leading to healthier vines and more flavourful grapes.

In home winemaking, this connection between biodiversity and wine quality underscores the importance of sustainable practices. By prioritising biodiversity conservation, home winemakers can produce wines that reflect the unique terroir of their region while minimising their ecological footprint and minimising waste. Country winemaking can accommodate surplus or imperfect fruits that might otherwise go to waste. Freezing fruits for later use is another way of minimising waste.

Country winemaking often fosters a strong sense of community and connection to the land. Through farmers' markets, community events, and wine circles/forums, winemakers can raise awareness about environmental issues and inspire others to adopt sustainable practices. Even if it is only a small contribution, winemakers can align with environmental and sustainability issues, and collectively we can make a difference.

Final Thoughts on Craft Winemaking at Home:

Congratulations! You have reached the final section of this book on home winemaking. Throughout this journey, we have delved into the art and science of transforming grapes or other fruits into delicious wines right in the comfort of your own home. We have explored how wine kits can play an important role in the hobby and can be used for blending wines. Modern home winemakers are likely to seamlessly integrate wine kit production with craft wines made from fruits, flowers, and other ingredients. They are also likely to extend their skills into making liqueurs, spirits, and cocktails.

Take a moment to reflect on how far you've come since beginning your winemaking journey. Perhaps you started with simple wine kits or experimented with small batches of fruit wines. Along the way, you've likely encountered challenges, celebrated successes, and honed your skills as a winemaker. Remember that winemaking is a continuous learning process. Even experienced winemakers encounter new techniques, varietals, and challenges with each batch they produce. Take the opportunity to learn from your experiences, whether they result in a perfect bottle of wine or a valuable lesson for improving future batches.

It is important thing to nurture your passion for the craft. Explore new wine kit styles, techniques, fruit varieties, and experiment with different fermentation methods. Mead, for example, is a style that is experiencing a renaissance. If you would like to develop a stronger interest in mead making, you should read the book 'The Art of Mead Making: A Comprehensive Guide'. This book explores this fascinating area in more detail.

It is easy to seek inspiration from fellow winemakers. Consider joining an online group, (such as the Facebook group 'Pure Brew'), where you can get advice and share experiences with others that are interested in brewing, winemaking, mead making, and producing spirits/cocktails. One of the joys of winemaking is sharing your creations fellow enthusiasts, by participating in local winemaking clubs and online communities. Sharing your wines and experiences with others, not only enhances the pleasure, but also fosters connections and appreciation for the craft.

Therefore, as you develop your skills, consider giving back to the winemaking community by sharing your knowledge and experiences with others. Offer guidance to beginners, contribute to online forums and social media groups, or volunteer at local winemaking events. By paying it forward, you contribute to the collective growth and enjoyment of future winemakers.

In conclusion, raise a glass to toast your winemaking journey. Whether you are just beginning or have been crafting wines for years, remember that every bottle tells a story, and is an expression of your creativity, dedication, and passion for winemaking. May your future batches be filled with success, joy, and the satisfaction of a well-crafted wine. Use this book as a point of reference whenever you need to and try out some of the recipes that follow. They have been thoroughly researched and honed over many years to produce wines that have won prizes at regional and national winemaking competitions. Cheers to your continued adventures in home winemaking!

Chapter 16. Prizewinning Craft Wine Recipes:

As you develop your skills and build up stocks of kit wines, you may wish to progress and supplement your cellar stocks with some craft-based country wines. These wines are fun to make and offer some interesting flavours. Fruit based craft wines are excellent in their own right but also make a great foundation for blending (both with other craft wines and also with kit wines). With some careful planning you will be able to schedule your production to coincide with fruits and crops coming into season, and this can be extremely cost effective. If you are not harvesting your own fruits, then look out for produce reaching the end of its shelf life in shops and supermarkets. Often this can be purchased cheaply and will make an inexpensive wine. Remember, you can select fruit and then freeze it until you are ready to make your wine. The process of freezing and thawing out fruit helps to break it down and release flavours. Therefore, it is actually beneficial to wine production.

The recipes in this section showcase wines that have won prizes in competitions and are compiled to produce the highest quality wines. If you allow them to fully mature, then you will make wines which are worthy of a competition entry. Unless otherwise stated the recipes are geared to making 4.5 litre (1-gallon) batches. It is simple to scale up the quantities to make larger volumes. Advice on this is indicated in the recipe.

It is possible to substitute fresh fruit with dried or canned fruit in some recipes. This allows you to extend your production outside of the normal growing season. Where this is possible, the recipe will indicate the equivalent quantities to use. If using dried or canned fruit, remember to avoid supplies that have preservatives included as this may inhibit yeast growth and fermentation.

Feel free to adapt these recipes to formulate your own styles and innovative flavours. Remember to keep a log of your activities and formulations for future reference. Part of the enjoyment of home winemaking is sharing your successes with others. Try wherever possible to reach out to other winemakers and share your ideas and recipes. There are some excellent and social media groups and forums, such as the Facebook group "Pure Brew", where you can keep in touch with other winemakers that share your passion.

The main thing is to have fun, so dip into these recipes and start building your own wine cellar. You may find that you suddenly become very popular amongst your family and friends.

Cheers!

Apple Wine.

This wine offers a tantalising fusion of fruity sweetness, refreshing acidity, and crisp tartness. Each sip unveils the essence of freshly picked apples, with bright and crisp nuances.

Ingredients:

At Start:

3Kg (6½lb) Apples
(Use 1kg dried or 800g canned fruit if fresh is unavailable)
250ml or 245g White Grape Concentrate
1 Kg Bag of Sugar
1 sachet of Harris Premium Wine Yeast
1 sachet of Pure Brew (or 1 Teaspoon Yeast Nutrient)
1 teaspoon Acid Blend
10 drops Pectinaze
1 Crushed Campden Tablet

After Fermentation:

½ teaspoonful of Potassium Sorbate
1 crushed Campden Tablet
1 sachet of Winefine Finings (one sachet will clear between 1 and 5 gallons)
10g Oak Barrel Chips (optional)
3½ litres (6 Pints) Cold Water

Directions:

Chop the apples and crush them in a pre-sterilised white plastic bucket. Pour over the grape concentrate, which will add depth and body to the wine. Add the oak barrel chips (optional). This will support a delicious chardonnay style flavour in the final wine. Then dissolve the sugar in a little hot water and add this to the bucket.

Pour the cold water over the contents together with the acid blend, and pectinaze. Crush a Campden tablet into the mix and stir well. Cover with a cloth and leave for 24 hours in a cool place. This process will kill any wild yeast and bacteria that may be present on the fruit. The next day add the yeast & Pure Brew sachet (or nutrient). This is now called the 'must'. Stir thoroughly for 1-2 minutes to oxygenate the must. Cover the bucket with a cloth and leave to ferment in a warm place for 5 days, stirring the contents of the bucket occasionally. Then strain into a demijohn (4½ litres) or fermenter, through a nylon straining bag. Press as much of the juice as possible and discard the pulp. It may be necessary to top up with a little extra cold water to achieve 4½ litres. Fit a bung and airlock and leave in a warm place to continue to ferment out completely.

Finishing your Wine:

Fermentation should be complete in 2-5 weeks. At this stage CO2 bubbles should have stopped being released through the airlock. Your wine should then be checked with a hydrometer. The hydrometer will indicate the remaining sugar level and finishing levels are as follows:

Dry = 0.990 – 0.996   Medium = 0.996 – 1.009   Sweet = 1.009 – 1.018

At the end of fermentation add 1 crushed Campden tablet and half teaspoon of potassium sorbate per gallon. Leave in a cool place (15C) for 3 days to kill off the yeast. Then syphon the wine from the sediment into a second fermenter. Shake or stir the wine to degas it then add wine finings to ensure your wine will clear. Leave for 5 days in a cool place then syphon the wine from the sediment. Finally, pass it through a Vinbrite filter to obtain a professional finish before bottling.

Apples contain a high level of pectin which can make it difficult to clear your wine. Therefore, it is important to add pectinaze (you cannot overdose so add a little extra if necessary), and to add finings to support the clearing process. Filtering will remove all colloidal suspended particles and will ensure that your efforts are rewarded with a professional clarity and a pure taste.

The wine should now be bottled and stored in a cool dark place to mature for at least 6 months. During this time any rough tastes will be smoothed out and the wine will improve in bouquet and flavour.

This recipe makes 1 gallon (4.5 litres) of wine. For larger quantities simply multiply the quantities of ingredients except for the Pure Brew, Yeast and Winefine. One sachet of each of these will be sufficient for any quantity between 1 and 5 gallons.

Apple Cider.

This timeless classic recipe captures the essence of autumn in a single sip. Made from freshly chopped apples, it exudes a delicious blend of sweet, tart, and crisp flavours, reminiscent of orchard-fresh goodness. With its vibrant amber hue and lively effervescence, this apple cider offers a refreshing tang and fruity aroma.

For best results try to select a mix of apple types including some tart cooking varieties. Choose good quality fruit without blemishes. It is possible to substitute apple juice for apples to simplify the process.

Ingredients:

At Start:

7.25kg (16 lbs) Apples
(Use 4.5 litres/ 1 gallon of apple juice instead of fresh apples if preferred)
10 drops Pectinaze
1 tsp Yeast Nutrient
1 sachet of Harris Cider Yeast

After Fermentation:

1 sachet of Cider Brite Finings (if you prefer a clear Cider)
½ teaspoon Potassium Sorbate (only used for a still scrumpy style)
1 crushed Campden Tablet (only used for a still scrumpy style)

Directions:

First cut apples into small pieces, which will help in juice extraction. Crush, press, and add juice to a bucket (fermenter). A wine press is recommended for maximum juice extraction and to make the process easy.

Add water or more apple juice if necessary to reach the final desired volume. Now take a specific gravity reading with a hydrometer and if necessary, add some sugar dissolved in a little hot water to increase the gravity. As a guide, your original gravity should be around 1050-1060. The higher the gravity, the stronger the cider will be. Add the Pectinaze and Yeast & Nutrient. Then stir well for 1-2 minutes to oxygenate the cider. Secure a lid fitted with an airlock and ferment in a warm place (24C).

Pressing Tip: if you do not have access to a fruit press chop the fruit into small pieces and crush with a wooden block or put through a blender. Put the crushed fruit into a nylon straining bag and tie it. Add the separated juice to the bucket, and the bag of pulp. After 3 days remove the bag from the bucket and discard the pulp.

Continue to ferment in the bucket (fermenter) until the bubbles stop emerging from the airlock. Take a hydrometer reading again. The finishing gravity should be below 1.010. Fermentation should take around two weeks to complete.

Finishing the Cider:

There are a number of options that you can take to finish your cider, depending on the style you prefer:

Sparkling Cider (Clear):

When the fermentation is complete, add Cider Brite finings to your bucket and gently stir. Leave in a cool place with the lid fitted for 2-3 days for the cider to clear. Then syphon the cider into pressurised bottles (preferably plastic beer bottles), add 1-2 Brew Fizz Carbonation Drops per 500ml bottle and secure the cap. Then store the bottles in a warm place (24C) for 5 days to carbonate through secondary fermentation. There will inevitably be a little sediment on the bottom of the bottles, but the finings should make this stick to the bottom if poured carefully. Leave the cider in a cool place for 2-3 weeks to mature and serve chilled from a fridge.

Still Cider (Cloudy Scrumpy Style):

If you do not wish to carbonate your cider and prefer it served flat, you should add 1/2 tsp of Potassium Sorbate and 1 Campden tablet per gallon of cider at the end of fermentation, to stabilise the yeast. If you prefer the cider to be still but clear, add a dose of Cider Brite Finings at this stage. Then leave for 48 hours before tasting and if necessary, you can sweeten your cider with Glycerine or Wine Sweetener. Bottle or keg the cider and allow it to mature for 4 weeks in a cool place to mature before sampling.

This recipe makes 1 gallon (4.5 litres) of cider. For larger quantities simply multiply the quantities of ingredients except for the Yeast and Cider Brite finings. One sachet of each of these will be sufficient for any quantity between 1 and 5 gallons.

Apple Cider 2 (Sweet Woodpecker Style)

Follow the same method as for making standard cider but add Harris Cider Sweetener with the apple juice. For a medium sweet cider add 125g, for a woodpecker style sweet cider add 250g. The cider sweetener is unfermentable so the sweetness will be retained in the final drink.

Apricot Wine:

This is a delicious white wine that is perfect served chilled at summer barbeques. Apricots must be ripe to release their full flavour. Always choose clean, fresh fruit and if you are picking the fruit yourself avoid roadside locations. Thoroughly wash the fruit in cold water before use and remove all stalks.

Ingredients:

At Start:

2 Kg (4½lb) Apricots
(Use 500g dried or 425g canned fruit if fresh is unavailable)
250ml or 245g White Grape Concentrate
1 Kg of Sugar
1 crushed Campden Tablet
1 sachet of Harris Premium Wine Yeast
1 teaspoon of Yeast Nutrient
½ teaspoon of Wine Tannin
1 teaspoon of Acid Blend
10 drops Pectinaze
3½ litres (6 Pints) Cold Water

After Fermentation:

½ teaspoon of Potassium Sorbate
1 crushed Campden Tablet
1 sachet of Winefine Finings (one sachet will clear between 1 and 5 gallons)
3½ litres (6 Pints) Cold Water

Directions:

Crush the Apricots in a pre-sterilised white plastic bucket and remove all stones. Pour over the grape concentrate, which will add depth and body to the wine. Then dissolve the sugar in a little hot water and add this to the bucket.

Pour the cold water over the contents together with the acid blend, and pectinaze. Crush a Campden tablet into the mix and stir well. Cover with a cloth and leave for 24 hours in a cool place. This process will kill any wild yeast and bacteria that may be present on the fruit. The next day add the yeast and yeast nutrient. Stir thoroughly for 1-2 minutes to oxygenate the must. Cover the bucket with a cloth and leave to ferment in a warm place for 5 days, stirring the contents of the bucket occasionally. Then strain into a demijohn (4½ litres) or fermenter, through a nylon straining bag. Press as much of the juice as possible and discard the pulp. It may be necessary to top up with a little extra cold water to achieve 4½ litres. Fit a bung and airlock and leave in a warm place to continue to ferment out completely.

Finishing your Wine:

Fermentation should be complete in 2-5 weeks. At this stage CO2 bubbles should have stopped being released through the airlock. Your wine should then be checked with a hydrometer. The hydrometer will indicate the remaining sugar level and finishing levels are as follows:

Dry = 0.990 – 0.996   Medium = 0.996 – 1.009   Sweet = 1.009 – 1.018

At the end of fermentation add 1 crushed Campden tablet and half teaspoon of potassium sorbate per gallon. Leave in a cool place (15C) for 3 days to kill off the yeast. Then syphon the wine from the sediment into a second fermenter. Shake or stir the wine to degas it then add wine finings to ensure your wine will clear. Leave for 5 days in a cool place then syphon the wine from the sediment. Finally, pass it through a Vinbrite filter to obtain a professional finish before bottling. Filtering will remove all colloidal suspended particles and will ensure that your efforts are rewarded with a professional clarity and a pure taste.

The wine should now be bottled and stored in a cool dark place to mature for at least 6 months. During this time any rough tastes will be smoothed out and the wine will improve in bouquet and flavour.

This recipe makes 1 gallon (4.5 litres) of wine. For larger quantities simply multiply the quantities of ingredients except for the Yeast and Winefine. One sachet of each of these will be sufficient for any quantity between 1 and 5 gallons.

Banana Wine:

This recipe produces a rich banana wine with a smooth and pleasing mouthfeel. It has a relatively light body that allows the banana flavour to shine through. The addition of wheat gives the wine extra robustness, and it makes and ideal dessert wine if extra sugar is added.

Ingredients:

At Start:

2 Kg (4½lb) Fresh peeled Bananas (discard skins)
250ml or 245g White Grape Concentrate
500g (1.1lb) of Wheat
1.35 Kg (3lb) of Sugar
1 crushed Campden Tablet
1 sachet of Gervin GV2 Wine Yeast
1 teaspoon of Yeast Nutrient
¼ teaspoon of Wine Tannin
2 teaspoons of Acid Blend
10 drops of Amylase
3½ litres (6 Pints) Cold Water

After Fermentation:

½ teaspoon of Potassium Sorbate
1 crushed Campden Tablet
1 sachet of Winefine Finings (one sachet will clear between 1 and 5 gallons)

Directions:

Peel the Bananas and mash them into a large pan. Add 2 litres of water to the mashed bananas in the pan and bring the mixture to a gentle boil. Simmer for about 15-20 minutes to extract flavours from the bananas. Stir in the sugar until it completely dissolves. You can add 1/2kg extra sugar if you prefer a stronger dessert wine. Allow the banana mixture to cool to room temperature then pour it into a pre-sterilised white plastic bucket and add the Wheat (rinse in a sieve under a cold tap first but do not crush). Pour over the grape concentrate, which will add depth and body to the wine. Then pour the remining 1.5 litres of cold water over the contents together with the acid blend, and Amylase. Add the yeast and yeast nutrient then stir thoroughly for 1-2 minutes to oxygenate the must. Cover the bucket with a cloth and leave to ferment in a warm place for 5 days, stirring the contents of the bucket occasionally. Then strain into a demijohn (4½ litres) or fermenter, through a nylon straining bag. Discard the pulp. It may be necessary to top up with a little extra cold water to achieve 4½ litres. Fit a bung and airlock and leave in a warm place to continue to ferment out completely.

Finishing your Wine:

Fermentation should be complete in 2-5 weeks. At this stage CO2 bubbles should have stopped being released through the airlock. Your wine should then be checked with a hydrometer. The hydrometer will indicate the remaining sugar level and finishing levels are as follows:

Dry = 0.990 – 0.996   Medium = 0.996 – 1.009   Sweet = 1.009 – 1.018

At the end of fermentation add 1 crushed Campden tablet and half teaspoon of potassium sorbate per gallon. Leave in a cool place (15C) for 3 days to kill off the yeast. Then syphon the wine from the sediment into a second fermenter. Shake or stir the wine to degas it then add wine finings to ensure your wine will clear. Leave for 5 days in a cool place then syphon the wine from the sediment. Finally, pass it through a Vinbrite filter to obtain a professional finish before bottling. Filtering will remove all colloidal suspended particles and will ensure that your efforts are rewarded with a professional clarity and a pure taste.

The wine should now be bottled and stored in a cool dark place to mature for at least 6 months. During this time any rough tastes will be smoothed out and the wine will improve in bouquet and flavour.

This recipe makes 1 gallon (4.5 litres) of wine. For larger quantities simply multiply the quantities of ingredients except for the Yeast and Winefine. One sachet of each of these will be sufficient for any quantity between 1 and 5 gallons.

Beetroot (Spiced) Wine:

This spiced beetroot wine recipe combines the earthy sweetness of beetroots with the aromatic and warm flavours of spices, resulting in a deep, complex wine. Spiced beetroot wine has a rich and aromatic aroma, with hints of earthy beetroots and cinnamon. The scent is inviting and complex, drawing you in with its enticing fragrance. It provides an ideal base for a seasonal mulled wine, due the inclusion of cassia bark, ginger, and star anise. Star anise has a potent and distinctive flavour, so use it sparingly to avoid overpowering the other flavours in your beetroot wine. As a general guideline, you should start with around 1-2 whole star anise pods for a gallon (4.5 litres) of wine.

The colour will be a deep red but note that Beetroot colour is not stable. It is important to use either a dark demijohn, or to wrap your fermenter in black plastic to avoid light intrusion. Then use dark bottles to store the wine. If beetroot wine is exposed to prolonged light, your final colour will be more golden than ruby red!

Beetroots can be harvested throughout the growing season, but they are typically at their peak flavour in late summer to early autumn.

Ingredients:

At Start:

2kg (4.5lb) of Beetroots
500g (1lb) of Wheat.
250ml or 245g Red Grape Concentrate
28 g (1oz) Root Ginger (bruise it by hitting with a rolling pin before use)
2 Star Anise pods
1 Cassia Bark stick
1.5 Kg (3.3lb) of Dark Soft Brown Sugar
1 crushed Campden Tablet
1 Sachet of Lalvin EC-1118 Wine Yeast
1 teaspoon of Yeast Nutrient

½ teaspoon of Wine Tannin
1 teaspoon of Acid Blend
10 drops of Amylaze
3½ litres (6 Pints) Cold Water

<u>After Fermentation:</u>

½ teaspoon of Potassium Sorbate
1 crushed Campden Tablet
1 sachet of Winefine Finings (one sachet will clear between 1 and 5 gallons)

<u>Directions:</u>

Wash the beetroots under a cold tap to remove all soil, before use, then cut them into cubes.

Bring the water to boil in a large pan on a stove. Once the water is boiling, add the beetroot pieces and sugar to the pan. Stir until the sugar is completely dissolved. Let the mixture simmer for about 20 minutes to fully extract flavour from the beetroots.

Remove the pan from heat and allow the beetroot mixture to cool to room temperature. Once cooled, strain the liquid into a pre-sterilised white plastic bucket and discard the beetroots (they can be eaten to avoid waste).

Then rinse the wheat and spices in a sieve with a kettle of boiling water to kill any bacteria and wild yeast cells. Add the wheat (whole, do not crush, or crack the husks), ginger, star anise, and cassia bark stick. Then pour over the grape concentrate, which will add depth and body to the wine. Add the acid blend, tannin, and Amylaze. Then add the yeast & yeast nutrient and stir thoroughly for 1-2 minutes to oxygenate the must. Cover the bucket with a cloth and leave to ferment in a warm place for 5 days, stirring the contents of the bucket occasionally. Then strain into a demijohn (4½ litres) or fermenter, through a nylon straining bag. Discard the wheat husks/spices. It may be necessary to top up with a little extra cold water to achieve 4½ litres. Fit a bung and airlock and leave in a warm place to continue to ferment out completely.

Finishing your Wine:

Fermentation should be complete in 2-5 weeks. At this stage CO2 bubbles should have stopped being released through the airlock. Your wine should then be checked with a hydrometer. The hydrometer will indicate the remaining sugar level and finishing levels are as follows:

Dry = 0.990 – 0.996   Medium = 0.996 – 1.009   Sweet = 1.009 – 1.018

At the end of fermentation add 1 crushed Campden tablet and half teaspoon of potassium sorbate per gallon. Leave in a cool place (15C) for 3 days to kill off the yeast. Then syphon the wine from the sediment into a second fermenter. Shake or stir the wine to degas it then add wine finings to ensure your wine will clear. Leave for 5 days in a cool place then syphon the wine from the sediment. Finally, pass it through a Vinbrite filter to obtain a professional finish before bottling. Filtering will remove all colloidal suspended particles and will ensure that your efforts are rewarded with a professional clarity and a pure taste. Sweeten to taste with brewers glycerine before bottling.

The wine should now be bottled in dark bottles to avoid colour loss and stored in a cool dark place to mature for at 12 months. During this time any rough tastes will be smoothed out and the wine will improve in bouquet and flavour.

This recipe makes 1 gallon (4.5 litres) of wine. For larger quantities simply multiply the quantities of ingredients except for the Yeast and Winefine. One sachet of each of these will be sufficient for any quantity between 1 and 5 gallons.

Blackberry Wine:

This is a quintessential English smooth red fruit wine. Blackberry wine offers a symphony of bold flavours and luscious aromas, which captures the essence of sun-ripened berries in every sip. When crafted from the plump, juicy fruit of blackberry bushes, this wine exudes a rich, deep hue reminiscent of midnight skies. With a perfect balance of sweetness and tartness, it provides layers of ripe berry flavours, tinged with hints of earthiness and spice. Each glass of blackberry wine is a journey through tangled brambles and sunlit fields, evoking memories of lazy summer days and the bounty of nature's harvest. Blackberries should be ripe to release their full flavour. Always choose clean, fresh fruit and avoid roadside locations when picking fruit. Thoroughly wash the fruit in cold water before use.

Ingredients:

At Start:

2 Kg (4½lb) Blackberries
(Use 450g of canned fruit if fresh is unavailable)

250ml or 245g Red Grape Concentrate
1 Kg of Sugar
1 crushed Campden Tablet
1 sachet of Lalvin K1-V1116 Wine Yeast
1 teaspoon of Yeast Nutrient
½ teaspoon of Wine Tannin
1 teaspoon of Acid Blend
10 drops of Pectinaze
3½ litres (6 Pints) Cold Water

After Fermentation:

½ teaspoon of Potassium Sorbate
1 crushed Campden Tablet
1 sachet of Winefine Finings (one sachet will clear between 1 and 5 gallons)

Directions:

Crush the Blackberries into a pre-sterilised white plastic bucket and pour over the grape concentrate, which will add depth and body to the wine. Then dissolve the sugar in a little hot water and add this to the bucket.

Pour the cold water over the contents together with the acid blend, tannin, and pectinaze. Crush a Campden tablet into the mix and stir well. Cover with a cloth and leave for 24 hours in a cool place. This process will kill any wild yeast and bacteria that may be present on the fruit. The next day add the yeast and yeast nutrient. Stir thoroughly for 1-2 minutes to oxygenate the must. Cover the bucket with a cloth and leave to ferment in a warm place for 5 days, stirring the contents of the bucket occasionally. Then strain into a demijohn (4½ litres) or fermenter, through a nylon straining bag. Press as much of the juice as possible and discard the pulp. It may be necessary to top up with a little extra cold water to achieve 4½ litres. Fit a bung and airlock and leave in a warm place to continue to ferment out completely.

Finishing your Wine:

Fermentation should be complete in 2-5 weeks. At this stage CO2 bubbles should have stopped being released through the airlock. Your wine should then be checked with a hydrometer. The hydrometer will indicate the remaining sugar level and finishing levels are as follows:

Dry = 0.990 – 0.996   Medium = 0.996 – 1.009   Sweet = 1.009 – 1.018

At the end of fermentation add 1 crushed Campden tablet and half teaspoon of potassium sorbate per gallon. Leave in a cool place (15C) for 3 days to kill off the yeast. Then syphon the wine from the sediment into a second fermenter. Shake or stir the wine to degas it then add wine finings to ensure your wine will clear. Leave for 5 days in a cool place then syphon the wine from the sediment. Finally, pass it through a Vinbrite filter to obtain a professional finish before bottling. Filtering will remove all colloidal suspended particles and will ensure that your efforts are rewarded with a professional clarity and a pure taste.

The wine should now be bottled and stored in a cool dark place to mature for at least 6 months. During this time any rough tastes will be smoothed out and the wine will improve in bouquet and flavour.

This recipe makes 1 gallon (4.5 litres) of wine. For larger quantities simply multiply the quantities of ingredients except for the Yeast and Winefine. One sachet of each of these will be sufficient for any quantity between 1 and 5 gallons.

Blackcurrant Wine:

Blackcurrants produce a wine with a deep hue coupled with an intense flavour and captivating aroma. From the first sip, the robustness of the berries punch through with a harmonious balance of sweetness and tartness.

Ingredients:

At Start:

1.5 Kg (3½lb) Blackcurrants
(Use 500g of canned fruit if fresh is unavailable)
250ml or 245g Red Grape Concentrate
1 Kg of Sugar
1 crushed Campden Tablet
1 sachet of Lalvin 71B Wine Yeast
1 teaspoon of Yeast Nutrient
½ teaspoon of Wine Tannin
1 teaspoon of Acid Blend
10 drops of Pectinaze
3½ litres (6 Pints) Cold Water

After Fermentation:

½ teaspoon of Potassium Sorbate
1 crushed Campden Tablet
1 sachet of Winefine Finings (one sachet will clear between 1 and 5 gallons)

Directions:

Crush the Blackcurrants into a pre-sterilised white plastic bucket and pour over the grape concentrate, which will add depth and body to the wine. Then dissolve the sugar in a little hot water and add this to the bucket.

Pour the cold water over the contents together with the acid blend, tannin, and pectinaze. Crush a Campden tablet into the mix and stir well. Cover with a cloth and leave for 24 hours in a cool place. This process will kill any wild yeast and bacteria that may be present on the fruit. The next day add the yeast and yeast nutrient. Stir thoroughly for 1-2 minutes to oxygenate the must. Cover the bucket with a cloth and leave to ferment in a warm place for 5 days, stirring the contents of the bucket occasionally. Then strain into a demijohn (4½ litres) or fermenter, through a nylon straining bag. Press as much of the juice as possible and discard the pulp. It may be necessary to top up with a little extra cold water to achieve 4½ litres. Fit a bung and airlock and leave in a warm place to continue to ferment out completely.

Finishing your Wine:

Fermentation should be complete in 2-5 weeks. At this stage CO_2 bubbles should have stopped being released through the airlock. Your wine should then be checked with a hydrometer. The hydrometer will indicate the remaining sugar level and finishing levels are as follows:

Dry = 0.990 – 0.996   Medium = 0.996 – 1.009   Sweet = 1.009 – 1.018

At the end of fermentation add 1 crushed Campden tablet and half teaspoon of potassium sorbate per gallon. Leave in a cool place (15C) for 3 days to kill off the yeast. Then syphon the wine from the sediment into a second fermenter. Shake or stir the wine to degas it then add wine finings to ensure your wine will clear. Leave for 5 days in a cool place then syphon the wine from the sediment. Finally, pass it through a Vinbrite filter to obtain a professional finish before bottling. Filtering will remove all colloidal suspended particles and will ensure that your efforts are rewarded with a professional clarity and a pure taste.

The wine should now be bottled and stored in a cool dark place to mature for at least 6 months. During this time any rough tastes will be smoothed out and the wine will improve in bouquet and flavour.

This recipe makes 1 gallon (4.5 litres) of wine. For larger quantities simply multiply the quantities of ingredients except for the Yeast and Winefine. One sachet of each of these will be sufficient for any quantity between 1 and 5 gallons.

Blueberry & Apple Wine:

While blueberries are known for their sweetness, they also have a subtle tartness that adds complexity to the flavour of blueberry wine. They have a rich and aromatic aroma that is inviting and fruity, with hints of sweetness and acidity. Blueberries combine well with other fruits such as raspberries. Raspberries add a bright and tangy flavour to blueberry wine, balancing the sweetness of the blueberries with their natural acidity. The combination of blueberries and raspberries creates a vibrant and refreshing wine with complex berry aromas. To follow this alternative, use 1kg (2.2lb) of raspberries instead of the apples described in this recipe.

Blueberry and apples complement each other very well in winemaking. Apples add a crisp and refreshing addition to blueberry wine. They balance the richness of blueberries and add complexity to the wine's flavour profile. This recipe produces a wine which has a smooth and lingering finish, with a pleasant mouthfeel that coats the palate.

Ingredients:

At Start:

1.5 Kg (3½lb) Blueberries
1kg (2.2lb) Apples (cooking apples are best)
250ml or 245g Red Grape Concentrate
1 Kg of Sugar
1 crushed Campden Tablet
1 sachet of Harris Premium Wine Yeast
1 teaspoon of Yeast Nutrient
½ teaspoon of Wine Tannin
½ teaspoon of Acid Blend
10 drops of Pectinaze
3½ litres (6 Pints) Cold Water

After Fermentation:

½ teaspoon of Potassium Sorbate

1 crushed Campden Tablet
1 sachet of Winefine Finings (one sachet will clear between 1 and 5 gallons)

Directions:

Wash the apples and blueberries under a tap before use. Then slice the apples into quarters. Crush the Blueberries and Apple quarters into a pre-sterilised white plastic bucket and pour over the grape concentrate, which will add depth and body to the wine. Then dissolve the sugar in a little hot water and add this to the bucket.

Pour the cold water over the contents together with the acid blend, tannin, and pectinaze. Crush a Campden tablet into the mix and stir well. Cover with a cloth and leave for 24 hours in a cool place. This process will kill any wild yeast and bacteria that may be present on the fruit. The next day add the yeast and yeast nutrient. Stir thoroughly for 1-2 minutes to oxygenate the must. Cover the bucket with a cloth and leave to ferment in a warm place for 5 days, stirring the contents of the bucket occasionally. Then strain into a demijohn (4½ litres) or fermenter, through a nylon straining bag. Press as much of the juice as possible and discard the pulp. It may be necessary to top up with a little extra cold water to achieve 4½ litres. Fit a bung and airlock and leave in a warm place to continue to ferment out completely.

Finishing your Wine:

Fermentation should be complete in 2-5 weeks. At this stage CO2 bubbles should have stopped being released through the airlock. Your wine should then be checked with a hydrometer. The hydrometer will indicate the remaining sugar level and finishing levels are as follows:

Dry = 0.990 – 0.996   Medium = 0.996 – 1.009   Sweet = 1.009 – 1.018

At the end of fermentation add 1 crushed Campden tablet and half teaspoon of potassium sorbate per gallon. Leave in a cool place (15C) for 3 days to kill off the yeast. Then syphon the wine from the sediment into a second fermenter. Shake or stir the wine to degas it then add wine finings to ensure your wine will clear. Leave for 5 days in a cool place then syphon the wine from the sediment. Finally, pass it through a Vinbrite filter to obtain a professional finish before bottling. Filtering will remove all colloidal suspended particles and will ensure that your efforts are rewarded with a professional clarity and a pure taste.

The wine should now be bottled and stored in a cool dark place to mature for at least 6 months. During this time any rough tastes will be smoothed out and the wine will improve in bouquet and flavour.

This recipe makes 1 gallon (4.5 litres) of wine. For larger quantities simply multiply the quantities of ingredients except for the Yeast and Winefine. One sachet of each of these will be sufficient for any quantity between 1 and 5 gallons.

Caraway Seed & Tea Wine:

Caraway seed and tea wine is an interesting combination that can result in a unique and flavourful wine. Caraway seeds have a distinctive flavour that is slightly sweet, earthy, and aromatic with hints of anise and citrus. When infused into wine, they can impart these complex flavours, adding depth and character. The tea, depending on its type (black, green, herbal, etc.), will contribute additional flavours ranging from floral and grassy to fruity or spicy, depending on the blend. Caraway seeds have a strong and aromatic fragrance, reminiscent of liquorice and citrus. When combined with the aroma of tea, the resulting wine can have a complex bouquet with herbal, spicy, and floral notes. The colour of the wine will depend on the type of tea used in the recipe. Black tea will produce a deep amber hue, while green tea will result in a lighter golden colour. The caraway seeds will not significantly affect the wine's colour, but only add subtle flecks or undertones.

This caraway seed and tea wine recipe uses black tea and offers a complex flavour profile with herbal, spicy, and citrusy notes, along with a pleasant aroma and potentially rich colour. The unique combination will appeal to those looking for something different from traditional grape based wines.

Ingredients:

At Start:

12 Black Tea Bags
150g (5oz) of Caraway Seeds.
250ml or 245g White Grape Concentrate
1.5 Kg (3.3lb) of Sugar
1 crushed Campden Tablet
1 sachet of Gervin GV1 Yeast
1 teaspoon of Yeast Nutrient
½ teaspoon of Wine Tannin
1 teaspoon of Acid Blend
10 drops of Amylaze
3½ litres (6 Pints) Cold Water

After Fermentation:

½ teaspoon of Potassium Sorbate
1 crushed Campden Tablet
1 sachet of Winefine Finings (one sachet will clear between 1 and 5 gallons)

Directions:

Wash the caraway seeds under a cold tap in a sieve before use.

Bring the water to boil in a large pan on a stove. Once the water is boiling, add the tea bags and sugar to the pan. Stir until the sugar is completely dissolved. Let the mixture simmer for about 10 minutes to fully extract flavour from the tea.

Remove the pan from heat and allow the tea mixture to cool to room temperature. Once cooled, strain the liquid into a pre-sterilised white plastic bucket and discard the tea bags.

Then rinse the caraway seeds in a sieve with a kettle of boiling water to kill any bacteria and wild yeast cells, then add to the bucket). Pour over the grape concentrate, which will add depth and body to the wine. Add the acid blend, tannin, and Amylaze. Then add the yeast & yeast nutrient and stir thoroughly for 1-2 minutes to oxygenate the must. Cover the bucket with a cloth and leave to ferment in a warm place for 5 days, stirring the contents of the bucket occasionally. Then strain into a demijohn (4½ litres) or fermenter, through a nylon straining bag. Discard the caraway seeds. It may be necessary to top up with a little extra cold water to achieve 4½ litres. Fit a bung and airlock and leave in a warm place to continue to ferment out completely.

Finishing your Wine:

Fermentation should be complete in 2-5 weeks. At this stage CO2 bubbles should have stopped being released through the airlock. Your wine should then be checked with a hydrometer. The hydrometer will indicate the remaining sugar level and finishing levels are as follows:

Dry = 0.990 – 0.996   Medium = 0.996 – 1.009   Sweet = 1.009 – 1.018

At the end of fermentation add 1 crushed Campden tablet and half teaspoon of potassium sorbate per gallon. Leave in a cool place (15C) for 3 days to kill off the yeast. Then syphon the wine from the sediment into a second fermenter. Shake or stir the wine to degas it then add wine finings to ensure your wine will clear. Leave for 5 days in a cool place then syphon the wine from the sediment. Finally, pass it through a Vinbrite filter to obtain a professional finish before bottling. Filtering will remove all colloidal suspended particles and will ensure that your efforts are rewarded with a professional clarity and a pure taste. Sweeten to taste with brewers glycerine before bottling.

The wine should now be bottled and stored in a cool dark place to mature for at 12 months. During this time any rough tastes will be smoothed out and the wine will improve in bouquet and flavour.

This recipe makes 1 gallon (4.5 litres) of wine. For larger quantities simply multiply the quantities of ingredients except for the Yeast and Winefine. One sachet of each of these will be sufficient for any quantity between 1 and 5 gallons.

Carrot Wine:

Carrot wine has a unique taste that combines the natural sweetness and earthiness of carrots with the characteristics of a well-made wine through the addition of grape concentrate. This recipe produces a wine on the sweeter side, to compliment the carrots natural sugars.

Carrot wine has a pronounced earthy flavour that is reminiscent of root vegetables and adds depth to the overall taste profile of the wine. Despite its earthy and vegetable notes, carrot wine is typically light and refreshing, with a clean finish. It can be enjoyed chilled, making it a popular choice for warm weather or as a refreshing alternative to heavier wines.

Select carrots that have reached a good size for their type. Avoid harvesting carrots that are too small, as they may not have developed enough sugars to contribute to the flavour of the wine. They should have a vibrant and uniform colour when ripe. Ripe carrots should have a firm and crisp texture. Avoid carrots that feel soft or mushy, as they may be overripe or starting to deteriorate.

Ingredients:

At Start:

2kg (4.5lb) of Carrots
500g (1lb) of Long Grain Brown Rice.
250ml or 245g White Grape Concentrate
1.5 Kg (3.3lb) of Sugar
1 crushed Campden Tablet
1 sachet of Lalvin EC-1118 Wine Yeast
1 teaspoon of Yeast Nutrient
½ teaspoon of Wine Tannin
1 teaspoon of Acid Blend
10 drops of Amylaze
3½ litres (6 Pints) Cold Water
After Fermentation:

½ teaspoon of Potassium Sorbate
1 crushed Campden Tablet
1 sachet of Winefine Finings (one sachet will clear between 1 and 5 gallons)

Directions:

Wash the carrots under a cold tap in a sieve before use. Cut off and discard the base then dice the stems.

Bring the water to boil in a large pan on a stove. Once the water is boiling, add the carrot pieces and sugar to the pan. Stir until the sugar is completely dissolved. Let the mixture simmer for about 20 minutes to fully extract flavour from the carrots.

Remove the pan from heat and allow the carrot mixture to cool to room temperature. Once cooled, strain the liquid into a pre-sterilised white plastic bucket and discard the carrots (they can be eaten to avoid waste).

Then rinse the rice in a sieve with a kettle of boiling water to kill any bacteria and wild yeast cells. Add the rice whole, do not crush, or crack the husks). Pour over the grape concentrate, which will add depth and body to the wine. Add the acid blend, tannin, and Amylaze. Then add the yeast & yeast nutrient and stir thoroughly for 1-2 minutes to oxygenate the must. Cover the bucket with a cloth and leave to ferment in a warm place for 5 days, stirring the contents of the bucket occasionally. Then strain into a demijohn (4½ litres) or fermenter, through a nylon straining bag. Discard the rice husks. It may be necessary to top up with a little extra cold water to achieve 4½ litres. Fit a bung and airlock and leave in a warm place to continue to ferment out completely.

Finishing your Wine:

Fermentation should be complete in 2-5 weeks. At this stage CO2 bubbles should have stopped being released through the airlock. Your wine should then be checked with a hydrometer. The hydrometer will indicate the remaining sugar level and finishing levels are as follows:

Dry = 0.990 – 0.996   Medium = 0.996 – 1.009   Sweet = 1.009 – 1.018

At the end of fermentation add 1 crushed Campden tablet and half teaspoon of potassium sorbate per gallon. Leave in a cool place (15C) for 3 days to kill off the yeast. Then syphon the wine from the sediment into a second fermenter. Shake or stir the wine to degas it then add wine finings to ensure your wine will clear. Leave for 5 days in a cool place then syphon the wine from the sediment. Finally, pass it through a Vinbrite filter to obtain a professional finish before bottling. Filtering will remove all colloidal suspended particles and will ensure that your efforts are rewarded with a professional clarity and a pure taste. Sweeten to taste with brewers glycerine before bottling.

The wine should now be bottled and stored in a cool dark place to mature for at 12 months. During this time any rough tastes will be smoothed out and the wine will improve in bouquet and flavour.

This recipe makes 1 gallon (4.5 litres) of wine. For larger quantities simply multiply the quantities of ingredients except for the Yeast and Winefine. One sachet of each of these will be sufficient for any quantity between 1 and 5 gallons.

Cherry Wine:

Cherry wine has been described as a crimson jewel of the vineyard. It provides a delicious blend of sweet and tart flavours, capturing the essence of ripe cherries in every sip. This wine has a vibrant aroma and luscious depth. With a perfect balance of fruity sweetness and refreshing acidity, it unfolds on the palate with a burst of cherry goodness, tinged with hints of spice and earthiness.

Ingredients:

At Start:

2.5 Kg (5½lb) Cherries (Morello Cherries produce the best flavour)
(Use 500g of dried or 850g of canned fruit if fresh is unavailable)
250ml or 245g Red Grape Concentrate
1 Kg of Sugar
1 crushed Campden Tablet
1 sachet of Gervin GV2 Wine Yeast
1 teaspoon of Yeast Nutrient
1 teaspoon of Acid Blend
10 drops of Pectinaze
3½ litres (6 Pints) Cold Water

After Fermentation:
½ teaspoon of Potassium Sorbate
1 crushed Campden Tablet
1 sachet of Winefine Finings (one sachet will clear between 1 and 5 gallons)

Directions:

Remove all stones from the Cherries (an Olive/Cherry Pitter is an ideal tool to remove the stones) and crush them into a pre-sterilised white plastic bucket. Then pour over the grape concentrate, which will add depth and body to the wine. Then dissolve the sugar in a little hot water and add this to the bucket.

Pour the cold water over the contents together with the acid blend, and pectinaze. Crush a Campden tablet into the mix and stir well. Cover with a cloth and leave for 24 hours in a cool place. This process will kill any wild yeast and bacteria that may be present on the fruit. The next day add the yeast and yeast nutrient. Stir thoroughly for 1-2 minutes to oxygenate the must. Cover the bucket with a cloth and leave to ferment in a warm place for 5 days, stirring the contents of the bucket occasionally. Then strain into a demijohn (4½ litres) or fermenter, through a nylon straining bag. Press as much of the juice as possible and discard the pulp. It may be necessary to top up with a little extra cold water to achieve 4½ litres. Fit a bung and airlock and leave in a warm place to continue to ferment out completely.

Finishing your Wine:

Fermentation should be complete in 2-5 weeks. At this stage CO2 bubbles should have stopped being released through the airlock. Your wine should then be checked with a hydrometer. The hydrometer will indicate the remaining sugar level and finishing levels are as follows:

Dry = 0.990 – 0.996   Medium = 0.996 – 1.009   Sweet = 1.009 – 1.018

At the end of fermentation add 1 crushed Campden tablet and half teaspoon of potassium sorbate per gallon. Leave in a cool place (15C) for 3 days to kill off the yeast. Then syphon the wine from the sediment into a second fermenter. Shake or stir the wine to degas it then add wine finings to ensure your wine will clear. Leave for 5 days in a cool place then syphon the wine from the sediment. Finally, pass it through a Vinbrite filter to obtain a professional finish before bottling. Filtering will remove all colloidal suspended particles and will ensure that your efforts are rewarded with a professional clarity and a pure taste.

The wine should now be bottled and stored in a cool dark place to mature for at least 6 months. During this time any rough tastes will be smoothed out and the wine will improve in bouquet and flavour.

This recipe makes 1 gallon (4.5 litres) of wine. For larger quantities simply multiply the quantities of ingredients except for the Yeast and Winefine. One sachet of each of these will be sufficient for any quantity between 1 and 5 gallons.

Cherry Brandy Liqueur:

This recipe produces a delicious liqueur, which is popular at Christmas. Cherry brandy, also known as cherry liqueur or kirsch, is a sweet and flavourful alcoholic drink made from cherries. It has a rich and intense flavour that is both sweet and slightly tart, with a deep ruby colour hue. The taste of ripe cherries shines through, providing a burst of fruity sweetness with hints of acidity. Cherry brandy typically has an alcohol content, ranging from around 20% to 40% alcohol by volume (ABV).

Ingredients:

To make one 70cl bottle of Liqueur:
500g (1lb) of ripe Cherries
One 70cl bottle of Brandy (Your own Brandy produced from Still Spirits Air Still is ideal and saves you money).
500g (1lb) Sugar.

Directions:

Slit each cherry and remove the stone. This will ensure a smooth rich flavour (with no bitterness from the stone) and will allow you to use the cherries later to make liqueur chocolates.

Half fill a wide necked jar, such as a Kilner Jar, with the stoned cherries. Shake the jar so that the cherries fall into place (allow enough space for the brandy to be added).

Gently heat the brandy in a pan on the stove and pour in the sugar. Do not boil, just raise the temperature high enough to stir the sugar until it dissolves and then leave to cool.

Pour the cooled brandy/sugar solution into the jar and add more cherries until the jar is full, then seal down. Shake the jar to mix the ingredients then store for a minimum of eight weeks, preferably in a dark and dry place. Return and shake occasionally. The longer you leave it, the richer the flavour and deeper the colour will be.

After a minimum of eight weeks strain the liqueur through a muslin bag taking care not to crush the cherries too much. The liqueur should then be strained through a filter paper to ensure that it is clear and bright before bottling. Be patient. Cherry Brandy is quite gelatinous so it will drip slowly through the filter paper. Alternatively, you could filter it through a Vinbrite Filter fitted with a Prime Pad.

The brandy infused cherries that are strained from the liqueur make delicious Christmas liqueur chocolates.

Cherry Brandy Liqueur Chocolates:

To make cherry brandy liqueur chocolates you will need:

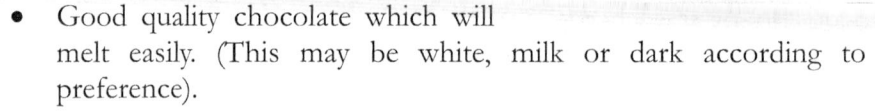

- An ice cube (or chocolate) mould
- Good quality chocolate which will melt easily. (This may be white, milk or dark according to preference).
- Brandy infused cherries from the cherry brandy.

Directions:

Break the chocolate into small pieces and place in a heat resistant bowl. Rest the bowl on a small saucepan of boiling water. The heat/steam will melt the chocolate as you stir. This method is known as a "bain-marie".

Pour a small amount of melted chocolate into each of the moulds to cover the bottom. Then add one cherry to each mould. Pour over more chocolate to completely cover the cherries.

Place the mould into a fridge to set the chocolates.

Once set they can be removed from the mould and placed into a box or sweet papers for display. The chocolates can also be dusted with cocoa or vanilla powder to add variety, or a nut of your choice can be placed on the top as a garnish.

Crab-Apple Wine.

This recipe produces a wine with crisp acidity and delicate sweetness, capturing the essence of tart crab apples in every sip. Crafted from the small, vibrant fruit of the crab apple tree, this wine offers a delightful balance of tangy notes and subtle fruitiness. Its pale golden hue evokes images of sunlit orchards, while its refreshing character leaves a lasting impression of orchard-fresh goodness.

Ingredients:

At Start:

2.5Kg (5½lb) Crab-Apples
250ml or 245g White Grape Concentrate
1 Kg Bag of Sugar
1 sachet of Harris Premium Wine Yeast
1 sachet of Pure Brew (or 1 Teaspoon Yeast Nutrient)
1 teaspoon of Acid Blend
10 drops of Pectinaze
1 Crushed Campden Tablet
3½ litres (6 Pints) Cold Water

After Fermentation:

½ teaspoon of Potassium Sorbate
1 crushed Campden Tablet
1 sachet of Winefine Finings (one sachet will clear between 1 and 5 gallons)
10g Oak Barrel Chips (optional)

Directions:

Chop the crab-apples and crush them in a pre-sterilised white plastic bucket. Pour over the grape concentrate, which will add depth and body to the wine. Add the oak barrel chips (optional). This will support a delicious chardonnay style flavour in the final wine. Then dissolve the sugar in a little hot water and add this to the bucket.

Pour the cold water over the contents together with the acid blend, and pectinaze. Crush a Campden tablet into the mix and stir well. Cover with a cloth and leave for 24 hours in a cool place. This process will kill any wild yeast and bacteria that may be present on the fruit. The next day add the yeast & Pure Brew sachet (or nutrient). This is now called the 'must'. Stir thoroughly for 1-2 minutes to oxygenate the must. Cover the bucket with a cloth and leave to ferment in a warm place for 5 days, stirring the contents of the bucket occasionally. Then strain into a demijohn (4½ litres) or fermenter, through a nylon straining bag. Press as much of the juice as possible and discard the pulp. It may be necessary to top up with a little extra cold water to achieve 4½ litres. Fit a bung and airlock and leave in a warm place to continue to ferment out completely.

Finishing your Wine:

Fermentation should be complete in 2-5 weeks. At this stage CO2 bubbles should have stopped being released through the airlock. Your wine should then be checked with a hydrometer. The hydrometer will indicate the remaining sugar level and finishing levels are as follows:

Dry = 0.990 – 0.996   Medium = 0.996 – 1.009   Sweet = 1.009 – 1.018

At the end of fermentation add 1 crushed Campden tablet and half teaspoon of potassium sorbate per gallon. Leave in a cool place (15C) for 3 days to kill off the yeast. Then syphon the wine from the sediment into a second fermenter. Shake or stir the wine to degas it then add wine finings to ensure your wine will clear. Leave for 5 days in a cool place then syphon the wine from the sediment. Finally, pass it through a Vinbrite filter to obtain a professional finish before bottling.

Crab-Apples contain a high level of pectin which can make it difficult to clear your wine. Therefore, it is important to add pectinaze (you cannot overdose so add a little extra if necessary), and to add finings to support the clearing process. Filtering will remove all colloidal suspended particles and will ensure that your efforts are rewarded with a professional clarity and a pure taste.

The wine should now be bottled and stored in a cool dark place to mature for at least 9 months. During this time any rough tastes will be smoothed out and the wine will improve in bouquet and flavour.

This recipe makes 1 gallon (4.5 litres) of wine. For larger quantities simply multiply the quantities of ingredients except for the Pure Brew, Yeast and Winefine. One sachet of each of these will be sufficient for any quantity between 1 and 5 gallons.

Damson Wine:

Damson wine is a quintessential English country wine made from the tart and juicy damson plums. With its deep ruby colour and rich, fruity flavour, it offers a delicious alternative to traditional grape wines.

Ingredients:

At Start:

2 Kg (4½lb) Damsons
250g (1/2lb) Barley (whole, do not crush or crack the husks)
250ml or 245g Red Grape Concentrate
1 Kg of Sugar
1 crushed Campden Tablet
1 sachet of Harris Premium Wine Yeast
1 teaspoon of Yeast Nutrient
1 teaspoon of Acid Blend
10 drops of Pectinaze
3½ litres (6 Pints) Water

After Fermentation:
½ teaspoon of Potassium Sorbate
1 crushed Campden Tablet
1 sachet of Winefine Finings (one sachet will clear between 1 and 5 gallons)

Directions:

Remove all stones from the Damsons (an Olive/Cherry Pitter is an ideal tool to remove the stones) and crush them into a pre-sterilised white plastic bucket. Rinse the barley in a sieve under a cold tap to clean it then add to the bucket (do not crush or crack the husks as they act as a filter to retain unwanted starch). Then add the grape concentrate, which will provide depth and body to the wine. Then dissolve the sugar in a little hot water and add this to the bucket.

Pour the cold water over the contents together with the acid blend, and pectinaze. Crush a Campden tablet into the mix and stir well. Cover with a cloth and leave for 24 hours in a cool place. This process will kill any wild yeast and bacteria that may be present on the fruit. The next day add the yeast and yeast nutrient. Stir thoroughly for 1-2 minutes to oxygenate the must. Cover the bucket with a cloth and leave to ferment in a warm place for 5 days, stirring the contents of the bucket occasionally. Then strain into a demijohn (4½ litres) or fermenter, through a nylon straining bag. Press as much of the juice as possible and discard the pulp. It may be necessary to top up with a little extra cold water to achieve 4½ litres. Fit a bung and airlock and leave in a warm place to continue to ferment out completely.

<u>Finishing your Wine:</u>

Fermentation should be complete in 2-5 weeks. At this stage CO2 bubbles should have stopped being released through the airlock. Your wine should then be checked with a hydrometer. The hydrometer will indicate the remaining sugar level and finishing levels are as follows:

Dry = 0.990 – 0.996   Medium = 0.996 – 1.009   Sweet = 1.009 – 1.018

At the end of fermentation add 1 crushed Campden tablet and half teaspoon of potassium sorbate per gallon. Leave in a cool place (15C) for 3 days to kill off the yeast. Then syphon the wine from the sediment into a second fermenter. Shake or stir the wine to degas it then add wine finings to ensure your wine will clear. Leave for 5 days in a cool place then syphon the wine from the sediment. Finally, pass it through a Vinbrite filter to obtain a professional finish before bottling. Damsons contain a high level of pectin which can make it difficult to clear your wine. Therefore, it is important to add pectinaze (you cannot overdose so add a little extra if necessary), and to add finings to support the clearing process. Filtering will remove all colloidal suspended particles and will ensure that your efforts are rewarded with a professional clarity and a pure taste.

The wine should now be bottled and stored in a cool dark place to mature for at least 6 months. During this time any rough tastes will be smoothed out and the wine will improve in bouquet and flavour.

This recipe makes 1 gallon (4.5 litres) of wine. For larger quantities simply multiply the quantities of ingredients except for the Yeast and Winefine. One sachet of each of these will be sufficient for any quantity between 1 and 5 gallons.

Damson Port:

Damson port wine is a luxurious and indulgent fortified wine crafted from the intense flavours of ripe damsons. With its deep, ruby-red hue and complex bouquet, it evokes images of opulent evenings by the fire. This unique wine is fortified with brandy following fermentation, resulting in a higher alcohol content and a rich, velvety texture. The flavours are a harmonious blend of sweet and tart, with notes of ripe plum, dark berries, and subtle spices. Damson port wine is often enjoyed as a decadent dessert wine, paired with rich chocolate desserts, sharp cheeses, or enjoyed on its own as a luxurious after-dinner indulgence.

Ingredients:

At Start:

2 Kg (4½lb) Damsons
500g (1lb) Wheat (whole, do not crush or crack the husks)
1 Banana
250ml or 245g Red Grape Concentrate
2Kg of Dextrose Brewing Sugar
1 crushed Campden Tablet
1 sachet of Lalvin EC-1118 Yeast
1 sachet of Harris Pure Brew
1 teaspoon of Acid Blend
10 drops of Pectinaze
3½ litres (6 Pints) Water

After Fermentation:
½ teaspoon of Potassium Sorbate
1 crushed Campden Tablet
1 sachet of Winefine Finings (one sachet will clear between 1 and 5 gallons)
150ml Brandy

Directions:

Remove all stones from the Damsons (an Olive/Cherry Pitter is an ideal tool to remove the stones) and crush them into a pre-sterilised white plastic bucket, together with the peeled banana. Rinse the wheat in a sieve under a cold tap to clean it then add to the bucket (do not crush or crack the husks as they act as a filter to retain unwanted starch). Then add the grape concentrate, which will provide depth and body to the wine. Then dissolve the brewing sugar in a little hot water and add this to the bucket.

Pour the cold water over the contents together with the acid blend, and pectinaze. Crush a Campden tablet into the mix and stir well. Cover with a cloth and leave for 24 hours in a cool place. This process will kill any wild yeast and bacteria that may be present on the fruit. The next day add the yeast and sachet of Pure Brew. Stir thoroughly for 1-2 minutes to oxygenate the must. Cover the bucket with a cloth and leave to ferment in a warm place for 5 days, stirring the contents of the bucket occasionally. Then strain into a demijohn (4½ litres) or fermenter, through a nylon straining bag. Press as much of the juice as possible and discard the pulp. It may be necessary to top up with a little extra cold water to achieve 4½ litres. Fit a bung and airlock and leave in a warm place to continue to ferment out completely.

Finishing your Wine:

Fermentation should be complete in 2-5 weeks. At this stage CO2 bubbles should have stopped being released through the airlock. Your wine should then be checked with a hydrometer. The hydrometer will indicate the remaining sugar level and finishing levels are as follows:

Dry = 0.990 – 0.996   Medium = 0.996 – 1.009   Sweet = 1.009 – 1.018

At the end of fermentation add 1 crushed Campden tablet and half teaspoon of potassium sorbate per gallon. Leave in a cool place (15C) for 3 days to kill off the yeast. Then syphon the wine from the sediment into a second fermenter. Shake or stir the wine to degas it then add wine finings to ensure your wine will clear. Leave for 5 days in a cool place then syphon the wine from the sediment. Finally, pass it through a Vinbrite filter to obtain a professional finish before bottling. Damsons contain a high level of pectin which can make it difficult to clear your wine. Therefore, it is important to add pectinaze (you cannot overdose so add a little extra if necessary), and to add finings to support the clearing process. Filtering will remove all colloidal suspended particles and will ensure that your efforts are rewarded with a professional clarity and a pure taste.

The wine should now be bottled. Add 25ml of Brandy to each bottle of wine to fortify it before corking the bottles. Then store in a cool dark place to mature for 6-12 months. During this time any rough tastes will be smoothed out and the wine will improve in bouquet and flavour.

This recipe makes 1 gallon (4.5 litres) of wine. For larger quantities simply multiply the quantities of ingredients except for the Pure Brew, Yeast and Winefine. One sachet of each of these will be sufficient for any quantity between 1 and 5 gallons.

Damson Vodka Liqueur:

This recipe produces a delicious liqueur, which is popular at Christmas. Damsons are small, oval-shaped plums that have an indigo skin and yellow-green flesh. They are larger and less tart than Sloes (which can be substituted to make a Sloe Vodka). Damsons make excellent pies and jams and are perfect for this delicious liqueur, which is a Christmas favourite.

Ingredients:

To make one 70cl bottle of Liqueur:
500g (1lb) of ripe Damsons
One 70cl bottle of Vodka (Your own Vodka produced from Still Spirits Air Still is ideal and saves you money).
500g (1lb) Sugar.

Directions:

Slit each damson and remove the stone. Then, if possible, prick them with a fork. This will ensure a smooth rich flavour and will allow you to use the damsons later to make liqueur chocolates.

Half fill a wide necked jar, such as a Kilner Jar, with the stoned damsons. Shake the jar so that the damsons fall into place (allow enough space for the vodka to be added).

Gently heat the vodka in a pan on the stove and pour in the sugar. Do not boil, just raise the temperature high enough to stir the sugar until it dissolves and then leave to cool.

Pour the cooled vodka/sugar solution into the jar and add more damsons until the jar is full, then seal down. Shake the jar to mix the ingredients then store for a minimum of eight weeks, preferably in a dark and dry place. Return and shake occasionally. The longer you leave it, the richer the flavour and deeper the colour will be.

After a minimum of eight weeks strain the liqueur through a muslin bag taking care not to crush the damsons too much. The liqueur should then be strained through a filter paper to ensure that it is clear and bright before bottling. Be patient. Damson Vodka is quite gelatinous so it will drip slowly through the filter paper. Alternatively, you could filter it through a Vinbrite Filter fitted with a Prime Pad.

The vodka infused damsons that are strained from the liqueur make delicious Christmas liqueur chocolates.

Damson Liqueur Chocolates:

To make damson liqueur chocolates you will need:

- An ice cube (or chocolate) mould
- Good quality chocolate which will melt easily. (This may be white, milk or dark according to preference).
- Vodka infused damsons from the damson vodka.

Directions:

Break the chocolate into small pieces and place in a heat resistant bowl. Rest the bowl on a small saucepan of boiling water. The heat/steam will melt the chocolate as you stir. This method is known as a "bain-marie".

Pour a small amount of melted chocolate into each of the moulds to cover the bottom. Then add one damson to each mould. Pour over more chocolate to completely cover the damsons.

Place the mould into a fridge to set the chocolates.

Once set they can be removed from the mould and placed into a box or sweet papers for display. The chocolates can also be dusted with cocoa or vanilla powder to add variety, or a nut of your choice can be placed on the top as a garnish.

Dandelion Wine:

Making dandelion wine is a traditional and delightful way to capture the essence of springtime. It produces a sweet, floral wine with subtle notes of honey. It is important to only pick the yellow petals, and not include green parts which will impart bitterness. This recipe uses honey instead of sugar to accentuate the floral notes of the dandelions.

Ingredients:

At Start:

1 litre (2 pints) of fresh yellow Dandelion petals
250ml or 245g White Grape Concentrate
1 Kg of clear honey
1 crushed Campden Tablet
1 sachet of Lalvin K1-V1116 Wine Yeast
1 teaspoon of Yeast Nutrient
1 teaspoon of Acid Blend
¼ teaspoon of Wine Tannin
10 drops of Pectinaze
3½ litres (6 Pints) Cold Water

After Fermentation:
½ teaspoon of Potassium Sorbate
1 crushed Campden Tablet
1 sachet of Winefine Finings (one sachet will clear between 1 and 5 gallons)

Directions:

Remove the petals from their stalks and rinse them in a sieve under a cold tap to remove any dirt. Then put them into a pre-sterilised white plastic bucket and pour over the grape concentrate, which will add depth and body to the wine. Then dissolve the honey in water and add this to the bucket (keep the water temperature to 40C to avoid destroying the fine flavours of the honey).

Pour the cold water over the contents together with the acid blend, tannin, and pectinaze. Crush a Campden tablet into the mix and stir well. Cover with a cloth and leave for 24 hours in a cool place. This process will kill any wild yeast and bacteria that may be present on the flowers. The next day add the yeast and yeast nutrient. Stir thoroughly for 1-2 minutes to oxygenate the must. Cover the bucket with a cloth and leave to ferment in a warm place for 5 days, stirring the contents of the bucket occasionally. Then strain into a demijohn (4½ litres) or fermenter, through a nylon straining bag and discard the flower pulp. It may be necessary to top up with a little extra cold water to achieve 4½ litres. Fit a bung and airlock and leave in a warm place to continue to ferment out completely.

Finishing your Wine:

Fermentation should be complete in 2-5 weeks. At this stage CO2 bubbles should have stopped being released through the airlock. Your wine should then be checked with a hydrometer. The hydrometer will indicate the remaining sugar level and finishing levels are as follows:

Dry = 0.990 – 0.996   Medium = 0.996 – 1.009   Sweet = 1.009 – 1.018

At the end of fermentation add 1 crushed Campden tablet and half teaspoon of potassium sorbate per gallon. Leave in a cool place (15C) for 3 days to kill off the yeast. Then syphon the wine from the sediment into a second fermenter. Shake or stir the wine to degas it then add wine finings to ensure your wine will clear. Leave for 5 days in a cool place then syphon the wine from the sediment. Finally, pass it through a Vinbrite filter to obtain a professional finish before bottling. Filtering will remove all colloidal suspended particles and will ensure that your efforts are rewarded with a professional clarity and a pure taste.

The wine should now be bottled and stored in a cool dark place to mature for at least 6 months. During this time any rough tastes will be smoothed out and the wine will improve in bouquet and flavour.

This recipe makes 1 gallon (4.5 litres) of wine. For larger quantities simply multiply the quantities of ingredients except for the Yeast and Winefine. One sachet of each of these will be sufficient for any quantity between 1 and 5 gallons.

Elderberry Wine:

This is possibly the fruit wine which has been made most in the UK. It is the quintessential English wine. Elderberries typically come from the elder tree (Sambucus), which produces small, dark purple to black berries. These berries are commonly used in various culinary and medicinal applications due to their tart flavour and high levels of antioxidants. Elderberries can have high tannin content which require longer maturation periods. One tip to remove excess tannin is to boil the elderberries in a pan before using them. A scum will develop on the surface, which can be scraped off and discarded. This is excess tannin, and the process can reduce maturation times by as much as 25%. Always pick dark black elderberries, which are fully ripe. Avoid using green berries, and always pick them from areas away from traffic pollution. The berries can be stripped from their stalks using a fork. Discard the stalks as they will impart bitterness to the wine. Rinse the berries under a cold tap (in a sieve) to remove any dirt.

Ingredients:

At Start:

1.5 Kg (3½lb) Elderberries
(Use 500g of dried fruit if fresh is unavailable)
250g (1/2lb) Wheat (whole, do not crush or crack the husks)
250ml or 245g Red Grape Concentrate
1 Kg of Sugar
1 crushed Campden Tablet
1 sachet of Harris Premium Wine Yeast
1 teaspoon of Yeast Nutrient
1 teaspoon of Acid Blend
10 drops of Pectinaze
3½ litres (6 Pints) Cold Water

After Fermentation:

½ teaspoon of Potassium Sorbate
1 crushed Campden Tablet
1 sachet of Winefine Finings (one sachet will clear between 1 and 5 gallons)

Directions:

Crush the Elderberries into a pre-sterilised white plastic bucket and pour over the grape concentrate, which will add depth and body to the wine. Rinse the wheat in a sieve under a cold tap then add to the bucket (do not crush or crack the grains as the husks act as a filter preventing the release of starch). Then dissolve the sugar in a little hot water and add this to the bucket.

Pour the cold water over the contents together with the acid blend, and pectinaze. Crush a Campden tablet into the mix and stir well. Cover with a cloth and leave for 24 hours in a cool place. This process will kill any wild yeast and bacteria that may be present on the fruit. The next day add the yeast and yeast nutrient. Stir thoroughly for 1-2 minutes to oxygenate the must. Cover the bucket with a cloth and leave to ferment in a warm place for 5 days, stirring the contents of the bucket occasionally. Then strain into a demijohn (4½ litres) or fermenter, through a nylon straining bag. Press as much of the juice as possible and discard the pulp. It may be necessary to top up with a little extra cold water to achieve 4½ litres. Fit a bung and airlock and leave in a warm place to continue to ferment out completely.

Finishing your Wine:

Fermentation should be complete in 2-5 weeks. At this stage CO_2 bubbles should have stopped being released through the airlock. Your wine should then be checked with a hydrometer. The hydrometer will indicate the remaining sugar level and finishing levels are as follows:

Dry = 0.990 – 0.996   Medium = 0.996 – 1.009   Sweet = 1.009 – 1.018

At the end of fermentation add 1 crushed Campden tablet and half teaspoon of potassium sorbate per gallon. Leave in a cool place (15C) for 3 days to kill off the yeast. Then syphon the wine from the sediment into a second fermenter. Shake or stir the wine to degas it then add wine finings to ensure your wine will clear. Leave for 5 days in a cool place then syphon the wine from the sediment. Finally, pass it through a Vinbrite filter to obtain a professional finish before bottling. Filtering will remove all colloidal suspended particles and will ensure that your efforts are rewarded with a professional clarity and a pure taste.

The wine should now be bottled and stored in a cool dark place to mature for at least 6 months. During this time any rough tastes will be smoothed out and the wine will improve in bouquet and flavour.

This recipe makes 1 gallon (4.5 litres) of wine. For larger quantities simply multiply the quantities of ingredients except for the Yeast and Winefine. One sachet of each of these will be sufficient for any quantity between 1 and 5 gallons.

Spiced Elderberry Port:

This recipe produces a deep, rich wine, with warming spices. It makes an excellent toddy on a cold winter's night. Alternatively, it makes an excellent base for a mulled wine. The final wine can be fortified with brandy to achieve a port-like finish.

Remember that elderberries can have high tannin content which require longer maturation periods. One tip to remove excess tannin is to boil the elderberries in a pan before using them. A scum will develop on the surface, which can be scraped off and discarded. This is excess tannin, and the process can reduce maturation times by as much as 25%.

Always pick dark black elderberries, which are fully ripe. Avoid using green berries, and always pick them from areas away from traffic pollution. The berries can be stripped from their stalks using a fork. Discard the stalks as they will impart bitterness to the wine. Rinse the berries under a cold tap (in a sieve) to remove any dirt.

Ingredients:

At Start:

2 Kg (4.4lb) Elderberries
(Use 500g of dried fruit if fresh is unavailable)
250g (1/2lb) Wheat (whole, do not crush or crack the husks)
250ml or 245g Red Grape Concentrate
1.5 Kg (3lb) of Sugar
1 ripe Banana
1 Cassia Bark stick
15g Root Ginger (Bruise it before use by hitting it with a rolling pin)
5 All-Spice pods
1 crushed Campden Tablet
1 sachet of Lalvin EC-1118 Wine Yeast
1 teaspoon of Yeast Nutrient
1 teaspoon of Acid Blend
10 drops of Pectinaze
3½ litres (6 Pints) Cold Water

After Fermentation:

½ teaspoon of Potassium Sorbate
1 crushed Campden Tablet
1 sachet of Winefine Finings (one sachet will clear between 1 and 5 gallons)
150ml Brandy (to fortify the wine)

Directions:

Crush the Elderberries and Banana into a pre-sterilised white plastic bucket and pour over the grape concentrate, which will add depth and body to the wine. Rinse the wheat and spices in a sieve under a cold tap then add to the bucket (do not crush or crack the grains as the husks act as a filter preventing the release of starch). Then dissolve the sugar in a little hot water and add this to the bucket.

Pour the cold water over the contents together with the acid blend, and pectinaze. Crush a Campden tablet into the mix and stir well. Cover with a cloth and leave for 24 hours in a cool place. This process will kill any wild yeast and bacteria that may be present on the fruit. The next day add the yeast and yeast nutrient. Stir thoroughly for 1-2 minutes to oxygenate the must. Cover the bucket with a cloth and leave to ferment in a warm place for 5 days, stirring the contents of the bucket occasionally. Then strain into a demijohn (4½ litres) or fermenter, through a nylon straining bag. Press as much of the juice as possible and discard the pulp. It may be necessary to top up with a little extra cold water to achieve 4½ litres. Fit a bung and airlock and leave in a warm place to continue to ferment out completely.

Finishing your Wine:

Fermentation should be complete in 2-5 weeks. At this stage CO2 bubbles should have stopped being released through the airlock. Your wine should then be checked with a hydrometer. The hydrometer will indicate the remaining sugar level and finishing levels are as follows:

Dry = 0.990 – 0.996   Medium = 0.996 – 1.009   Sweet = 1.009 – 1.018

At the end of fermentation add 1 crushed Campden tablet and half teaspoon of potassium sorbate per gallon. Leave in a cool place (15C) for 3 days to kill off the yeast. Then syphon the wine from the sediment into a second fermenter. Shake or stir the wine to degas it then add wine finings to ensure your wine will clear. Leave for 5 days in a cool place then syphon the wine from the sediment. Finally, pass it through a Vinbrite filter to obtain a professional finish before bottling. Filtering will remove all colloidal suspended particles and will ensure that your efforts are rewarded with a professional clarity and a pure taste. Back-sweeten the wine with brewers' glycerine or honey to achieve the desired level of sweetness.

The wine should now be bottled and stored in a cool dark place to mature for at least 6 months. During this time any rough tastes will be smoothed out and the wine will improve in bouquet and flavour. 25ml of brandy can optionally be added to each bottle to fortify the wine and give it a port-like consistency.

This recipe makes 1 gallon (4.5 litres) of wine. For larger quantities simply multiply the quantities of ingredients except for the Yeast and Winefine. One sachet of each of these will be sufficient for any quantity between 1 and 5 gallons.

Elderflower Wine:

The quantity of elderflowers needed for elderflower wine can vary depending on the preferred intensity of flavour, and the size of the elderflower heads. However, a common guideline is to use about 20-30 elderflower heads for every gallon (4.5 litres) of wine. It is essential to ensure that the elderflowers are freshly picked and free from any debris or insects. Also, avoid picking them from areas where there is traffic pollution.

Creamy elderflowers are elderflowers that are fully opened and have begun to develop their creamy white colour. They may offer a more pronounced aroma and flavour compared to younger, still-white elderflowers. Creamy elderflowers are often preferred by some winemakers for their stronger fragrance and potential for more intense flavour in the finished wine.

White elderflowers, on the other hand, are younger flowers that have not yet fully opened or turned creamy in colour. They may have a milder aroma and flavour compared to creamy elderflowers but can still produce delightful elderflower wine with a delicate floral character.

Ultimately, you can use either creamy elderflowers or white ones for elderflower wine, depending on what is available to you and your preference for the intensity of flavour and aroma. Some winemakers even choose to use a combination of both types of flowers to achieve a balance of flavours. Whichever you choose, be sure to harvest the elderflowers when they are fresh and at their aromatic peak for the best results.

It is possible to substitute dried elderflowers if fresh are out of season. Dried elderflowers have a more concentrated flavour compared to fresh ones, so you may want to adjust the quantity based on your taste preferences.

Ingredients:

At Start:

20 fresh Elderflower heads
(Use 28 grams (1 ounce) of dried elderflowers if fresh flowers are unavailable)
250ml or 245g White Grape Concentrate
1 Kg of Sugar
1 crushed Campden Tablet
1 sachet of Lalvin K1-V1116 Wine Yeast
1 teaspoon of Yeast Nutrient
1 teaspoon of Acid Blend
¼ teaspoon of Wine Tannin
10 drops of Pectinaze
3½ litres (6 Pints) Cold Water

After Fermentation:
½ teaspoon of Potassium Sorbate
1 crushed Campden Tablet
1 sachet of Winefine Finings (one sachet will clear between 1 and 5 gallons)

Directions:

Remove the flowers from their stalks with a fork and rinse them in a sieve under a cold tap to remove any dirt. Then put them into a pre-sterilised white plastic bucket and pour over the grape concentrate, which will add depth and body to the wine. Then dissolve the sugar in a little hot water and add this to the bucket.

Pour the cold water over the contents together with the acid blend, tannin, and pectinaze. Crush a Campden tablet into the mix and stir well. Cover with a cloth and leave for 24 hours in a cool place. This process will kill any wild yeast and bacteria that may be present on the flowers. The next day add the yeast and yeast nutrient. Stir thoroughly for 1-2 minutes to oxygenate the must. Cover the bucket with a cloth and leave to ferment in a warm place for 5 days, stirring the contents of the bucket occasionally. Then strain into a demijohn (4½ litres) or fermenter, through a nylon straining bag and discard the flower pulp. It may be necessary to top up with a little extra cold water to achieve 4½ litres. Fit a bung and airlock and leave in a warm place to continue to ferment out completely.

<u>Finishing your Wine:</u>

Fermentation should be complete in 2-5 weeks. At this stage CO2 bubbles should have stopped being released through the airlock. Your wine should then be checked with a hydrometer. The hydrometer will indicate the remaining sugar level and finishing levels are as follows:

Dry = 0.990 – 0.996   Medium = 0.996 – 1.009   Sweet = 1.009 – 1.018

At the end of fermentation add 1 crushed Campden tablet and half teaspoon of potassium sorbate per gallon. Leave in a cool place (15C) for 3 days to kill off the yeast. Then syphon the wine from the sediment into a second fermenter. Shake or stir the wine to degas it then add wine finings to ensure your wine will clear. Leave for 5 days in a cool place then syphon the wine from the sediment. Finally, pass it through a Vinbrite filter to obtain a professional finish before bottling. Filtering will remove all colloidal suspended particles and will ensure that your efforts are rewarded with a professional clarity and a pure taste.

The wine should now be bottled and stored in a cool dark place to mature for at least 6 months. During this time any rough tastes will be smoothed out and the wine will improve in bouquet and flavour.

This recipe makes 1 gallon (4.5 litres) of wine. For larger quantities simply multiply the quantities of ingredients except for the Yeast and Winefine. One sachet of each of these will be sufficient for any quantity between 1 and 5 gallons.

Elderflower Prosecco:

This recipe produces a light, floral, sparkling wine, which is an interesting alternative to Prosecco. It can be consumed chilled on its own or used as a basis for a delicious mixer drink.

Ingredients:

At Start:

20 fresh Elderflower heads
(Use 28 grams (1 ounce) of dried elderflowers if fresh flowers are unavailable)
250ml or 245g White Grape Concentrate
1kg (2.2lb) Sugar
1 crushed Campden Tablet
¼ teaspoon of Wine Tannin
1 teaspoon of Acid Blend
¼ teaspoon of Wine Tannin
1 sachet of Pure Brew
1 sachet of Gervin GV3 or Lalvin EC1118 Wine Yeast
1 gallon of water

After Fermentation:
1 sachet of Winefine Finings (one sachet will clear between 1 and 5 gallons)
Brew Fizz Carbonation Drops (optional)

Directions:

Remove the flowers from their stalks with a fork and rinse them in a sieve under a cold tap to remove any dirt. Then put them into a pre-sterilised white plastic bucket and pour over the grape concentrate, which will add depth and body to the wine. Then dissolve the sugar in a little hot water and add this to the bucket.

Pour the cold water over the contents together with the acid blend, tannin, and pectinaze. Crush a Campden tablet into the mix and stir well. Cover with a cloth and leave for 24 hours in a cool place. This process will kill any wild yeast and bacteria that may be present on the flowers. The next day add the yeast and yeast nutrient. Stir thoroughly for 1-2 minutes to oxygenate the must. Cover the bucket with a cloth and leave to ferment in a warm place for 5 days, stirring the contents of the bucket occasionally. Then strain into a demijohn (4½ litres) or fermenter, through a nylon straining bag and discard the flower pulp. It may be necessary to top up with a little extra cold water to achieve 4½ litres. Fit a bung and airlock and leave in a warm place to continue to ferment out completely.

Leave to ferment until gravity falls below 1.000. This should take around three weeks. Try to maintain a constant temperature of around 22-24C (71-75F) during fermentation.

Once the fermentation has completed it is important not to add any crushed Campden Tablets or Potassium Sorbate as this will prevent the yeast from creating a secondary fermentation, which produces the fizz. Just add a sachet of Winefine Finings and return to a cool place for a week to clear.

There are two methods you can follow to achieve a sparkling wine. The first is to conduct a secondary fermentation. Secondly you can force carbonate the mead with CO2.

To follow the secondary fermentation route, once clear, syphon the wine from the sediment into bottles that are designed to hold fizzy drinks. Your homebrew shop can supply either champagne style bottles with corks/cages or alternatively PET style beer bottles (which are a cheaper option if you are not gifting the wine). Leave a 2cm space at the top of the bottle and add 2 brew fizz carbonation drops. Secure the bottles, shake them, then store in a warm place (24C/75F) for 7-10 days. Then move the bottles to a cool room to age them for a minimum of 6 months. Bottles should be carefully placed upright in a fridge to chill for 24 hours before drinking. Open the bottles carefully and gently pour the contents into glasses or a decanter in one process. This will avoid pouring out any fine sediment at the bottom of the bottle, which will inevitably form because of the carbonation process.

For a commercial clarity you could consider following a force-carbonation process. Following the fining stage, filter your wine through a Vinbrite Wine Filter to achieve a professional clarity. Then syphon the wine into a 5-litre mini-keg, party keg or a corny keg and fit a regulator and CO_2 cylinder. Force-carbonate the wine to a pressure of around 25psi. Leave under pressure for 7-10 days. Allow the wine to bulk age in the keg for 3-6 months in a cool room. Then chill down the keg and return the pressure to 25psi for 2 days before drinking to allow the wine to absorb the gas. A useful calculator can be found at https://www.hopsteiner.com/uk/psi-calculator/.

The carbonation level of sparkling wines must reach a level greater than 2 volumes of CO_2 to be classed as 'sparkling wine'. As a guide, champagne normally contains 4 volumes of CO_2. The lower you can reduce the temperature; the more effective force-carbonation will be.

This recipe makes 1 gallon (4.5 litres) of sparkling elderflower prosecco. For larger quantities simply multiply the quantities of ingredients except for the Pure Brew, Yeast and Winefine. One sachet of each of these will be sufficient for any quantity between 1 and 5 gallons.

Elderflower Cordial:

Whilst not technically a wine, this recipe makes a delicious cordial at a fraction of the price of commercial ones. Furthermore, it is totally natural without any flavours or additives. Making elderflower cordial is a wonderful springtime experience that you can share with your family and children in particular love to make it. During the month of June, the creamy white heads can be harvested to make a home-made elderflower cordial, which makes a delicious fragrant summer drink, and can be as strong a tradition as blackberry or apple pie.

This traditional elderflower cordial recipe makes 750ml (a normal wine bottle).

Ingredients:

1 Lemon (Grate the rind and slice the fruit).
35g Citric Acid
900g Sugar
10 Elderflower heads
750ml Water

Direction:

Put the sugar in a large bowl or fermenting bucket and pour 750ml of boiling water over to dissolve into a syrup. Add the grated lemon rind, and the rest of the lemon, the citric acid, and the flower heads. Cover and leave for 24 hours, stirring occasionally. Sieve through a muslin bag, pour into clean bottles and seal with screw cap tops.

The cordial keeps for 6 months, or you can freeze it as ice cubes or in plastic bottles (leaving room for expansion).

Elderflower cordial is made following this method on a commercial basis which results in various distinctive tastes. Some companies use cold water sieving to remove impurities, whereas others pasteurise but the essential ingredients are the same, namely, sugar, flower heads, water, citric acid, and lemons.

Despite its homely origins, commercial elderflower cordial is seen as a sophisticated adult cordial/soft drink and sells in most supermarkets. It is added in small quantities to sparkling wine and soda water, as a mixer.

Fig & Date Dessert Wine:

Fig wine tends to have a rich, fruity flavour with undertones of honey and caramel. Some describe it as having a jammy quality. If you enjoy sweet wines with complex flavours, you may find this fig & date wine appealing. It can be enjoyed on its own as a dessert wine or paired with various foods. It can complement cheeses, nuts, and desserts like fruit tarts or chocolate.

The addition of dates in the recipe contributes to the body and mouthfeel of the wine. Wines made with dates have a fuller texture and a more viscous mouthfeel. There is a larger quantity of dates in the recipe as figs produce a powerful flavour which can overpower the balance if used in large amounts.

Dates have a distinct taste characterised by caramel-like sweetness and rich, fruity notes. When incorporated into wine, dates add complexity and depth to the final wine. Dates contain various nutrients and minerals, including potassium, magnesium, and vitamins. These nutrients provide the yeast with essential elements necessary for fermentation, helping to ensure a healthy and vigorous fermentation process.

Ingredients:

At Start:

225g (8oz) Dried Figs
400g (14oz) Dried Dates (Medjool are the best type)
500g (16oz) Raisins
1 Kg of Light Soft Brown Sugar
500g Clear Honey
1 crushed Campden Tablet
1 sachet of Lalvin EC-1118 Wine Yeast
1 teaspoon Yeast Nutrient
1 teaspoon of Acid Blend
10 drops of Pectinaze

3½ litres (6 Pints) Cold Water

After Fermentation:

½ teaspoon of Potassium Sorbate
1 crushed Campden Tablet
1 sachet of Winefine Finings (one sachet will clear between 1 and 5 gallons)

Directions:

Chop or mince the raisins, figs, and dates and rinse them under a cold tap in a sieve. Then put them into a pre-sterilised white plastic bucket and pour the cold water over the contents, cover, and leave overnight for the fruit to infuse with the water.

The next day pour the contents into a large pan on a stove and bring to the boil. Simmer for 15 minutes to extract the flavour then leave to cool to room temperature. Once cool, strain the liquid into a pre-sterilised white plastic bucket and discard the fruit (you can eat it if desired to avoid waste). Dissolve the sugar in a little hot water and add this to the bucket, together with the honey. Add the acid blend, and pectinaze. Ensure the liquid is around 22C then add the yeast and yeast nutrient. Stir thoroughly for 1-2 minutes to oxygenate the must. Then transfer the wine must into a demijohn (4½ litres) or fermenter. If necessary, top up with a little extra cold water to achieve 4½ litres. Fit a bung and airlock and leave in a warm place to continue to ferment out completely.

Finishing your Wine:

Fermentation should be complete in 2-5 weeks. At this stage CO2 bubbles should have stopped being released through the airlock. Your wine should then be checked with a hydrometer. The hydrometer will indicate the remaining sugar level and finishing levels are as follows:

Dry = 0.990 – 0.996   Medium = 0.996 – 1.009   Sweet = 1.009 – 1.018

At the end of fermentation add 1 crushed Campden tablet and half teaspoon of potassium sorbate per gallon. Leave in a cool place (15C) for 3 days to kill off the yeast. Then syphon the wine from the sediment into a second fermenter. Shake or stir the wine to degas it then add wine finings to ensure your wine will clear. Leave for 5 days in a cool place then syphon the wine from the sediment. Finally, pass it through a Vinbrite filter to obtain a professional finish before bottling. Filtering will remove all colloidal suspended particles and will ensure that your efforts are rewarded with a professional clarity and a pure taste.

This is a dessert wine recipe so your final gravity should be 1.009-1.018 as a guide. Back-sweeten the wine with brewers' glycerine or honey to achieve the desired taste and consistency. The wine should now be bottled and stored in a cool dark place to mature for at least 12 months. During this time any rough tastes will be smoothed out and the wine will improve in bouquet and flavour.

This recipe makes 1 gallon (4.5 litres) of wine. For larger quantities simply multiply the quantities of ingredients except for the Yeast and Winefine. One sachet of each of these will be sufficient for any quantity between 1 and 5 gallons.

Gooseberry Wine:

This recipe captures the essence of tart and tangy gooseberries in every sip. Crafted from the juicy fruit of the gooseberry bush, this wine boasts a pale golden hue and a vibrant aroma redolent of summer orchards. With a perfect balance of sweetness and acidity, it tantalises the palate with its crisp, fruity flavours, accented by subtle herbal notes. Gooseberry wine can be enjoyed on its own as a refreshing aperitif, served chilled on a warm day, or paired with a variety of dishes, from light salads to seafood and poultry. Its lively acidity and bright fruit character make it a versatile companion to a wide range of cuisines, while its clean, refreshing finish leaves a lasting impression. Whether enjoyed casually with friends or savoured during special occasions, gooseberry wine promises a delightful and memorable drinking experience.

Ingredients:

At Start:

2.5 Kg (5½lb) Gooseberries
(Use 550g of canned fruit if fresh is unavailable)

250ml or 245g White Grape Concentrate
1 Kg of Sugar
1 crushed Campden Tablet
1 sachet of Harris Premium Wine Yeast
1 teaspoon of Yeast Nutrient
1 teaspoon of Acid Blend
10 drops of Pectinaze
3½ litres (6 Pints) Cold Water

After Fermentation:

½ teaspoon of Potassium Sorbate
1 crushed Campden Tablet

1 sachet of Winefine Finings (one sachet will clear between 1 and 5 gallons)

Directions:

Top and tail the Gooseberries and rinse them under a cold tap in a sieve. Then crush them into a pre-sterilised white plastic bucket and pour over the grape concentrate, which will add depth and body to the wine. Then dissolve the sugar in a little hot water and add this to the bucket.

Pour the cold water over the contents together with the acid blend, and pectinaze. Crush a Campden tablet into the mix and stir well. Cover with a cloth and leave for 24 hours in a cool place. This process will kill any wild yeast and bacteria that may be present on the fruit. The next day add the yeast and yeast nutrient. Stir thoroughly for 1-2 minutes to oxygenate the must. Cover the bucket with a cloth and leave to ferment in a warm place for 5 days, stirring the contents of the bucket occasionally. Then strain into a demijohn (4½ litres) or fermenter, through a nylon straining bag. Press as much of the juice as possible and discard the pulp. It may be necessary to top up with a little extra cold water to achieve 4½ litres. Fit a bung and airlock and leave in a warm place to continue to ferment out completely.

Finishing your Wine:

Fermentation should be complete in 2-5 weeks. At this stage CO2 bubbles should have stopped being released through the airlock. Your wine should then be checked with a hydrometer. The hydrometer will indicate the remaining sugar level and finishing levels are as follows:

Dry = 0.990 – 0.996   Medium = 0.996 – 1.009   Sweet = 1.009 – 1.018

At the end of fermentation add 1 crushed Campden tablet and half teaspoon of potassium sorbate per gallon. Leave in a cool place (15C) for 3 days to kill off the yeast. Then syphon the wine from the sediment into a second fermenter. Shake or stir the wine to degas it then add wine finings to ensure your wine will clear. Leave for 5 days in a cool place then syphon the wine from the sediment. Finally, pass it through a Vinbrite filter to obtain a professional finish before bottling. Filtering will remove all colloidal suspended particles and will ensure that your efforts are rewarded with a professional clarity and a pure taste.

The wine should now be bottled and stored in a cool dark place to mature for at least 6 months. During this time any rough tastes will be smoothed out and the wine will improve in bouquet and flavour.

This recipe makes 1 gallon (4.5 litres) of wine. For larger quantities simply multiply the quantities of ingredients except for the Yeast and Winefine. One sachet of each of these will be sufficient for any quantity between 1 and 5 gallons.

Sparkling Gooseberry Fizz:

This recipe produces a light, slightly tart, sparkling wine, which can be consumed chilled on its own, or used as a basis for a delicious mixer drink. Gooseberry fizz is a lively and effervescent drink that combines the tartness of gooseberries with the refreshing sparkle of carbonation. It offers a burst of fruity flavour with a crisp, bubbly texture. Its vibrant greenish-yellow colour and tangy aroma evoke images of sun-drenched beach days and summer picnics. Gooseberry fizz is a wonderful thirst-quencher on a hot day, offering a refreshing balance of sweet and tart flavours that invigorate the palate.

Ingredients:

At Start:

2.5 Kg (5½lb) Gooseberries
(Use 550g of canned fruit if fresh is unavailable)

250ml or 245g White Grape Concentrate
1kg (2.2lb) Sugar
1 crushed Campden Tablet
¼ teaspoon of Wine Tannin
1 teaspoon of Acid Blend
¼ teaspoon of Wine Tannin
1 sachet of Pure Brew
1 sachet of Gervin GV3 or Lalvin EC1118 Wine Yeast
1 gallon of water

After Fermentation:
1 sachet of Winefine Finings (one sachet will clear between 1 and 5 gallons)

Brew Fizz Carbonation Drops (optional)

Directions:

Top and tail the Gooseberries and rinse them in a sieve under a cold tap to remove any dirt. Then put them into a pre-sterilised white plastic bucket and pour over the grape concentrate, which will add depth and body to the wine. Then dissolve the sugar in a little hot water and add this to the bucket.

Pour the cold water over the contents together with the acid blend, and pectinaze. Crush a Campden tablet into the mix and stir well. Cover with a cloth and leave for 24 hours in a cool place. This process will kill any wild yeast and bacteria that may be present on the fruit. The next day add the yeast and yeast nutrient. Stir thoroughly for 1-2 minutes to oxygenate the must. Cover the bucket with a cloth and leave to ferment in a warm place for 5 days, stirring the contents of the bucket occasionally. Then strain into a demijohn (4½ litres) or fermenter, through a nylon straining bag and discard the fruit pulp. It may be necessary to top up with a little extra cold water to achieve 4½ litres. Fit a bung and airlock and leave in a warm place to continue to ferment out completely.

Leave to ferment until gravity falls below 1.000. This should take around three weeks. Try to maintain a constant temperature of around 22-24C (71-75F) during fermentation.

Once the fermentation has completed it is important not to add any crushed Campden Tablets or Potassium Sorbate as this will prevent the yeast from creating a secondary fermentation, which produces the fizz. Just add a sachet of Winefine Finings and return to a cool place for a week to clear.

There are two methods you can follow to achieve a sparkling wine. The first is to conduct a secondary fermentation. Secondly you can force carbonate the mead with CO_2.

To follow the secondary fermentation route, once clear, syphon the wine from the sediment into bottles that are designed to hold fizzy drinks. Your homebrew shop can supply either champagne style bottles with corks/cages or alternatively PET style beer bottles (which are a cheaper option if you are not gifting the wine). Leave a 2cm space at the top of the bottle and add 2 brew fizz carbonation drops. Secure the bottles, shake them, then store in a warm place (24C/75F) for 7-10 days. Then move the bottles to a cool room to age them for a minimum of 6 months. Bottles should be carefully placed upright in a fridge to chill for 24 hours before drinking. Open the bottles carefully and gently pour the contents into glasses or a decanter in one process. This will avoid pouring out any fine sediment at the bottom of the bottle, which will inevitably form because of the carbonation process.

For a commercial clarity you could consider following a force-carbonation process. Following the fining stage, filter your wine through a Vinbrite Wine Filter to achieve a professional clarity. Then syphon the wine into a 5-litre mini-keg, party keg or a corny keg and fit a regulator and CO2 cylinder. Force-carbonate the wine to a pressure of around 25psi. Leave under pressure for 7-10 days. Allow the wine to bulk age in the keg for 3-6 months in a cool room. Then chill down the keg and return the pressure to 25psi for 2 days before drinking to allow the wine to absorb the gas. A useful calculator can be found at https://www.hopsteiner.com/uk/psi-calculator/.

The carbonation level of sparkling wines must reach a level greater than 2 volumes of CO2 to be classed as 'sparkling wine'. As a guide, champagne normally contains 4 volumes of CO2. The lower you can reduce the temperature; the more effective force-carbonation will be.

This recipe makes 1 gallon (4.5 litres) of sparkling Gooseberry Fizz. For larger quantities simply multiply the quantities of ingredients except for the Pure Brew, Yeast and Winefine. One sachet of each of these will be sufficient for any quantity between 1 and 5 gallons.

Grape Wine (White):

White grape wine, a classic and versatile wine, which embodies the essence of sun-kissed vines and the craftsmanship of winemaking. This recipe showcases a spectrum of flavours, from crisp and refreshing to rich and complex depending on the grapes chosen. With pale straw to golden hues, white grape wine offers a visual feast for the senses, followed by a taste that provides a harmonious balance of fruitiness and acidity.

Ingredients:

At Start:

6.4 Kg (14lb) White Grapes
250ml or 245g White Grape Concentrate
Sugar Syrup (made by dissolving 1kg of sugar and 1 teaspoon of acid blend into 1 litre of water).
1 crushed Campden Tablet
1 sachet of Gervin GV1 Wine Yeast
1 Teaspoon Yeast Nutrient
Acid Blend (the precise amount is determined by the acidity in the grapes)
Ph Testing papers (range pH2.8-44) for testing the grapes acidity.
10 drops of Pectinaze
Cold Water as necessary to increase the juice volume to 4.5 litres (1 gallon).

After Fermentation:

½ teaspoon of Potassium Sorbate
1 crushed Campden Tablet
1 sachet of Winefine Finings (one sachet will clear between 1 and 5 gallons)

Directions:

Remove any stalks and rinse the grapes under a cold tap in a sieve. Then crush them through a fruit press to collect as much juice as possible. Alternatively crush the grapes using a sanitised wooden post (or potato masher) and squeeze juice through a straining bag into a pre-sterilised white plastic bucket. Then pour over the grape concentrate, which will add depth and body to the wine. Add cold water to bring the volume near to 4.5 litres (1 gallon). At this point stir the must and take a hydrometer reading. Your target original specific gravity (OG) should be 1.085 to achieve a wine around 11% ABV. Add sugar syrup slowly stirring the mix thoroughly after each addition. Take further hydrometer readings until the target gravity is reached.

Next take dip a pH test strip into the wine and take a reading (the colour of the strip will match a colour scale on the pack). You should aim for a pH of 3.5 for this recipe. If necessary, add Acid Blend to achieve the correct acidity level. One teaspoon will increase the acidity by approximately 1 point on the scale (4.5-3.5). Therefore, add the acid in small quantities and re-take pH tests until the target acidity level is reached. In the unlikely event that there is too much acid present, the acidity level can be reduced by adding acid reducer (precipitated chalk).

Once the correct acid and sugar levels are achieved, add the pectinaze. Crush a Campden tablet into the mix and stir well. Cover with a cloth and leave for 24 hours in a cool place. This process will kill any wild yeast and bacteria that may be present in the grape juice. The next day add the yeast and yeast nutrient. Stir thoroughly for 1-2 minutes to oxygenate the must. Seal the lid and fit an airlock, then leave to ferment in a warm place to continue to ferment out completely.

Finishing your Wine:

Fermentation should be complete in 2-5 weeks. At this stage CO2 bubbles should have stopped being released through the airlock. Your wine should then be checked with a hydrometer. The hydrometer will indicate the remaining sugar level and finishing levels are as follows:

Dry = 0.990 – 0.996   Medium = 0.996 – 1.009   Sweet = 1.009 – 1.018

At the end of fermentation add 1 crushed Campden tablet and half teaspoon of potassium sorbate per gallon. Leave in a cool place (15C) for 3 days to kill off the yeast. Then syphon the wine from the sediment into a second fermenter. Shake or stir the wine to degas it then add wine finings to ensure your wine will clear. Leave for 5 days in a cool place then syphon the wine from the sediment. Finally, pass it through a Vinbrite filter to obtain a professional finish before bottling. Filtering will remove all colloidal suspended particles and will ensure that your efforts are rewarded with a professional clarity and a pure taste.

The wine should now be bottled and stored in a cool dark place to mature for at least 6 months. During this time any rough tastes will be smoothed out and the wine will improve in bouquet and flavour.

Grape Wine (Orange Wine):

White wine that is fermented on the skins is often referred to as "orange wine" or "skin-contact white wine." This ancient style of wine is made by fermenting white grape juice with the grape skins, seeds, and sometimes stems, similar to the process used for red wines.

During fermentation, the grape skins impart colour, tannins, and additional flavour compounds to the wine, resulting in a wine with more complexity and texture compared to traditional white wines. Depending on the length of skin contact and other winemaking techniques, orange wines can range from pale amber to deep gold in colour.

Orange wines have gained popularity in recent years due to their unique flavour profiles, which can include notes of citrus, stone fruit, floral, and spice, as well as a distinct tannic structure. They are often described as having a more robust and savoury character compared to conventional white wines, making them popular among adventurous wine enthusiasts and those seeking alternative wine styles. They often exhibit a broader range of pH values compared to traditional white wines due to the influence of skin contact. The extended contact with grape skins can introduce additional compounds and acidity to the wine, affecting its overall pH level. They typically have a pH that falls within the range of 3.2 to 3.6 and an ABV between 10-14%. This recipe will produce a 12% ABV orange wine.

Ingredients:

At Start:

7.25 Kg (16lb) Green Grapes
250ml or 245g White Grape Concentrate
Sugar Syrup (made by dissolving 1kg of sugar and 1 teaspoon of acid blend into 1 litre of water).
1 crushed Campden Tablet
1 sachet of Harris Premium Wine Yeast

1 teaspoon of Yeast Nutrient
Acid Blend (the precise amount is determined by the acidity in the grapes)
Ph Testing papers (range pH2.8-44) for testing the grapes acidity.
10 drops of Pectinaze
Cold Water as necessary to increase the juice volume to 4.5 litres (1 gallon).

After Fermentation:

½ teaspoon of Potassium Sorbate
1 crushed Campden Tablet
1 sachet of Winefine Finings (one sachet will clear between 1 and 5 gallons)

Directions:

Remove any stalks and rinse the grapes under a cold tap in a sieve. Then crush them through a fruit press to collect as much juice as possible. Alternatively crush the grapes using a sanitised wooden post (or potato masher) and squeeze juice through a straining bag into a pre-sterilised white plastic bucket. Keep the grape skins/pulp on one side. Then pour over the grape concentrate, which will add depth and body to the wine. Add cold water to bring the volume near to 4.5 litres (1 gallon). At this point stir the must and take a hydrometer reading. Your target original specific gravity (OG) should be 1.100 to achieve a wine around 12% ABV. Add sugar syrup slowly stirring the mix thoroughly after each addition. Take further hydrometer readings until the target gravity is reached.

Next take dip a pH test strip into the wine and take a reading (the colour of the strip will match a colour scale on the pack). You should aim for a pH of 3.5 for this recipe. If necessary, add Acid Blend to achieve the correct acidity level. One teaspoon will increase the acidity by approximately 1 point on the scale (4.5-3.5). Therefore, add the acid in small quantities and re-take pH tests until the target acidity level is reached. In the unlikely event that there is too much acid present, the acidity level can be reduced by adding acid reducer (precipitated chalk).

Once the correct acid and sugar levels are achieved, add the pectinaze. Then add the grape skins back into the bucket. Crush a Campden tablet into the mix and stir well. Cover with a cloth and leave for 24 hours in a cool place. This process will kill any wild yeast and bacteria that may be present in the grape juice. The next day add the yeast and yeast nutrient. Stir thoroughly for 1-2 minutes to oxygenate the must. Stir thoroughly for 1-2 minutes to oxygenate the must. Cover the bucket with a cloth and leave to ferment in a warm place for 5 days, stirring the contents of the bucket occasionally. Then strain into a demijohn (4½ litres) or fermenter, through a nylon straining bag. Press as much of the juice as possible and discard the pulp. It may be necessary to top up with a little extra cold water to achieve 4½ litres. Fit a bung and airlock and leave in a warm place to continue to ferment out completely.

Finishing your Wine:

Fermentation should be complete in 2-5 weeks. At this stage CO2 bubbles should have stopped being released through the airlock. Your wine should then be checked with a hydrometer. The hydrometer will indicate the remaining sugar level and finishing levels are as follows:

Dry = 0.990 – 0.996   Medium = 0.996 – 1.009   Sweet = 1.009 – 1.018

At the end of fermentation add 1 crushed Campden tablet and half teaspoon of potassium sorbate per gallon. Leave in a cool place (15C) for 3 days to kill off the yeast. Then syphon the wine from the sediment into a second fermenter. Shake or stir the wine to degas it then add wine finings to ensure your wine will clear. Leave for 5 days in a cool place then syphon the wine from the sediment. Finally, pass it through a Vinbrite filter to obtain a professional finish before bottling. Filtering will remove all colloidal suspended particles and will ensure that your efforts are rewarded with a professional clarity and a pure taste.

The wine should now be bottled and stored in a cool dark place to mature for at least 6 months. During this time any rough tastes will be smoothed out and the wine will improve in bouquet and flavour.

Grape Wine (Red Wine):

Red wine is produced by using red or black grapes that are fermented on their skins, seeds, and sometimes stems. During fermentation, the grape skins impart colour, tannins, and additional flavour compounds to the wine, resulting in a wine with more complexity and texture compared to traditional white wines. Red wines can vary from being light and acidic (such as Beaujolais styles), to full bodied deep colours (such as Shiraz styles). The acidity content of red wines tends to be in the 3.5-4 pH range. They often have a slightly higher ABV than white wines, in the 12-14% range (although some may be lower). This recipe produces a deep full-bodied wine with a target ABV of 13% and acidity of pH 3.8.

Ingredients:

At Start:

7.25 Kg (16lb) Black Grapes
250ml or 245g Red Grape Concentrate
Sugar Syrup (made by dissolving 1kg of sugar and 1 teaspoon of acid blend into 1 litre of water).
1 crushed Campden Tablet
1 sachet of Lalvin 71B Wine Yeast
1 teaspoon of Yeast Nutrient
Acid Blend (the precise amount is determined by the acidity in the grapes)
Ph Testing papers (range pH2.8-44) for testing the grapes acidity.
10 drops of Pectinaze
Cold Water as necessary to increase the juice volume to 4.5 litres (1 gallon).

After Fermentation:

½ teaspoon of Potassium Sorbate
1 crushed Campden Tablet

1 sachet of Winefine Finings (one sachet will clear between 1 and 5 gallons)

Directions:

Remove any stalks and rinse the grapes under a cold tap in a sieve. Then crush them through a fruit press to collect as much juice as possible. Alternatively crush the grapes using a sanitised wooden post (or potato masher) and squeeze juice through a straining bag into a pre-sterilised white plastic bucket. Keep the grape skins/pulp on one side. Then pour over the grape concentrate, which will add depth and body to the wine. Add cold water to bring the volume near to 4.5 litres (1 gallon). At this point stir the must and take a hydrometer reading. Your target original specific gravity (OG) should be 1.110 to achieve a wine around 13% ABV. Add sugar syrup slowly stirring the mix thoroughly after each addition. Take further hydrometer readings until the target gravity is reached.

Next take dip a pH test strip into the wine and take a reading (the colour of the strip will match a colour scale on the pack). You should aim for a pH of 3.8 for this recipe. If necessary, add Acid Blend to achieve the correct acidity level. One teaspoon will increase the acidity by approximately 1 point on the scale (4.8-3.8). Therefore, add the acid in small quantities and re-take pH tests until the target acidity level is reached. In the unlikely event that there is too much acid present, the acidity level can be reduced by adding acid reducer (precipitated chalk).

Once the correct acid and sugar levels are achieved, add the pectinaze. Then add the grape skins back into the bucket. Crush a Campden tablet into the mix and stir well. Cover with a cloth and leave for 24 hours in a cool place. This process will kill any wild yeast and bacteria that may be present in the grape juice. The next day add the yeast and yeast nutrient. Stir thoroughly for 1-2 minutes to oxygenate the must. Stir thoroughly for 1-2 minutes to oxygenate the must. Cover the bucket with a cloth and leave to ferment in a warm place for 5 days, stirring the contents of the bucket occasionally. Then strain into a demijohn (4½ litres) or fermenter, through a nylon straining bag. Press as much of the juice as possible and discard the pulp. It may be necessary to top up with a little extra cold water to achieve 4½ litres. Fit a bung and airlock and leave in a warm place to continue to ferment out completely.

Finishing your Wine:

Fermentation should be complete in 2-5 weeks. At this stage CO_2 bubbles should have stopped being released through the airlock. Your wine should then be checked with a hydrometer. The hydrometer will indicate the remaining sugar level and target finishing levels are as follows:

Dry = 0.990 – 0.996   Medium = 0.996 – 1.009   Sweet = 1.009 – 1.018

At the end of fermentation add 1 crushed Campden tablet and half teaspoon of potassium sorbate per gallon. Leave in a cool place (15C) for 3 days to kill off the yeast. Then syphon the wine from the sediment into a second fermenter. Shake or stir the wine to degas it then add wine finings to ensure your wine will clear. Leave for 5 days in a cool place then syphon the wine from the sediment. Finally, pass it through a Vinbrite filter to obtain a professional finish before bottling. Filtering will remove all colloidal suspended particles and will ensure that your efforts are rewarded with a professional clarity and a pure taste.

The wine should now be bottled and stored in a cool dark place to mature for at least 6 months. During this time any rough tastes will be smoothed out and the wine will improve in bouquet and flavour.

Grape Wine (Provençal Rosé Wine):

Making rosé wine typically involves a process called "limited skin contact," where red grape skins are left in contact with the grape juice for a short period to impart colour, flavour, and aroma to the wine. Rosé wines can vary considerably from producing a light, dry wine (such as Provençal Rosé) to a sweeter fuller bodied Rosé (such as White Zinfandel). The typical total acidity (TA) of rosé wines, measured in grams per litre of tartaric acid, can range from around 5 g/L to 8 g/L or even higher in some cases. This acidity level helps balance the wine's flavour profile, providing brightness and vibrancy on the palate. If measured on the pH scale this equates to acidity levels typically falling between 3.1 and 3.6.

This recipe produces a lighter drier Provençal style of Rosé, typical of the wines produced in the Provence region of southeastern France. Provence is one of the oldest wine-producing regions in France and is renowned for its high-quality rosé wines, which are among the most sought-after rosés in the world. They are known for their pale pink to salmon colour, which is often referred to as "pale Provence pink." The colour is achieved through a short maceration period with the grape skins, resulting in delicate colour extraction. Provençal rosés typically exhibit delicate aromas of fresh red berries, citrus fruits, and floral notes. The aromas are often subtle and elegant, contributing to the wine's refreshing character. They are characterised by their bright and crisp acidity, which provides a refreshing and lively palate. The acidity balances the wine's fruitiness and contributes to its overall freshness. Most Provençal rosés are dry, with minimal residual sugar. They are known for their refreshing and thirst-quenching qualities, making them perfect for warm-weather drinking.

Ingredients:

At Start:

6.35 Kg (14lb) Black Grapes

250ml or 245g White Grape Concentrate
Sugar Syrup (made by dissolving 1kg of sugar and 1 teaspoon of acid blend into 1 litre of water).
1 crushed Campden Tablet
1 sachet of Lalvin 71B Wine Yeast
1 teaspoon of Yeast Nutrient
Acid Blend (the precise amount is determined by the acidity in the grapes)
Ph Testing papers (range pH2.8-44) for testing the grapes acidity.
10 drops of Pectinaze
Cold Water as necessary to increase the juice volume to 4.5 litres (1 gallon).

After Fermentation:

½ teaspoon of Potassium Sorbate
1 crushed Campden Tablet
1 sachet of Winefine Finings (one sachet will clear between 1 and 5 gallons)

Directions:

Remove any stalks and rinse the grapes under a cold tap in a sieve. Then crush them through a fruit press to collect as much juice as possible. Alternatively crush the grapes using a sanitised wooden post (or potato masher) and squeeze juice through a straining bag into a pre-sterilised white plastic bucket. Keep the grape skins/pulp on one side. Then pour over the grape concentrate, which will add depth and body to the wine. Add cold water to bring the volume near to 4.5 litres (1 gallon). At this point stir the must and take a hydrometer reading. Your target original specific gravity (OG) should be 1.0822 to achieve a wine around 10% ABV. Add sugar syrup slowly stirring the mix thoroughly after each addition. Take further hydrometer readings until the target gravity is reached.

Next take dip a pH test strip into the wine and take a reading (the colour of the strip will match a colour scale on the pack). You should aim for a pH of 3.8 for this recipe. If necessary, add Acid Blend to achieve the correct acidity level. One teaspoon will increase the acidity by approximately 1 point on the scale (4.8-3.8). Therefore, add the acid in small quantities and re-take pH tests until the target acidity level is reached. In the unlikely event that there is too much acid present, the acidity level can be reduced by adding acid reducer (precipitated chalk).

Once the correct acid and sugar levels are achieved, add the pectinaze. Then add the grape skins back into the bucket. Crush a Campden tablet into the mix and stir well. Cover with a cloth and leave for 24 hours in a cool place. This process will kill any wild yeast and bacteria that may be present in the grape juice. The next day add the yeast and yeast nutrient. Stir thoroughly for 1-2 minutes to oxygenate the must. Stir thoroughly for 1-2 minutes to oxygenate the must. Cover the bucket with a cloth and leave to ferment in a warm place for 2 days, stirring the contents of the bucket occasionally. The longer you leave the skins in the must the deeper the colour will be. This is a light rosé so the skins should be left in the must for no more than 2 days.

Then strain into a demijohn (4½ litres) or fermenter, through a nylon straining bag. Press as much of the juice as possible and discard the pulp. It may be necessary to top up with a little extra cold water to achieve 4½ litres. Fit a bung and airlock and leave in a warm place to continue to ferment out completely.

Finishing your Wine:

Fermentation should be complete in 2-5 weeks. At this stage CO_2 bubbles should have stopped being released through the airlock. Your wine should then be checked with a hydrometer. The hydrometer will indicate the remaining sugar level and target finishing levels are as follows:

Dry = 0.990 – 0.996   Medium = 0.996 – 1.009

At the end of fermentation add 1 crushed Campden tablet and half teaspoon of potassium sorbate per gallon. Leave in a cool place (15C) for 3 days to kill off the yeast. Then syphon the wine from the sediment into a second fermenter. Shake or stir the wine to degas it then add wine finings to ensure your wine will clear. Leave for 5 days in a cool place then syphon the wine from the sediment. Finally, pass it through a Vinbrite filter to obtain a professional finish before bottling. Filtering will remove all colloidal suspended particles and will ensure that your efforts are rewarded with a professional clarity and a pure taste.

Grape Wine (White Zinfandel style Rosé Wine):

White Zinfandel is a style of rosé wine made primarily from the Zinfandel grape variety, which is a red wine grape. The wine gets its name from its colour, which is lighter than traditional red Zinfandel wine, resembling that of a rosé or blush wine. White Zinfandel typically has a pale pink to salmon colour, which may be a little deeper than Provençal rosé wines. The colour is achieved through a brief maceration period where the grape skins are in contact with the juice, extracting some colour but not enough to make a fully red wine.

White Zinfandel is known for its fruity and slightly sweet flavour profile. It often exhibits aromas and flavours of strawberries, raspberries, watermelon, and sometimes a hint of citrus. The sweetness level can vary depending on the winemaking style, with some White Zinfandels being off-dry to slightly sweet. While White Zinfandel tends to have moderate acidity, it is generally less acidic compared to traditional dry rosé wines. This characteristic contributes to its easy-drinking and approachable nature. White Zinfandel is typically light to medium-bodied, with a smooth and easy-drinking texture. It lacks the heavy tannins found in red Zinfandel wines, making it a popular choice for those who prefer lighter wine styles.

White Zinfandel rose-style wines gained popularity in the United States in the latter half of the 20th century and became widely consumed due to their approachable flavour profile and affordability. White Zinfandel remains a preferred choice for many younger wine drinkers, particularly those seeking a sweeter and fruit-forward wine option.

Ingredients:

At Start:

6.8 Kg (15lb) Black Grapes
0.45kg (1lb) Strawberries

250ml or 245g White Grape Concentrate
Sugar Syrup (made by dissolving 1kg of sugar and 1 teaspoon of acid blend into 1 litre of water).
1 crushed Campden Tablet
1 sachet of Lalvin 71B Wine Yeast
1 teaspoon of Yeast Nutrient
Acid Blend (the precise amount is determined by the acidity in the grapes)
Ph Testing papers (range pH2.8-44) for testing the grapes acidity.
10 drops of Pectinaze
Cold Water as necessary to increase the juice volume to 4.5 litres (1 gallon).

After Fermentation:

½ teaspoon of Potassium Sorbate
1 crushed Campden Tablet
1 sachet of Winefine Finings (one sachet will clear between 1 and 5 gallons)

Directions:

Remove any stalks and rinse the grapes and strawberries under a cold tap in a sieve. Then crush them through a fruit press to collect as much juice as possible. Alternatively crush them using a sanitised wooden post (or potato masher) and squeeze juice through a straining bag into a pre-sterilised white plastic bucket. Keep the grape skins/fruit pulp on one side. Then pour over the grape concentrate, which will add depth and body to the wine. Add cold water to bring the volume near to 4.5 litres (1 gallon). At this point stir the must and take a hydrometer reading. Your target original specific gravity (OG) should be 1.0822 to achieve a wine around 12% ABV. Add sugar syrup slowly stirring the mix thoroughly after each addition. Take further hydrometer readings until the target gravity is reached.

Next take dip a pH test strip into the wine and take a reading (the colour of the strip will match a colour scale on the pack). You should aim for a pH of 3.6 for this recipe. If necessary, add Acid Blend to achieve the correct acidity level. One teaspoon will increase the acidity by approximately 1 point on the scale (4.6-3.6). Therefore, add the acid in small quantities and re-take pH tests until the target acidity level is reached. In the unlikely event that there is too much acid present, the acidity level can be reduced by adding acid reducer (precipitated chalk).

Once the correct acid and sugar levels are achieved, add the pectinaze. Then add the grape skins back into the bucket. Crush a Campden tablet into the mix and stir well. Cover with a cloth and leave for 24 hours in a cool place. This process will kill any wild yeast and bacteria that may be present in the grape juice. The next day add the yeast and yeast nutrient. Stir thoroughly for 1-2 minutes to oxygenate the must. Stir thoroughly for 1-2 minutes to oxygenate the must. Cover the bucket with a cloth and leave to ferment in a warm place for 2-3 days, stirring the contents of the bucket occasionally. The longer you leave the skins in the must the deeper the colour will be. This is a medium-coloured rosé so the skins should be left in the must for no more than 3 days.

Then strain into a demijohn (4½ litres) or fermenter, through a nylon straining bag. Press as much of the juice as possible and discard the pulp. It may be necessary to top up with a little extra cold water to achieve 4½ litres. Fit a bung and airlock and leave in a warm place to continue to ferment out completely.

Finishing your Wine:

Fermentation should be complete in 2-5 weeks. At this stage CO2 bubbles should have stopped being released through the airlock. Your wine should then be checked with a hydrometer. The hydrometer will indicate the remaining sugar level and target finishing levels are as follows:

Dry = 0.990 – 0.996   Medium = 0.996 – 1.009   Sweet = 1.009 – 1.018

At the end of fermentation add 1 crushed Campden tablet and half teaspoon of potassium sorbate per gallon. Leave in a cool place (15C) for 3 days to kill off the yeast. Then syphon the wine from the sediment into a second fermenter. Shake or stir the wine to degas it then add wine finings to ensure your wine will clear. Leave for 5 days in a cool place then syphon the wine from the sediment. Finally, pass it through a Vinbrite filter to obtain a professional finish before bottling. Filtering will remove all colloidal suspended particles and will ensure that your efforts are rewarded with a professional clarity and a pure taste. At this point the wine can be back sweetened to taste as necessary. Glycerine is recommended as it will provide a smooth finish without imparting too much sweetness.

The wine should now be bottled and stored in a cool dark place to mature for at least 6 months. During this time any rough tastes will be smoothed out and the wine will improve in bouquet and flavour.

Grape Juice Recipes:

This recipe allows you to make grape wine without the fuss, using grape juices. It is important to use juices which do not contain any preservatives, as they may inhibit the fermentation. Try to use good quality organic juices if possible.

Ingredients for White wine:

At Start:

2 litres White Grape Juice
250ml or 245g White Grape Concentrate
1 kg Sugar
1 teaspoon of Acid Blend
1 sachet of Harris Premium Wine Yeast
1 teaspoon of Yeast Nutrient
10 drops of Pectinaze
Cold Water as necessary to increase the juice volume to 4.5 litres (1 gallon).

After Fermentation:

½ teaspoon of Potassium Sorbate
1 crushed Campden Tablet
1 sachet of Winefine Finings (one sachet will clear between 1 and 5 gallons)

Ingredients for Rosé wine:

At Start:

2 litres White Grape Juice
250ml or 245g Red Grape Concentrate
1 kg Sugar
1 teaspoon of Acid Blend
1 sachet of Harris Premium Wine Yeast

1 teaspoon of Yeast Nutrient
10 drops of Pectinaze
Cold Water as necessary to increase the juice volume to 4.5 litres (1 gallon).

After Fermentation:

½ teaspoon of Potassium Sorbate
1 crushed Campden Tablet
1 sachet of Winefine Finings (one sachet will clear between 1 and 5 gallons)

Ingredients for Red wine:

At Start:

2 litres Red Grape Juice
250ml or 245g Red Grape Concentrate
1 kg Sugar
1 teaspoon of Acid Blend
1 sachet of Harris Premium Wine Yeast
1 teaspoon of Yeast Nutrient
10 drops of Pectinaze
Cold Water as necessary to increase the juice volume to 4.5 litres (1 gallon).

After Fermentation:

½ teaspoon of Potassium Sorbate
1 crushed Campden Tablet
1 sachet of Winefine Finings (one sachet will clear between 1 and 5 gallons)

Directions:

Pour the juice into a pre-sterilised 4.5 litres (1 gallon) demijohn or fermenter and pour over the grape concentrate, which will add depth and body to the wine. Then dissolve the sugar in a little hot water and add this to the fermenter.

Pour the cold water over the contents together with the acid blend, and pectinaze. Then add the yeast and yeast nutrient. Stir thoroughly for 1-2 minutes to oxygenate the must. Fit a bung and airlock to the fermenter and leave in a warm place to continue to ferment out completely.

<u>Finishing your Wine:</u>

Fermentation should be complete in 2-5 weeks. At this stage CO2 bubbles should have stopped being released through the airlock. Your wine should then be checked with a hydrometer. The hydrometer will indicate the remaining sugar level and finishing levels are as follows:

Dry = 0.990 – 0.996   Medium = 0.996 – 1.009   Sweet = 1.009 – 1.018

At the end of fermentation add 1 crushed Campden tablet and half teaspoon of potassium sorbate per gallon. Leave in a cool place (15C) for 3 days to kill off the yeast. Then syphon the wine from the sediment into a second fermenter. Shake or stir the wine to degas it then add wine finings to ensure your wine will clear. Leave for 5 days in a cool place then syphon the wine from the sediment. Finally, pass it through a Vinbrite filter to obtain a professional finish before bottling. Filtering will remove all colloidal suspended particles and will ensure that your efforts are rewarded with a professional clarity and a pure taste.

The wine should now be bottled and stored in a cool dark place to mature for at least 6 months. During this time any rough tastes will be smoothed out and the wine will improve in bouquet and flavour. This recipe makes a general-purpose grape wine which is ideal for blending purposes. The recipe makes 1 gallon (4.5 litres) of wine. For larger quantities simply multiply the quantities of ingredients except for the Yeast and Winefine. One sachet of each of these will be sufficient for any quantity between 1 and 5 gallons.

Hedgerow Wine:

This recipe uses a mixture of hedgerow fruits. You can adapt the recipe as required substituting the fruits. Try to avoid raspberries making up more than one-third of the fruit base in order to keep the flavour profile in balance. Always choose clean, fresh fruit and avoid roadside locations when picking fruit. Thoroughly wash the fruit in cold water before use. You can collect fruit at different times and freeze it until you are ready to make the wine. This avoids you having to choose fruits that come into harvest at the same time.

Ingredients:

At Start:

1 Kg (2.2lb) Blackberries
(Use 250g of canned fruit if fresh is unavailable)
500g (17oz) Raspberries
(Use 250g of canned fruit if fresh is unavailable)
500g (17oz) Hawthorn Berries
1kg (2.2lb) Sloes
(Use 250g of dried fruit if fresh is unavailable)
500g Rosehips
(Use 250g of dried fruit if fresh is unavailable)
250ml or 245g Red Grape Concentrate
1 Kg of Sugar
1 crushed Campden Tablet
1 sachet of Harris Premium Wine Yeast
1 teaspoon of Yeast Nutrient
½ teaspoon of Wine Tannin
1 teaspoon of Acid Blend
10 drops of Pectinaze
3½ litres (6 Pints) Cold Water

After Fermentation:

½ teaspoon of Potassium Sorbate
1 crushed Campden Tablet
1 sachet of Winefine Finings (one sachet will clear between 1 and 5 gallons)

Directions:

Crush the fruit into a pre-sterilised white plastic bucket and pour over the grape concentrate, which will add depth and body to the wine. Then dissolve the sugar in a little hot water and add this to the bucket.

Pour the cold water over the contents together with the acid blend, tannin, and pectinaze. Crush a Campden tablet into the mix and stir well. Cover with a cloth and leave for 24 hours in a cool place. This process will kill any wild yeast and bacteria that may be present on the fruit. The next day add the yeast and yeast nutrient. Stir thoroughly for 1-2 minutes to oxygenate the must. Cover the bucket with a cloth and leave to ferment in a warm place for 5 days, stirring the contents of the bucket occasionally. Then strain into a demijohn (4½ litres) or fermenter, through a nylon straining bag. Press as much of the juice as possible and discard the pulp. It may be necessary to top up with a little extra cold water to achieve 4½ litres. Fit a bung and airlock and leave in a warm place to continue to ferment out completely.

Finishing your Wine:

Fermentation should be complete in 2-5 weeks. At this stage CO2 bubbles should have stopped being released through the airlock. Your wine should then be checked with a hydrometer. The hydrometer will indicate the remaining sugar level and finishing levels are as follows:

Dry = 0.990 – 0.996   Medium = 0.996 – 1.009   Sweet = 1.009 – 1.018

At the end of fermentation add 1 crushed Campden tablet and half teaspoon of potassium sorbate per gallon. Leave in a cool place (15C) for 3 days to kill off the yeast. Then syphon the wine from the sediment into a second fermenter. Shake or stir the wine to degas it then add wine finings to ensure your wine will clear. Leave for 5 days in a cool place then syphon the wine from the sediment. Finally, pass it through a Vinbrite filter to obtain a professional finish before bottling. Filtering will remove all colloidal suspended particles and will ensure that your efforts are rewarded with a professional clarity and a pure taste.

The wine should now be bottled and stored in a cool dark place to mature for at least 6 months. During this time any rough tastes will be smoothed out and the wine will improve in bouquet and flavour.

This recipe makes 1 gallon (4.5 litres) of wine. For larger quantities simply multiply the quantities of ingredients except for the Yeast and Winefine. One sachet of each of these will be sufficient for any quantity between 1 and 5 gallons.

Mead (Traditional Mead Recipe):

Traditional mead, often referred to simply as "mead," is the oldest and most basic style of mead, dating back thousands of years. It is made primarily from honey, water, and yeast, without the addition of other flavourings or adjuncts. Balance is a key consideration when making a traditional mead. The balance of this recipe focuses on body, finish, and flavour intensity. It produces a dry to medium finish, with a clean, crisp mouthfeel, leaving behind a lingering impression of the honey's natural flavours.

Ingredients:

At Start:

1kg (2.2lb) Light Clear Honey
1 crushed Campden Tablet
¼ teaspoon of Wine Tannin
1 teaspoon of Acid Blend
1 sachet of Pure Brew
1 sachet of Harris Mead Yeast
1 gallon of water (filtered or spring if possible)

After Fermentation:
1 crushed Campden Tablet
½ teaspoon Potassium Sorbate
1 sachet of Winefine Finings (one sachet will clear between 1 and 5 gallons)

Directions:

Sterilise all equipment prior to use with Suresan No Rinse Sanitiser.

Pour the honey into the sanitised bucket and add four pints of warm water (40C/104F). Stir until dissolved. Then add one crushed Campden

Tablet and stir well. Cover the bucket and leave for 24 hours. This process will eliminate any bacteria or wild yeast contained in the honey.

The next day, top up to one gallon with cold water and stir well.

Then add the Tannin, Acid Blend, and a dose of Pure Brew. Stir well then add the sachet of yeast. Stir well for a further minute to oxygenate the mead.

Snap on the lid and fit an airlock filled with water.

Leave to ferment until gravity falls below 1.000. This should take around three weeks. Try to maintain a constant temperature of around 22-24C (71-75F) during fermentation.

Once the fermentation has completed add one crushed Campden Tablet and a dose of Potassium Sorbate. Stir gently and leave for 24 hours in a cool place.

Then add a sachet of Winefine Finings and return to a cool place for a week to clear.

Once clear, syphon the mead from the sediment and bottle. For a commercial clarity and professional finish, it is strongly recommended that you filter your mead through a Vinbrite Wine Filter before bottling.

Your mead should now be left to mature before drinking in a cool place. It should be ready for sampling after 3-6 months but will benefit from leaving for up to one year.

This recipe makes 1 gallon (4.5 litres) of mead. For larger quantities simply multiply the quantities of ingredients except for the Pure Brew, Yeast and Winefine. One sachet of each of these will be sufficient for any quantity between 1 and 5 gallons.

Mead (Dry Oaked Mead Recipe).

Dry oaked mead contains little to no residual sweetness. The fermentation process should consume most of the sugars present in the honey, resulting in a dry taste profile. This recipe ferments the honey completely, leaving the mead with a crisp and less sweet flavour profile. Oak ageing using oak chunks imparts distinct flavours and aromas to the mead, such as vanilla, caramel, and a hint of spice.

Ingredients:

At Start:

1.5 kg (3.3lb) Clear Honey
1 crushed Campden Tablet
¼ teaspoon of Wine Tannin
1 teaspoon of Acid Blend
1 sachet of Pure Brew
1 sachet of Harris Mead Yeast
1 gallon of water (filtered or spring if possible)
2 Oak Barrel Chunks

After Fermentation:
1 crushed Campden Tablet
½ teaspoon of Potassium Sorbate
1 sachet of Winefine Finings (one sachet will clear between 1 and 5 gallons)

Directions:

Sterilise all equipment prior to use with Suresan No Rinse Sanitiser.

Pour the honey into the sanitised bucket and add four pints of warm water (40C/104F). Stir until dissolved. Then add one crushed Campden Tablet and stir well. Cover the bucket and leave for 24 hours. This process will eliminate any bacteria or wild yeast contained in the honey.

The next day, top up to one gallon with cold water and stir well.

Then add the Tannin, Acid Blend, and a dose of Pure Brew. Stir well then add the sachet of yeast. Stir well for a further minute to oxygenate the mead.

Snap on the lid and fit an airlock filled with water.

Leave to ferment for 7 days then add 2 oak barrel chunks. (pre-sanitise the chunks by soaking them in boiling water for 10 minutes before use).

Continue to ferment the mead out until bubbles stop emerging from the airlock and the gravity remains constant (around 1.000 or below). This should take around three weeks. Try to maintain a constant temperature of around 22-24C (71-75F) during fermentation.

Once the fermentation has completed add one crushed Campden Tablet and Potassium Sorbate. Stir gently and leave for 24 hours in a cool place.

Then add a sachet of Winefine Finings and return to a cool place for a week to clear.

Once clear, syphon the mead from the sediment/oak chunks and bottle. For a commercial clarity and professional finish, it is strongly recommended that you filter your mead through a Vinbrite Wine Filter before bottling.

Your mead should now be left to mature before drinking in a cool place. It should be ready for sampling after 3-6 months but will benefit from leaving for up to one year.

This recipe makes 1gallon (4.5 litres) of mead. For larger quantities multiply the quantities of ingredients except for the Pure Brew, Yeast and Winefine.

Mead (Sweet Sack Mead Recipe):

Sack mead is a type of mead characterised by its sweetness and higher alcohol content compared to traditional meads. The term "sack" is believed to have originated from the Spanish word "sacar," meaning to draw out, referring to the practice of drawing out a portion of the must or wort before fermentation and replacing it with honey or sugar to increase the alcohol content. This recipe produces a full bodied, robust mead, with a sweet finish. It is delicious drunk chilled on its own or pairs well with desserts and puddings.

Ingredients

At Start:

2kg (4.4lb) Clover Honey
1 crushed Campden Tablet
¼ teaspoon of Wine Tannin
1 teaspoon of Acid Blend
1 sachet of Pure Brew
1 sachet of Lalvin EC-1118 Yeast (or Harris Mead Yeast)
1 gallon of water

After Fermentation:
1 crushed Campden Tablet
½ teaspoon of Potassium Sorbate
1 sachet of Winefine Finings (one sachet will clear between 1 and 5 gallons)

Directions:

Sterilise all equipment prior to use with Suresan No Rinse Sanitiser.

Pour 1.5kg honey into the sanitised bucket and add four pints of warm water (40C/104F). Stir until dissolved. Then add one crushed Campden Tablet and stir well. Cover the bucket and leave for 24 hours. This process will eliminate any bacteria or wild yeast contained in the honey.

The next day, top up to 6 pints with cold water and stir well.

Then add the Tannin, Acid Blend, and dose of Pure Brew. Stir well then add the sachet of yeast. Stir well for a further minute to oxygenate the mead.

Snap on the lid and fit an airlock filled with water.

Leave to ferment until gravity reaches 1.010. This should take around two weeks. Try to maintain a constant temperature of around 22-24C (71-75F) during fermentation.

Dissolve a further 500g of honey into 2 pints of warm water and stir until dissolved. Then add to the bulk of the mead to make up to 1 gallon.

Refit the airlock and continue the fermentation process.

Once the fermentation has completed add one crushed Campden Tablet and a dose of Potassium Sorbate. Stir gently and leave for 24 hours in a cool place.

Then add a sachet of Winefine Finings and return to a cool place for a week to clear.

Once clear, syphon the mead from the sediment and bottle. For a commercial clarity and professional finish, it is strongly recommended that you filter your mead through a Vinbrite Wine Filter before bottling.

Your mead should now be left to mature before drinking in a cool place. It should be ready for sampling after 6 months but will benefit from leaving for 1-2 years.

This recipe makes 1 gallon (4.5 litres) of mead. For larger quantities simply multiply the quantities of ingredients except for the Pure Brew, Yeast and Winefine. One sachet of each of these will be sufficient for any quantity between 1 and 5 gallons.

Mead (Sparkling Mead):

This recipe produces a light, floral, sparkling mead, which is an interesting alternative to Prosecco. It can be consumed chilled on its own or used as a basis for a delicious mixer drink.

Ingredients:

At Start:

1kg (2.2lb) Orange Blossom Honey
1 crushed Campden Tablet
¼ teaspoon of Wine Tannin
1 teaspoon of Acid Blend
1 sachet of Pure Brew
1 sachet of Lalvin EC-1118 Yeast
1 gallon of water

After Fermentation:
1 sachet of Winefine Finings (one sachet will clear between 1 and 5 gallons)
Brew Fizz Carbonation Drops (optional)

Directions:

Sterilise all equipment prior to use with Suresan No Rinse Sanitiser.

Pour the honey into the sanitised bucket and add four pints of warm water (40C/104F). Stir until dissolved. Then add one crushed Campden Tablet and stir well. Cover the bucket and leave for 24 hours. This process will eliminate any bacteria or wild yeast contained in the honey.

The next day, top up to one gallon with cold water and stir well.

Then add the Tannin, Acid Blend, and a dose of Pure Brew. Stir well then add the sachet of yeast. Stir well for a further minute to oxygenate the mead.

Snap on the lid and fit an airlock filled with water.

Leave to ferment until gravity falls below 1.000. This should take around three weeks. Try to maintain a constant temperature of around 22-24C (71-75F) during fermentation.

Once the fermentation has completed it is important not to add any crushed Campden Tablets or Potassium Sorbate as this will prevent the yeast from creating a secondary fermentation, which produces the fizz. Just add a sachet of Winefine Finings and return to a cool place for a week to clear.

There are two methods you can follow to achieve a sparkling mead. The first is to conduct a secondary fermentation. Secondly you can force carbonate the mead with CO2.

To follow the secondary fermentation route, once clear, syphon the mead from the sediment into bottles that are designed to hold fizzy drinks. Your homebrew shop can supply either champagne style bottles with corks/cages or alternatively PET style beer bottles (which are a cheaper option if you are not gifting the mead). Leave a 2cm space at the top of the bottle and add 2 brew fizz carbonation drops. Secure the bottles, shake them, then store in a warm place (24C/75F) for 7-10 days. Then move the bottles to a cool room to age them for a minimum of 3-6 months. Bottles should be carefully placed upright in a fridge to chill for 24 hours before drinking. Open the bottles carefully and gently pour the contents into glasses or a decanter in one process. This will avoid pouring out any fine sediment at the bottom of the bottle, which will inevitably form because of the carbonation process.

For a commercial clarity you could consider following a force-carbonation process. Following the fining stage, filter your mead through a Vinbrite Wine Filter to achieve a professional clarity. Then syphon the mead into a 5-litre mini-keg, party keg or a corny keg and fit a regulator and CO2 cylinder. Force-carbonate the mead to a pressure of around 25psi. Leave under pressure for 7-10 days. Allow the mead to bulk age in the keg for 3-6 months in a cool room. Then chill down the keg and return the pressure to 25psi for 2 days before drinking to allow the mead to absorb the gas. A useful calculator can be found at https://www.hopsteiner.com/uk/psi-calculator/. The carbonation level of sparkling wines must reach a level greater than 2 volumes of CO2 to be classed as 'sparkling wine'. As a guide, champagne normally contains 4 volumes of CO2. The lower you can reduce the temperature; the more effective force-carbonation will be.

It is possible to experiment and turn any matured mead into a sparkling mead using the force-carbonation technique. Simply pour the mead as quickly and smoothly as possible into a pressurised keg. Then purge any air from kegs immediately the mead is transferred into them. This is achieved by adding CO2 and then releasing the purge valve for a second or two. The first burst of gas out will be air and only CO2 should then remain over the mead, preventing any subsequent oxygen or bacterial spoilage which could otherwise occur from the air contact.

This recipe makes 1 gallon (4.5 litres) of mead. For larger quantities simply multiply the quantities of ingredients except for the Pure Brew, Yeast and Winefine. One sachet of each of these will be sufficient for any quantity between 1 and 5 gallons.

Mead (Christmas Spiced Metheglin Recipe):

Metheglin distinguishes itself by the inclusion of spices and herbs during the fermentation process. The result is a mead with a nuanced and often complex profile, where the aromatic and flavourful qualities of the added spices complement the natural sweetness of the honey. This spiced mead is an ideal complement for Christmas festivities.

Ingredients

At Start:

3lb Clover Honey
1 crushed Campden Tablet
¼ teaspoon of Wine Tannin
1 teaspoon of Acid Blend
1 sachet of Pure Brew
1 sachet of Harris Mead Yeast
1 gallon of water

After Fermentation:
1 crushed Campden Tablet
1 Harris Homecraft Spiced Mead Infusion Pack
½ teaspoon of Potassium Sorbate
1 sachet of Winefine Finings (one sachet will clear between 1 and 5 gallons)

Directions:

Sterilise all equipment prior to use with Suresan No Rinse Sanitiser.

Pour the honey into the sanitised bucket and add four pints of warm water (40C/104F). Stir until dissolved. Then add one crushed Campden Tablet and stir well. Cover the bucket and leave for 24 hours. This process will eliminate any bacteria or wild yeast contained in the honey.

The next day, top up to one gallon with cold water and stir well.

Then add the Tannin, Acid Blend, and a dose of Pure Brew. Stir well then add the sachet of yeast. Stir well for a further minute to oxygenate the mead.

Snap on the lid and fit an airlock filled with water.

Leave to ferment until bubbles stop emerging from the airlock and the gravity falls below 1.000. This should take around three weeks. Try to maintain a constant temperature of around 22-24C (71-75F) during fermentation.

Once the fermentation has completed add one crushed Campden Tablet and a dose of Potassium Sorbate. Stir gently and leave for 24 hours in a cool place.

Then add a sachet of Winefine Finings and return to a cool place for a week to clear.

Once clear, syphon the mead from the sediment. Then add the Metheglin Spice Infusion to the tea/spice bag and knot the bag. Put the bag into a teacup and cover with boiling water. Leave for 10 minutes (this will sanitise the infusion) then add the bag and liquid to the mead. Leave for 24 hours then taste a sample. Then remove the bag (you can leave the bag immersed for longer if necessary until you reach your preferred taste).

For a commercial clarity and professional finish, it is strongly recommended that you now filter your mead through a Vinbrite Wine Filter before bottling.

Your mead should now be left to mature before drinking in a cool place. It should be ready for sampling after 6 months but will benefit from leaving for up to one year.

This recipe makes 1 gallon (4.5 litres) of mead. For larger quantities simply multiply the quantities of ingredients except for the Pure Brew, Yeast and Winefine. One sachet of each of these will be sufficient for any quantity between 1 and 5 gallons.

Mulled Wine 1 (Party Recipe, makes one gallon):

Mulled wine has grown in popularity over recent years. This recipe makes a delicious, mulled wine that is perfect for bonfire parties, Christmas & New Year festivities and Diwali parties. It is a tried and tested recipe that never fails to win praise from party guests. The recipe makes 4.5 litres (one gallon) but can be easily scaled up or down.

Ingredients

At Start:

4.5 litres (1 gallon) of home-made Red Wine.
340g (0.75lb) Clear Honey
3 large Oranges
1 large Root of Ginger
2 teaspoons of Cinnamon powder
½ teaspoon of Ginger powder
2 Star Anise pods
2 Cassia Bark sticks
1 teaspoon of Nutmeg powder
250ml Brandy (your own made brandy keeps the cost down)

Directions:

Slice the oranges and put them in a large pan on a stove. Pour over the wine and apply heat. Bring the pan temperature up to 80C (176F). Stir in the honey until dissolved then add the spices. Allow the Ginger and Cassia Bark, and Star Anise to float in the wine as a garnish. Allow the infusions to simmer in the wine for 30 minutes then add the brandy. Stir well and once the liquid has returned to temperature serve the wine hot in mugs or insulated cups.

The mulled wine can be bottled to use it at a later date. Simply allow it to cool then strain the wine through a sieve and discard the spices and oranges. Then bottle in sanitised wine bottles, fit a cork, and label your mulled wine. Filter the mulled wine to achieve a high clarity if necessary.

Mulled Wine 2 (Traditional Glühwein, makes one 75cl bottle):

This recipe follows a more traditional (drier) Glühwein style, made popular in Germany and Nordic countries, where it is a staple part of their winter survival kit! There are different regional variations of mulled wine, and the recipe itself can be adjusted to your personal taste. Glühwein is traditionally served at stalls at Christmas markets across Germany and Austria to keep people warm as they shop and socialise.

This recipe is for the German Glühwein, which literally translates to glow-wine, describing how you feel after you've been drinking mugs of it outside in winter. The recipe makes one bottle (75cl) but can be easily scaled up or down.

Ingredients

At Start:

1 bottle (75cl) of dry Red Wine.
1 large Orange
50g (2oz) of Sugar
½ teaspoon of Cinnamon powder
2 Star Anise pods
2 Cassia Bark sticks
5 Cloves
1 shot of Rum or Amaretto (optional to each glass to fortify the mulled wine)

Directions:

Slice the orange and put into a large pan on a stove. Pour over the wine and apply heat. Bring the pan temperature up to 80C (176F). Stir in the sugar until dissolved then add the spices. Allow the spices to simmer in the wine for 30 minutes before serving the wine hot in mugs or insulated cups. Taste the wine before serving and if you prefer a sweeter taste add a little more sugar and stir until dissolved. Add a shot of Rum or Amaretto (your own made versions are ideal and keep the cost down) to add an extra warming kick to the drink.

Mulled Wine 3 (Easy Mulled Wine, makes one 75cl bottle):

This mulled wine recipe is extremely easy to make and is excellent for impromptu celebrations. It makes one bottle of delicious Glühwein.

Ingredients

At Start:

One bottle (75cl) of home-made Red Wine.
2 tablespoons of Clear Honey (optional-leave the honey out if you want a dry finish)
1 Orange
1 Harris Homecraft Mulled Wine Infusion Pack
1 measure of Brandy (your own made brandy keeps the cost down)

Directions:

Slice the orange and put into a large pan on a stove, together with a bottle of red wine. Apply heat and bring the pan temperature up to 80C (176F). Stir in the honey until dissolved then add the spice infusion pack and brandy (optional to give the mulled wine a warming kick!). Simmer for 30 minutes then remove the infusion pack and serve the mulled wine in mugs or insulated cups.

Orange Wine:

This recipe produces a vibrant citrusy wine that can be enjoyed young. The wine has a fresh, clean, and light flavour. It is a great wine to enjoy on a summer picnic and is an idea base for a citrus spritzer.

Ingredients:

At Start:

10 large Oranges
(Use 450g of dried or 425g of canned fruit if fresh is unavailable)
250ml or 245g White Grape Concentrate
1 Kg of Sugar
1 crushed Campden Tablet
1 sachet of Harris Premium Wine Yeast
1 teaspoon of Yeast Nutrient
½ teaspoon of Wine Tannin
½ teaspoon of Acid Blend
10 drops of Pectinaze
3½ litres (6 Pints) Cold Water

After Fermentation:

½ teaspoon of Potassium Sorbate
1 crushed Campden Tablet
1 sachet of Winefine Finings (one sachet will clear between 1 and 5 gallons)

Directions:

Peel the oranges and discard the peelings. Crush the fruit into a pre-sterilised white plastic bucket and pour over the grape concentrate, which will add depth and body to the wine. Then dissolve the sugar in a little hot water and add this to the bucket.

Pour the cold water over the contents together with the acid blend, tannin, and pectinaze. Crush a Campden tablet into the mix and stir well. Cover with a cloth and leave for 24 hours in a cool place. This process will kill any wild yeast and bacteria that may be present on the fruit. The next day add the yeast and yeast nutrient. Stir thoroughly for 1-2 minutes to oxygenate the must. Cover the bucket with a cloth and leave to ferment in a warm place for 5 days, stirring the contents of the bucket occasionally. Then strain into a demijohn (4½ litres) or fermenter, through a nylon straining bag. Press as much of the juice as possible and discard the pulp. It may be necessary to top up with a little extra cold water to achieve 4½ litres. Fit a bung and airlock and leave in a warm place to continue to ferment out completely.

Finishing your Wine:

Fermentation should be complete in 2-5 weeks. At this stage CO2 bubbles should have stopped being released through the airlock. Your wine should then be checked with a hydrometer. The hydrometer will indicate the remaining sugar level and finishing levels are as follows:

Dry = 0.990 – 0.996   Medium = 0.996 – 1.009   Sweet = 1.009 – 1.018

At the end of fermentation add 1 crushed Campden tablet and half teaspoon of potassium sorbate per gallon. Leave in a cool place (15C) for 3 days to kill off the yeast. Then syphon the wine from the sediment into a second fermenter. Shake or stir the wine to degas it then add wine finings to ensure your wine will clear. Leave for 5 days in a cool place then syphon the wine from the sediment. Finally, pass it through a Vinbrite filter to obtain a professional finish before bottling. Filtering will remove all colloidal suspended particles and will ensure that your efforts are rewarded with a professional clarity and a pure taste.

The wine should now be bottled and stored in a cool dark place to mature for at least 6 months. During this time any rough tastes will be smoothed out and the wine will improve in bouquet and flavour.

This recipe makes 1 gallon (4.5 litres) of wine. For larger quantities simply multiply the quantities of ingredients except for the Yeast and Winefine. One sachet of each of these will be sufficient for any quantity between 1 and 5 gallons.

Parsnip Sherry:

This recipe produces a flavourful and aromatic parsnip wine that captures the essence of the popular root vegetable. It has a distinct earthy flavour reminiscent of root vegetables and adds depth to the overall taste profile. Like many vegetable wines, parsnip wine tends to be on the sweeter side. The natural sugars present in the parsnips ferment into alcohol during the winemaking process, resulting in a pleasantly sweet flavour that balances the earthy notes. It has a rich and full-bodied mouthfeel, with a texture that coats the palate. This richness adds to the overall complexity of the wine and lends itself to sipping. Parsnip wine is often used for blending purposes.

Use fresh parsnips that are firm and without blemishes. The best time to make this wine is in January after the parsnips have been subjected to frost, since this enhances their flavour. When parsnips are exposed to frost, their starches are converted into sugars through a process called cold sweetening. This can result in sweeter, firmer, and more flavourful parsnips, making them better for winemaking. Try to select parsnips with small to medium widths. Larger roots tend to become woody and fibrous.

Ingredients:

At Start:

2kg (4.5lb) of Parsnips
250ml or 245g White Grape Concentrate
500g (1lb) Wheat
1.5 Kg (3.3lb) of Light Soft Brown Sugar
1 crushed Campden Tablet
1 sachet of Lalvin EC-1118 Wine Yeast
1 teaspoon of Yeast Nutrient
½ teaspoon of Wine Tannin
1 teaspoon of Acid Blend
10 drops of Amylaze

3½ litres (6 Pints) Cold Water
After Fermentation:

½ teaspoon of Potassium Sorbate
1 crushed Campden Tablet
1 sachet of Winefine Finings (one sachet will clear between 1 and 5 gallons)
150ml Brandy (optional to further fortify the wine)
Directions:

Wash the parsnips under a cold tap in a sieve before use. Cut off and discard the base of the leaves and dice the stems.

Bring the water to boil in a large pan on a stove. Once the water is boiling, add the parsnip pieces and sugar to the pan. Stir until the sugar is completely dissolved. Let the mixture simmer for about 20 minutes to fully extract flavour from the parsnips.

Remove the pan from heat and allow the parsnip mixture to cool to room temperature. Once cooled, strain the liquid into a pre-sterilised white plastic bucket and discard the parsnips (they can be eaten to avoid waste).

Then rinse the wheat in a sieve with a kettle of boiling water to kill any bacteria and wild yeast cells. Add the wheat whole, do not crush, or crack the husks). Pour over the grape concentrate, which will add depth and body to the wine. Add the acid blend, tannin, and Amylaze. Then add the yeast & yeast nutrient and stir thoroughly for 1-2 minutes to oxygenate the must. Cover the bucket with a cloth and leave to ferment in a warm place for 5 days, stirring the contents of the bucket occasionally. Then strain into a demijohn (4½ litres) or fermenter, through a nylon straining bag. Discard the wheat husks. It may be necessary to top up with a little extra cold water to achieve 4½ litres. Fit a bung and airlock and leave in a warm place to continue to ferment out completely.

Finishing your Wine:

Fermentation should be complete in 2-5 weeks. At this stage CO_2 bubbles should have stopped being released through the airlock. Your wine should then be checked with a hydrometer. The hydrometer will indicate the remaining sugar level and finishing levels are as follows:

Dry = 0.990 – 0.996   Medium = 0.996 – 1.009   Sweet = 1.009 – 1.018

At the end of fermentation add 1 crushed Campden tablet and half teaspoon of potassium sorbate per gallon. Leave in a cool place (15C) for 3 days to kill off the yeast. Then syphon the wine from the sediment into a second fermenter. Shake or stir the wine to degas it then add wine finings to ensure your wine will clear. Leave for 5 days in a cool place then syphon the wine from the sediment. Finally, pass it through a Vinbrite filter to obtain a professional finish before bottling. Filtering will remove all colloidal suspended particles and will ensure that your efforts are rewarded with a professional clarity and a pure taste.

The wine should now be bottled and stored in a cool dark place to mature for at 12 months. During this time any rough tastes will be smoothed out and the wine will improve in bouquet and flavour. When bottling you can fortify the wine by adding 25ml of brandy to each bottle, in order to enhance the sherry-like qualities.

This recipe makes 1 gallon (4.5 litres) of wine. For larger quantities simply multiply the quantities of ingredients except for the Yeast and Winefine. One sachet of each of these will be sufficient for any quantity between 1 and 5 gallons.

Peach Wine:

This recipe offers a flavour is dominated by the sweetness of the peaches, with a subtle tartness in the background. The aroma carries hints of ripe fruit and floral notes. Peach wine is a simple, refreshing wine, best enjoyed chilled on a warm day or as a casual accompaniment to light meals or tapas style snacks. It can also form the basis of a delicious spritzer when mixed with soda water.

Ingredients:

At Start:

1.5kg (3.5lb) of ripe Peaches
(Use 500g of dried or 400g of canned fruit if fresh is unavailable)
250ml or 245g White Grape Concentrate
1 Kg of Sugar
1 crushed Campden Tablet
1 sachet of Harris Premium Wine Yeast
1 teaspoon of Yeast Nutrient
½ teaspoon of Wine Tannin
1 teaspoon of Acid Blend
10 drops of Pectinaze
3½ litres (6 Pints) Cold Water

After Fermentation:

½ teaspoon of Potassium Sorbate
1 crushed Campden Tablet
1 sachet of Winefine Finings (one sachet will clear between 1 and 5 gallons)

Directions:

Rinse the fruit under a cold tap in a sieve before use. Remove and discard the stones from the peaches. Then crush the fruit into a pre-sterilised white plastic bucket and pour over the grape concentrate, which will add depth and body to the wine. Then dissolve the sugar in a little hot water and add this to the bucket.

Pour the cold water over the contents together with the acid blend, tannin, and pectinaze. Crush a Campden tablet into the mix and stir well. Cover with a cloth and leave for 24 hours in a cool place. This process will kill any wild yeast and bacteria that may be present on the fruit. The next day add the yeast and yeast nutrient. Stir thoroughly for 1-2 minutes to oxygenate the must. Cover the bucket with a cloth and leave to ferment in a warm place for 5 days, stirring the contents of the bucket occasionally. Then strain into a demijohn (4½ litres) or fermenter, through a nylon straining bag. Press as much of the juice as possible and discard the pulp. It may be necessary to top up with a little extra cold water to achieve 4½ litres. Fit a bung and airlock and leave in a warm place to continue to ferment out completely.

Finishing your Wine:

Fermentation should be complete in 2-5 weeks. At this stage CO_2 bubbles should have stopped being released through the airlock. Your wine should then be checked with a hydrometer. The hydrometer will indicate the remaining sugar level and finishing levels are as follows:

Dry = 0.990 – 0.996   Medium = 0.996 – 1.009   Sweet = 1.009 – 1.018

At the end of fermentation add 1 crushed Campden tablet and half teaspoon of potassium sorbate per gallon. Leave in a cool place (15C) for 3 days to kill off the yeast. Then syphon the wine from the sediment into a second fermenter. Shake or stir the wine to degas it then add wine finings to ensure your wine will clear. Leave for 5 days in a cool place then syphon the wine from the sediment. Finally, pass it through a Vinbrite filter to obtain a professional finish before bottling. Filtering will remove all colloidal suspended particles and will ensure that your efforts are rewarded with a professional clarity and a pure taste.

The wine should now be bottled and stored in a cool dark place to mature for at least 6 months. During this time any rough tastes will be smoothed out and the wine will improve in bouquet and flavour.

This recipe makes 1 gallon (4.5 litres) of wine. For larger quantities simply multiply the quantities of ingredients except for the Yeast and Winefine.

Pear Wine:

With its pale straw to golden hue, this wine captures the essence of orchard-fresh pears. On the palate, pear wine delivers a delicate balance of sweetness and acidity, reminiscent of the fruit's natural flavours. Its aroma is subtle, with hints of pear blossom and fresh fruit.

Ingredients:

At Start:

3Kg (6½lb) Pears
(Use 800g of canned fruit if fresh is unavailable)
250ml or 245g White Grape Concentrate
1 Kg Bag of Sugar
1 sachet of Lalvin ICV-D47 Wine Yeast
1 sachet of Pure Brew (or 1 Teaspoon Yeast Nutrient)
1 teaspoon of Acid Blend
10 drops of Pectinaze
1 Crushed Campden Tablet

After Fermentation:

½ teaspoon of Potassium Sorbate
1 crushed Campden Tablet
1 sachet of Winefine Finings (one sachet will clear between 1 and 5 gallons)
3½ litres (6 Pints) Cold Water

Directions:

Chop the pears and crush them in a pre-sterilised white plastic bucket. Pour over the grape concentrate, which will add depth and body to the wine. Then dissolve the sugar in a little hot water and add this to the bucket.

Pour the cold water over the contents together with the acid blend, and pectinaze. Crush a Campden tablet into the mix and stir well. Cover with a cloth and leave for 24 hours in a cool place. This process will kill any wild yeast and bacteria that may be present on the fruit. The next day add the yeast & Pure Brew sachet (or nutrient). This is now called the 'must'. Stir thoroughly for 1-2 minutes to oxygenate the must. Cover the bucket with a cloth and leave to ferment in a warm place for 5 days, stirring the contents of the bucket occasionally. Then strain into a demijohn (4½ litres) or fermenter, through a nylon straining bag. Press as much of the juice as possible and discard the pulp. It may be necessary to top up with a little extra cold water to achieve 4½ litres. Fit a bung and airlock and leave in a warm place to continue to ferment out completely.

Finishing your Wine:

Fermentation should be complete in 2-5 weeks. At this stage CO2 bubbles should have stopped being released through the airlock. Your wine should then be checked with a hydrometer. The hydrometer will indicate the remaining sugar level and finishing levels are as follows:

Dry = 0.990 – 0.996   Medium = 0.996 – 1.009   Sweet = 1.009 – 1.018

At the end of fermentation add 1 crushed Campden tablet and half teaspoon of potassium sorbate per gallon. Leave in a cool place (15C) for 3 days to kill off the yeast. Then syphon the wine from the sediment into a second fermenter. Shake or stir the wine to degas it then add wine finings to ensure your wine will clear. Leave for 5 days in a cool place then syphon the wine from the sediment. Finally, pass it through a Vinbrite filter to obtain a professional finish before bottling.

Pears contain a high level of pectin which can make it difficult to clear your wine. Therefore, it is important to add pectinaze (you cannot overdose so add a little extra if necessary), and to add finings to support the clearing process. Filtering will remove all colloidal suspended particles and will ensure that your efforts are rewarded with a professional clarity and a pure taste.

The wine should now be bottled and stored in a cool dark place to mature for at least 6 months. During this time any rough tastes will be smoothed out and the wine will improve in bouquet and flavour.

This recipe makes 1 gallon (4.5 litres) of wine. For larger quantities simply multiply the quantities of ingredients except for the Pure Brew, Yeast and Winefine. One sachet of each of these will be sufficient for any quantity between 1 and 5 gallons.

Perry.

Perry is a delicious alternative to apple cider. In terms of flavour, cider tends to have a broader range of tastes depending on the apple varieties used, ranging from sweet to tart, with varying levels of acidity and tannins. On the other hand, perry typically has a lighter and more delicate flavour profile, with a subtle sweetness and floral notes characteristic of pears. It provides a refreshing fruity taste with a subtle citrusy tartness in the background.

For best results try to select a mix of pear types. Choose good quality fruit without blemishes. It is possible to substitute pear juice for pears to simplify the process.

Ingredients:

At Start:

7.25kg (16 lbs) Pears (or 1 gallon of pear juice)
(Use 800g of canned fruit if fresh is unavailable)
10 drops Pectinaze
1 teaspoon of Yeast Nutrient
1 sachet of Harris Cider Yeast

After Fermentation:

1 sachet of Cider Brite Finings (if you prefer a clear perry)
½ teaspoon of Potassium Sorbate (only used for a still scrumpy style)
1 crushed Campden Tablet (only used for a still scrumpy style)

Directions:

First cut the pears into small pieces, which will help in juice extraction. Crush, press, and add the juice to a bucket (fermenter). A wine press is recommended for maximum juice extraction and to make the process easy.

Add water or more pear juice if necessary to reach the final desired volume. Now take a specific gravity reading with a hydrometer and if necessary, add some sugar dissolved in a little hot water to increase the gravity. As a guide, your original gravity should be around 1050-1060. The higher the gravity, the stronger the perry will be. Add the Pectinaze and Yeast & Nutrient. Then stir well for 1-2 minutes to oxygenate the perry. Secure a lid fitted with an airlock and ferment in a warm place (24C).

Pressing Tip: if you do not have access to a fruit press chop the fruit into small pieces and crush with a wooden block or put through a blender. Put the crushed fruit into a nylon straining bag and tie it. Add the separated juice to the bucket, and the bag of pulp. After 3 days remove the bag from the bucket and discard the pulp.

Continue to ferment in the bucket (fermenter) until the bubbles stop emerging from the airlock. Take a hydrometer reading again. The finishing gravity should be below 1.010. Fermentation should take around two weeks to complete.

Finishing the Perry:

There are a number of options that you can take to finish your cider, depending on the style you prefer:

Sparkling Perry (Clear):

When the fermentation is complete, add Cider Brite finings to your bucket and gently stir. Leave in a cool place with the lid fitted for 2-3 days for the perry to clear. Then syphon the perry into pressurised bottles (preferably plastic beer bottles), add 1-2 Brew Fizz Carbonation Drops per 500ml bottle and secure the cap. Then store the bottles in a warm place (24C) for 5 days to carbonate through secondary fermentation. There will inevitably be a little sediment on the bottom of the bottles, but the finings should make this stick to the bottom if poured carefully. Leave the perry in a cool place for 2-3 weeks to mature and serve chilled from a fridge.

Still Perry (Cloudy Scrumpy Style):

If you do not wish to carbonate your perry and prefer it served flat, you should add 1/2 tsp of Potassium Sorbate and 1 Campden tablet per gallon of perry at the end of fermentation, to stabilise the yeast. If you prefer the perry to be still but clear, add a dose of Cider Brite Finings at this stage. Then leave for 48 hours before tasting and if necessary, you can sweeten your perry with Glycerine or Wine Sweetener. Bottle or keg the perry and allow it to mature for 4 weeks in a cool place to mature before sampling.

This recipe makes 1 gallon (4.5 litres) of Perry. For larger quantities simply multiply the quantities of ingredients except for the Yeast and Cider Brite finings. One sachet of each of these will be sufficient for any quantity between 1 and 5 gallons.

Plum Wine:

This recipe captures the essence of ripe plums in every sip. Crafted from the juice of succulent plums, the wine boasts a rich and deep hue, reflecting the vibrant colours of the fruit. On the palate, plum wine offers a harmonious blend of sweet and tart flavours, with the natural sweetness of the plums balanced by a refreshing acidity.

Ingredients:

At Start:

2kg (4.5lb) Plums
(Use 2kg of dried or 1.1kg of canned fruit if fresh is unavailable)
250ml or 245g White Grape Concentrate
1 Kg of Sugar
1 crushed Campden Tablet
1 sachet of Gervin GV2 Wine Yeast
1 teaspoon of Yeast Nutrient
½ teaspoon of Wine Tannin
1 teaspoon of Acid Blend
10 drops of Pectinaze
3½ litres (6 Pints) Cold Water

After Fermentation:

½ teaspoon of Potassium Sorbate
1 crushed Campden Tablet
1 sachet of Winefine Finings (one sachet will clear between 1 and 5 gallons)

Directions:

Rinse the plums under a cold tap in a sieve before use. Remove and discard the stones. Then crush the fruit into a pre-sterilised white plastic bucket and pour over the grape concentrate, which will add depth and body to the wine. Then dissolve the sugar in a little hot water and add this to the bucket.

Pour the cold water over the contents together with the acid blend, tannin, and pectinaze. Crush a Campden tablet into the mix and stir well. Cover with a cloth and leave for 24 hours in a cool place. This process will kill any wild yeast and bacteria that may be present on the fruit. The next day add the yeast and yeast nutrient. Stir thoroughly for 1-2 minutes to oxygenate the must. Cover the bucket with a cloth and leave to ferment in a warm place for 5 days, stirring the contents of the bucket occasionally. Then strain into a demijohn (4½ litres) or fermenter, through a nylon straining bag. Press as much of the juice as possible and discard the pulp. It may be necessary to top up with a little extra cold water to achieve 4½ litres. Fit a bung and airlock and leave in a warm place to continue to ferment out completely.

Finishing your Wine:

Fermentation should be complete in 2-5 weeks. At this stage CO2 bubbles should have stopped being released through the airlock. Your wine should then be checked with a hydrometer. The hydrometer will indicate the remaining sugar level and finishing levels are as follows:

Dry = 0.990 – 0.996   Medium = 0.996 – 1.009   Sweet = 1.009 – 1.018

At the end of fermentation add 1 crushed Campden tablet and half teaspoon of potassium sorbate per gallon. Leave in a cool place (15C) for 3 days to kill off the yeast. Then syphon the wine from the sediment into a second fermenter. Shake or stir the wine to degas it then add wine finings to ensure your wine will clear. Leave for 5 days in a cool place then syphon the wine from the sediment. Finally, pass it through a Vinbrite filter to obtain a professional finish before bottling. Filtering will remove all colloidal suspended particles and will ensure that your efforts are rewarded with a professional clarity and a pure taste.

Plum wine can contain a large amount of pectin, so it is essential to use pectinaze. If the wine does not clear it may be necessary to test for pectin and add more pectinaze. You cannot overdose with pectinaze so be generous at the start. The wine can then be re-filtered after treating it.

The wine should now be bottled and stored in a cool dark place to mature for at least 6 months. During this time any rough tastes will be smoothed out and the wine will improve in bouquet and flavour.

This recipe makes 1 gallon (4.5 litres) of wine. For larger quantities simply multiply the quantities of ingredients except for the Yeast and Winefine. One sachet of each of these will be sufficient for any quantity between 1 and 5 gallons.

Raspberry Wine:

This recipe makes a delicious light red fruit wine. Raspberries should be ripe to release their full flavour. Always choose clean, fresh fruit and avoid roadside locations when picking fruit. Thoroughly wash the fruit in cold water before use.

Ingredients:

At Start:

1.5 Kg (3½lb) Raspberries
(Use 400g of canned fruit if fresh is unavailable)
250ml or 245g Red Grape Concentrate
1 Kg of Sugar
1 crushed Campden Tablet
1 sachet of Harris Premium Wine Yeast
1 teaspoon of Yeast Nutrient
1 teaspoon of Wine Tannin
1 teaspoon of Acid Blend
10 drops of Pectinaze
3½ litres (6 Pints) Cold Water

After Fermentation:

½ teaspoon of Potassium Sorbate
1 crushed Campden Tablet
1 sachet of Winefine Finings (one sachet will clear between 1 and 5 gallons)

Directions:

Crush the Raspberries into a pre-sterilised white plastic bucket and pour over the grape concentrate, which will add depth and body to the wine. Then dissolve the sugar in a little hot water and add this to the bucket.

Pour the cold water over the contents together with the acid blend, tannin, and pectinaze. Crush a Campden tablet into the mix and stir well. Cover with a cloth and leave for 24 hours in a cool place. This process will kill any wild yeast and bacteria that may be present on the fruit. The next day add the yeast and yeast nutrient. Stir thoroughly for 1-2 minutes to oxygenate the must. Cover the bucket with a cloth and leave to ferment in a warm place for 5 days, stirring the contents of the bucket occasionally. Then strain into a demijohn (4½ litres) or fermenter, through a nylon straining bag. Press as much of the juice as possible and discard the pulp. It may be necessary to top up with a little extra cold water to achieve 4½ litres. Fit a bung and airlock and leave in a warm place to continue to ferment out completely.

Finishing your Wine:

Fermentation should be complete in 2-5 weeks. At this stage CO2 bubbles should have stopped being released through the airlock. Your wine should then be checked with a hydrometer. The hydrometer will indicate the remaining sugar level and finishing levels are as follows:

Dry = 0.990 – 0.996   Medium = 0.996 – 1.009   Sweet = 1.009 – 1.018

At the end of fermentation add 1 crushed Campden tablet and half teaspoon of potassium sorbate per gallon. Leave in a cool place (15C) for 3 days to kill off the yeast. Then syphon the wine from the sediment into a second fermenter. Shake or stir the wine to degas it then add wine finings to ensure your wine will clear. Leave for 5 days in a cool place then syphon the wine from the sediment. Finally, pass it through a Vinbrite filter to obtain a professional finish before bottling. Filtering will remove all colloidal suspended particles and will ensure that your efforts are rewarded with a professional clarity and a pure taste.

The wine should now be bottled and stored in a cool dark place to mature for at least 6 months. During this time any rough tastes will be smoothed out and the wine will improve in bouquet and flavour.

This recipe makes 1 gallon (4.5 litres) of wine. For larger quantities simply multiply the quantities of ingredients except for the Yeast and Winefine. One sachet of each of these will be sufficient for any quantity between 1 and 5 gallons.

Redcurrant Wine:

Redcurrant wine is a unique and vibrant wine that captures the essence of tart and tangy redcurrants in every sip. Crafted from the juice of these tiny, flavourful berries, it showcases a brilliant ruby hue that sparkles in the glass. On the palate, it offers a delightful balance of sweetness and acidity, with the tartness of the redcurrants tempered by a subtle fruitiness and crisp finish. Its aroma is bright and refreshing, with hints of red berries and floral undertones.

Ingredients:

At Start:

1.5 Kg (3½lb) Redcurrants
500g Long Grain Brown Rice (whole, do not crush)
250ml or 245g White Grape Concentrate
1 Kg of Sugar
1 crushed Campden Tablet
1 sachet of Harris Premium Wine Yeast
1 teaspoon of Yeast Nutrient
½ teaspoon of Wine Tannin
1 teaspoon of Acid Blend
10 drops of Pectinaze
3½ litres (6 Pints) Cold Water

After Fermentation:

½ teaspoon of Potassium Sorbate
1 crushed Campden Tablet
1 sachet of Winefine Finings (one sachet will clear between 1 and 5 gallons)

Directions:

Crush the Redcurrants into a pre-sterilised white plastic bucket. Rinse the rice thoroughly in a sieve under cold water to remove starch. Then add to the bucket (do not crush or crack the husks) and pour over the grape concentrate, which will add depth and body to the wine. Then dissolve the sugar in a little hot water and add this to the bucket.

Pour the cold water over the contents together with the acid blend, tannin, and pectinaze. Crush a Campden tablet into the mix and stir well. Cover with a cloth and leave for 24 hours in a cool place. This process will kill any wild yeast and bacteria that may be present on the fruit. The next day add the yeast and yeast nutrient. Stir thoroughly for 1-2 minutes to oxygenate the must. Cover the bucket with a cloth and leave to ferment in a warm place for 5 days, stirring the contents of the bucket occasionally. Then strain into a demijohn (4½ litres) or fermenter, through a nylon straining bag. Press as much of the juice as possible and discard the pulp. It may be necessary to top up with a little extra cold water to achieve 4½ litres. Fit a bung and airlock and leave in a warm place to continue to ferment out completely.

Finishing your Wine:

Fermentation should be complete in 2-5 weeks. At this stage CO2 bubbles should have stopped being released through the airlock. Your wine should then be checked with a hydrometer. The hydrometer will indicate the remaining sugar level and finishing levels are as follows:

Dry = 0.990 – 0.996   Medium = 0.996 – 1.009   Sweet = 1.009 – 1.018

At the end of fermentation add 1 crushed Campden tablet and half teaspoon of potassium sorbate per gallon. Leave in a cool place (15C) for 3 days to kill off the yeast. Then syphon the wine from the sediment into a second fermenter. Shake or stir the wine to degas it then add wine finings to ensure your wine will clear. Leave for 5 days in a cool place then syphon the wine from the sediment. Finally, pass it through a Vinbrite filter to obtain a professional finish before bottling. Filtering will remove all colloidal suspended particles and will ensure that your efforts are rewarded with a professional clarity and a pure taste.

The wine should now be bottled and stored in a cool dark place to mature for at least 6 months. During this time any rough tastes will be smoothed out and the wine will improve in bouquet and flavour.

This recipe makes 1 gallon (4.5 litres) of wine. For larger quantities simply multiply the quantities of ingredients except for the Yeast and Winefine. One sachet of each of these will be sufficient for any quantity between 1 and 5 gallons.

Rhubarb Wine:

This is another traditional English wine. Rhubarb wine typically has a unique and distinctive flavour profile that is both tangy and slightly sweet. Rhubarb is naturally tart, and this tartness is often present in rhubarb wine. The tangy acidity of the rhubarb provides a refreshing and palate-cleansing sensation. The taste can vary slightly depending on the variety used but it generally has a fruity flavour reminiscent of apples or strawberries. This fruity character adds complexity and depth to the flavour profile. It is typically light to medium-bodied, with a crisp and refreshing mouthfeel. It is often enjoyed for its easy-drinking nature and suitability for warm-weather occasions. Rhubarb wine is often chosen for blending purposes.

Rhubarb stalks should be ripe to release their full flavour. The best time to pick and make the wine is in May as the younger Rhubarb makes better wine. Always clean the water by rinsing under a tap before use. Rhubarb contains Oxalic acid in the leaves which is unwanted and can be released when exposed to hot water. Therefore, it is important to only use a cold-water flavour extraction technique when making Rhubarb wine. Never use the leaves and always refrain from using the top 2cm of the stalk attached to the leaf.

Ingredients:

At Start:

2 Kg (4½lb) Rhubarb (use young stalks and avoid the area close to the leaf)
(Use 1.1kg of canned fruit if fresh is unavailable)
250ml or 245g White Grape Concentrate
1.36 Kg (3lbs) of Sugar
1 crushed Campden Tablet
1 sachet of Lalvin 71B Wine Yeast
1 teaspoon of Yeast Nutrient
½ teaspoon of Wine Tannin
10 drops of Pectinaze

3½ litres (6 Pints) Cold Water

After Fermentation:

½ teaspoon of Potassium Sorbate
1 crushed Campden Tablet
1 sachet of Winefine Finings (one sachet will clear between 1 and 5 gallons)

Directions:

Clean the Rhubarb stalks and cut into cubes. Crush them into a pre-sterilised white plastic bucket and pour over the grape concentrate, which will add depth and body to the wine. Then dissolve the sugar in a little hot water and add this to the bucket.

Pour the cold water over the contents together with the tannin, and pectinaze. Crush a Campden tablet into the mix and stir well. Cover with a cloth and leave for 24 hours in a cool place. This process will kill any wild yeast and bacteria that may be present on the fruit. The next day add the yeast and yeast nutrient. Stir thoroughly for 1-2 minutes to oxygenate the must. Cover the bucket with a cloth and leave to ferment in a warm place for 5 days, stirring the contents of the bucket occasionally. Then strain into a demijohn (4½ litres) or fermenter, through a nylon straining bag. Press as much of the juice as possible and discard the pulp. It may be necessary to top up with a little extra cold water to achieve 4½ litres. Fit a bung and airlock and leave in a warm place to continue to ferment out completely.

Finishing your Wine:

Fermentation should be complete in 2-5 weeks. At this stage CO_2 bubbles should have stopped being released through the airlock. Your wine should then be checked with a hydrometer. The hydrometer will indicate the remaining sugar level and finishing levels are as follows:

Dry = 0.990 – 0.996   Medium = 0.996 – 1.009   Sweet = 1.009 – 1.018

At the end of fermentation add 1 crushed Campden tablet and half teaspoon of potassium sorbate per gallon. Leave in a cool place (15C) for 3 days to kill off the yeast. Then syphon the wine from the sediment into a second fermenter. Shake or stir the wine to degas it then add wine finings to ensure your wine will clear. Leave for 5 days in a cool place then syphon the wine from the sediment. Finally, pass it through a Vinbrite filter to obtain a professional finish before bottling. Filtering will remove all colloidal suspended particles and will ensure that your efforts are rewarded with a professional clarity and a pure taste.

The wine should now be bottled and stored in a cool dark place to mature for at least 6 months. During this time any rough tastes will be smoothed out and the wine will improve in bouquet and flavour.

This recipe makes 1 gallon (4.5 litres) of wine. For larger quantities simply multiply the quantities of ingredients except for the Yeast and Winefine. One sachet of each of these will be sufficient for any quantity between 1 and 5 gallons.

Rice & Raisin Wine:

Rice and raisin is a unique and flavourful wine that combines the delicate sweetness of raisins with the subtle earthiness of rice. Crafted from a blend of fermented rice and raisins, this wine offers a golden hue that reflects its rich and complex flavours. On the palate, it delivers a harmonious balance of sweetness and depth, with the natural sugars of the raisins complementing the mellow notes of the rice. The aroma is warm and inviting, with hints of dried fruit and nutty undertones. Rice and raisin wine is a versatile option, enjoyed on its own as a dessert wine or paired with a variety of dishes, from spicy Asian cuisine to creamy cheeses and nuts.

Ingredients:

At Start:

1.5 Kg (3½lb) Raisins
500g Long Grain Brown Rice (whole, do not crush)
250ml or 245g White Grape Concentrate
1 Kg of Clear Honey
1 crushed Campden Tablet
1 sachet of Lalvin EC-1118 Wine Yeast
1 teaspoon of Yeast Nutrient
½ teaspoon of Wine Tannin
1 teaspoon of Acid Blend
10 drops of Pectinaze
3½ litres (6 Pints) Cold Water

After Fermentation:

½ teaspoon of Potassium Sorbate
1 crushed Campden Tablet
1 sachet of Winefine Finings (one sachet will clear between 1 and 5 gallons)

Directions:

Chop or mince the Raisins and put them into a pre-sterilised white plastic bucket. Rinse the rice thoroughly in a sieve under cold water to remove starch. Then add to the bucket (do not crush or crack the husks) and pour over the grape concentrate, which will add depth and body to the wine. Then dissolve the honey in a little water (around 40C temperature) and add this to the bucket.

Pour the cold water over the contents together with the acid blend, tannin, and pectinaze. Crush a Campden tablet into the mix and stir well. Cover with a cloth and leave for 24 hours in a cool place. This process will kill any wild yeast and bacteria that may be present on the fruit. The next day add the yeast and yeast nutrient. Stir thoroughly for 1-2 minutes to oxygenate the must. Cover the bucket with a cloth and leave to ferment in a warm place for 5 days, stirring the contents of the bucket occasionally. Then strain into a demijohn (4½ litres) or fermenter, through a nylon straining bag. Press as much of the juice as possible and discard the pulp. It may be necessary to top up with a little extra cold water to achieve 4½ litres. Fit a bung and airlock and leave in a warm place to continue to ferment out completely.

Finishing your Wine:

Fermentation should be complete in 2-5 weeks. At this stage CO2 bubbles should have stopped being released through the airlock. Your wine should then be checked with a hydrometer. The hydrometer will indicate the remaining sugar level and finishing levels are as follows:

Dry = 0.990 – 0.996   Medium = 0.996 – 1.009   Sweet = 1.009 – 1.018

At the end of fermentation add 1 crushed Campden tablet and half teaspoon of potassium sorbate per gallon. Leave in a cool place (15C) for 3 days to kill off the yeast. Then syphon the wine from the sediment into a second fermenter. Shake or stir the wine to degas it then add wine finings to ensure your wine will clear. Leave for 5 days in a cool place then syphon the wine from the sediment. Finally, pass it through a Vinbrite filter to obtain a professional finish before bottling. Filtering will remove all colloidal suspended particles and will ensure that your efforts are rewarded with a professional clarity and a pure taste.

The wine should now be bottled and stored in a cool dark place to mature for at least 9 months. During this time any rough tastes will be smoothed out and the wine will improve in bouquet and flavour. Back sweeten the wine to taste with honey or brewers' glycerine before bottling.

This recipe makes 1 gallon (4.5 litres) of wine. For larger quantities simply multiply the quantities of ingredients except for the Yeast and Winefine. One sachet of each of these will be sufficient for any quantity between 1 and 5 gallons.

Rosehip Wine:

Rosehip wine has a distinctive flavour that is both fruity and tart, with floral and citrus undertones. It typically has a vibrant reddish-orange colour. The hue may vary depending on factors such as the variety of roses used and the length of fermentation. It is best to pick the Rosehips immediately after the first frosts in late Autumn. Rosehips are rich in vitamin C, antioxidants, and other beneficial compounds. As a result, rosehip wine may offer some health benefits, although the concentration of nutrients in the wine may vary depending on factors such as processing and fermentation.

Ingredients:

At Start:

1 Kg (2.2lb) Rosehips
(Use 500g of dried fruit if fresh is unavailable)
250ml or 245g White Grape Concentrate
1.36 Kg (3lbs) of Sugar
1 crushed Campden Tablet
1 sachet of Harris Premium Wine Yeast
1 teaspoon of Acid Blend
1 teaspoon of Yeast Nutrient
10 drops of Pectinaze
3½ litres (6 Pints) Cold Water

After Fermentation:

½ teaspoon of Potassium Sorbate
1 crushed Campden Tablet
1 sachet of Winefine Finings (one sachet will clear between 1 and 5 gallons)

Directions:

Rinse the Rosehips under a cold tap in a sieve then slice them into two sections. Crush them into a pre-sterilised white plastic bucket and pour over the grape concentrate, which will add depth and body to the wine. Then dissolve the sugar in a little hot water and add this to the bucket.

Pour the cold water over the contents together with the acid blend, and pectinaze. Crush a Campden tablet into the mix and stir well. Cover with a cloth and leave for 24 hours in a cool place. This process will kill any wild yeast and bacteria that may be present on the fruit. The next day add the yeast and yeast nutrient. Stir thoroughly for 1-2 minutes to oxygenate the must. Cover the bucket with a cloth and leave to ferment in a warm place for 7 days, stirring the contents of the bucket occasionally. Then strain into a demijohn (4½ litres) or fermenter, through a nylon straining bag. Press as much of the juice as possible and discard the pulp. It may be necessary to top up with a little extra cold water to achieve 4½ litres. Fit a bung and airlock and leave in a warm place to continue to ferment out completely.

Finishing your Wine:

Fermentation should be complete in 2-5 weeks. At this stage CO2 bubbles should have stopped being released through the airlock. Your wine should then be checked with a hydrometer. The hydrometer will indicate the remaining sugar level and finishing levels are as follows:

Dry = 0.990 – 0.996   Medium = 0.996 – 1.009   Sweet = 1.009 – 1.018

At the end of fermentation add 1 crushed Campden tablet and half teaspoon of potassium sorbate per gallon. Leave in a cool place (15C) for 3 days to kill off the yeast. Then syphon the wine from the sediment into a second fermenter. Shake or stir the wine to degas it then add wine finings to ensure your wine will clear. Leave for 5 days in a cool place then syphon the wine from the sediment. Finally, pass it through a Vinbrite filter to obtain a professional finish before bottling. Filtering will remove all colloidal suspended particles and will ensure that your efforts are rewarded with a professional clarity and a pure taste.

The wine should now be bottled and stored in a cool dark place to mature for at least 6 months. During this time any rough tastes will be smoothed out and the wine will improve in bouquet and flavour.

This recipe makes 1 gallon (4.5 litres) of wine. For larger quantities simply multiply the quantities of ingredients except for the Yeast and Winefine. One sachet of each of these will be sufficient for any quantity between 1 and 5 gallons. It is possible to substitute fresh Rosehips for 200ml Rosehip syrup if fresh fruit is not available.

Rose Petal & Raspberry Rosé Wine:

This recipe captures the delicate floral aroma of fresh rose petals in a wine that's light and fresh, perfect for summertime sipping. It has a delicate floral aroma and a light, fresh taste. The flavour of rose petal wine is deep and complex, bringing you back to warm summer days. The combination of Rose Petals and Raspberries makes a delicious deep Rose wine, which is best served chilled. The Raspberries contribute a sweet and slightly tart profile to the wine that complements the floral notes of the rose petals, adding complexity and depth to the overall taste. They have a distinct aroma that will enhance the fragrance of the wine. When combined with the delicate floral scent of rose petals, it will create a captivating bouquet. Raspberries are known for their vibrant red hue. Adding them to rose petal wine will intensify the colour, giving the wine a richer and more visually appealing appearance.

Ingredients:

At Start:

1 litre (2 pints) of fresh Rose Petals
(Use 2oz/50g of dried flowers if fresh are unavailable)
1.5kg (3.3lbs) of Raspberries
(Use 200g of canned fruit if fresh is unavailable)
250ml or 245g White Grape Concentrate
1 Kg of Light Clear Honey
1 crushed Campden Tablet
1 sachet of Lalvin K1-V1116 Wine Yeast
1 teaspoon of Yeast Nutrient
1 teaspoon of Acid Blend
¼ teaspoon of Wine Tannin
10 drops of Pectinaze
3½ litres (6 Pints) Cold Water

After Fermentation:
½ teaspoon of Potassium Sorbate
1 crushed Campden Tablet
1 sachet of Winefine Finings (one sachet will clear between 1 and 5 gallons)

Directions:

Remove the petals from their stalks and rinse them (together with the raspberries) in a sieve under a cold tap to remove any dirt. Then put them into a pre-sterilised white plastic bucket and crush the raspberries in. Pour over the grape concentrate, which will add depth and body to the wine. Then dissolve the honey in water and add this to the bucket (keep the water temperature to 40C to avoid destroying the fine flavours of the honey).

Pour the cold water over the contents together with the acid blend, tannin, and pectinaze. Crush a Campden tablet into the mix and stir well. Cover with a cloth and leave for 24 hours in a cool place. This process will kill any wild yeast and bacteria that may be present on the flowers. The next day add the yeast and yeast nutrient. Stir thoroughly for 1-2 minutes to oxygenate the must. Cover the bucket with a cloth and leave to ferment in a warm place for 5 days, stirring the contents of the bucket occasionally. Then strain into a demijohn (4½ litres) or fermenter, through a nylon straining bag and discard the flower pulp. It may be necessary to top up with a little extra cold water to achieve 4½ litres. Fit a bung and airlock and leave in a warm place to continue to ferment out completely.

Finishing your Wine:

Fermentation should be complete in 2-5 weeks. At this stage CO2 bubbles should have stopped being released through the airlock. Your wine should then be checked with a hydrometer. The hydrometer will indicate the remaining sugar level and finishing levels are as follows:

Dry = 0.990 – 0.996   Medium = 0.996 – 1.009   Sweet = 1.009 – 1.018

At the end of fermentation add 1 crushed Campden tablet and half teaspoon of potassium sorbate per gallon. Leave in a cool place (15C) for

3 days to kill off the yeast. Then syphon the wine from the sediment into a second fermenter. Shake or stir the wine to degas it then add wine finings to ensure your wine will clear. Leave for 5 days in a cool place then syphon the wine from the sediment. Finally, pass it through a Vinbrite filter to obtain a professional finish before bottling. Filtering will remove all colloidal suspended particles and will ensure that your efforts are rewarded with a professional clarity and a pure taste.

The wine should now be bottled and stored in a cool dark place to mature for at least 6 months. During this time any rough tastes will be smoothed out and the wine will improve in bouquet and flavour.

This recipe makes 1 gallon (4.5 litres) of wine. For larger quantities simply multiply the quantities of ingredients except for the Yeast and Winefine. One sachet of each of these will be sufficient for any quantity between 1 and 5 gallons.

Sloe Wine:

Sloe wine is a deep dark red wine that has a spiciness, a sweetness and a richness that provides depth and character. It captures the essence of tart and tangy sloe berries in every sip. The juice of these small, dark fruits provide a rich ruby hue that reflects the wines' intense flavour profile. On the palate, it offers a delightful balance of sweetness and acidity, with the tartness of the sloe berries complemented by a subtle fruitiness and depth. Its aroma is complex and inviting, with hints of ripe berries and floral undertones.

Ingredients:

At Start:

2 Kg (4½lb) Sloes
(Use 500g of dried fruit if fresh is unavailable)
250g (1/2lb) Wheat (whole, do not crush or crack the husks)
250ml or 245g Red Grape Concentrate
1 Kg of Sugar
1 crushed Campden Tablet
1 sachet of Harris Premium Wine Yeast
1 teaspoon of Yeast Nutrient
1 teaspoon of Acid Blend
10 drops of Pectinaze
3½ litres (6 Pints) Water

After Fermentation:
½ teaspoon of Potassium Sorbate
1 crushed Campden Tablet
1 sachet of Winefine Finings (one sachet will clear between 1 and 5 gallons)

Directions:

Remove all stones from the Sloes (an Olive/Cherry Pitter is an ideal tool to remove the stones) and crush them into a pre-sterilised white plastic bucket. Rinse the wheat in a sieve under a cold tap to clean it then add to the bucket (do not crush or crack the husks as they act as a filter to retain unwanted starch). Then add the grape concentrate, which will provide depth and body to the wine. Then dissolve the sugar in a little hot water and add this to the bucket.

Pour the cold water over the contents together with the acid blend, and pectinaze. Crush a Campden tablet into the mix and stir well. Cover with a cloth and leave for 24 hours in a cool place. This process will kill any wild yeast and bacteria that may be present on the fruit. The next day add the yeast and yeast nutrient. Stir thoroughly for 1-2 minutes to oxygenate the must. Cover the bucket with a cloth and leave to ferment in a warm place for 5 days, stirring the contents of the bucket occasionally. Then strain into a demijohn (4½ litres) or fermenter, through a nylon straining bag. Press as much of the juice as possible and discard the pulp. It may be necessary to top up with a little extra cold water to achieve 4½ litres. Fit a bung and airlock and leave in a warm place to continue to ferment out completely.

Finishing your Wine:

Fermentation should be complete in 2-5 weeks. At this stage CO2 bubbles should have stopped being released through the airlock. Your wine should then be checked with a hydrometer. The hydrometer will indicate the remaining sugar level and finishing levels are as follows:

Dry = 0.990 – 0.996   Medium = 0.996 – 1.009   Sweet = 1.009 – 1.018

At the end of fermentation add 1 crushed Campden tablet and half teaspoon of potassium sorbate per gallon. Leave in a cool place (15C) for 3 days to kill off the yeast. Then syphon the wine from the sediment into a second fermenter. Shake or stir the wine to degas it then add wine finings to ensure your wine will clear. Leave for 5 days in a cool place then syphon the wine from the sediment. Finally, pass it through a Vinbrite filter to obtain a professional finish before bottling. Sloes contain a high level of pectin which can make it difficult to clear your wine. Therefore, it is important to add pectinaze (you cannot overdose so add a little extra if necessary), and to add finings to support the clearing process. Filtering will remove all colloidal suspended particles and will ensure that your efforts are rewarded with a professional clarity and a pure taste.

The wine should now be bottled and stored in a cool dark place to mature for at least 6 months. During this time any rough tastes will be smoothed out and the wine will improve in bouquet and flavour.

This recipe makes 1 gallon (4.5 litres) of wine. For larger quantities simply multiply the quantities of ingredients except for the Yeast and Winefine. One sachet of each of these will be sufficient for any quantity between 1 and 5 gallons.

Sloe Gin Liqueur:

This recipe produces a delicious liqueur, which is popular at Christmas. Sloes are small, oval-shaped fruits that have a deep blue skin and yellow-green flesh. They are smaller and tarter than Damsons, which can be substituted to make a Damson Gin. This delicious liqueur is a Christmas favourite.

Ingredients:

To make one 70cl bottle of Liqueur:
500g (1lb) of ripe Sloes
One 70cl bottle of Gin (Your own Gin produced from Still Spirits Air Still is ideal and saves you money).
500g (1lb) Sugar.

Directions:

Wash the fruit under a cold tap then prick the sloes with a fork. This will ensure a smooth rich flavour.

Half fill a wide necked jar, such as a Kilner Jar, with the sloes. Shake the jar so that the sloes fall into place (allow enough space for the gin to be added).

Gently heat the gin in a pan on the stove and pour in the sugar. Do not boil, just raise the temperature high enough to stir the sugar until it dissolves and then leave to cool.

Pour the cooled gin/sugar solution into the jar and add more sloes until the jar is full, then seal down. Shake the jar to mix the ingredients then store for a minimum of eight weeks, preferably in a dark and dry place. Return and shake occasionally. The longer you leave it, the richer the flavour and deeper the colour will be.

After a minimum of eight weeks strain the liqueur through a muslin bag taking care not to crush the sloes too much. The liqueur should then be strained through a filter paper to ensure that it is clear and bright before bottling. Be patient. Sloe gin is quite gelatinous so it will drip slowly through the filter paper. Alternatively, you could filter it through a Vinbrite Filter fitted with a Prime Pad.

Strawberry Wine:

This recipe has a distinctively fruity and aromatic flavour that captures the essence of ripe strawberries. It has a subtle tartness, which come from the natural acidity of the strawberries, that adds complexity to the flavour profile. This Strawberry wine is refreshing and easy to drink. It strikes a balance between sweetness, fruitiness, and acidity. The sweetness of the strawberries is balanced by the natural acidity of the fruit and the additional acid added during winemaking, resulting in a harmonious and enjoyable wine. It is a Rose style that should be enjoyed chilled, making it a popular choice for warm weather or as a refreshing alternative to heavier wines.

Ingredients:

At Start:

2 Kg (4½lb) Strawberries
(Use 400g of canned fruit if fresh is unavailable)
250g (1/2lb) Long Grain Brown Rice (whole, do not crush or crack the husks)
250ml or 245g White Grape Concentrate
1 Kg of Sugar
1 crushed Campden Tablet
1 sachet of Gervin GV1 Wine Yeast
1 teaspoon of Yeast Nutrient
1 teaspoon of Acid Blend
1 teaspoon of Wine Tannin
10 drops of Pectinaze
3½ litres (6 Pints) Water

After Fermentation:
½ teaspoon of Potassium Sorbate
1 crushed Campden Tablet
1 sachet of Winefine Finings (one sachet will clear between 1 and 5 gallons)

Directions:

Always choose ripe strawberries and remove any stalks from the fruit. Rinse them under a cold tap in a sieve before use. Then crush them into a pre-sterilised white plastic bucket. Rinse the rice in a sieve under a cold tap to clean it then add to the bucket (do not crush or crack the husks as they act as a filter to retain unwanted starch). Then add the grape concentrate, which will provide depth and body to the wine. Then dissolve the sugar in a little hot water and add this to the bucket.

Pour the cold water over the contents together with the acid blend, and pectinaze. Crush a Campden tablet into the mix and stir well. Cover with a cloth and leave for 24 hours in a cool place. This process will kill any wild yeast and bacteria that may be present on the fruit. The next day add the yeast and yeast nutrient. Stir thoroughly for 1-2 minutes to oxygenate the must. Cover the bucket with a cloth and leave to ferment in a warm place for 5 days, stirring the contents of the bucket occasionally. Then strain into a demijohn (4½ litres) or fermenter, through a nylon straining bag. Press as much of the juice as possible and discard the pulp. It may be necessary to top up with a little extra cold water to achieve 4½ litres. Fit a bung and airlock and leave in a warm place to continue to ferment out completely.

Finishing your Wine:

Fermentation should be complete in 2-5 weeks. At this stage CO2 bubbles should have stopped being released through the airlock. Your wine should then be checked with a hydrometer. The hydrometer will indicate the remaining sugar level and finishing levels are as follows:

Dry = 0.990 – 0.996   Medium = 0.996 – 1.009   Sweet = 1.009 – 1.018

At the end of fermentation add 1 crushed Campden tablet and half teaspoon of potassium sorbate per gallon. Leave in a cool place (15C) for 3 days to kill off the yeast. Then syphon the wine from the sediment into a second fermenter. Shake or stir the wine to degas it then add wine finings to ensure your wine will clear. Leave for 5 days in a cool place then syphon the wine from the sediment. Finally, pass it through a Vinbrite filter to obtain a professional finish before bottling. Filtering will remove all colloidal suspended particles and will ensure that your efforts are rewarded with a professional clarity and a pure taste.

The wine should now be bottled and stored in a cool dark place to mature for at least 6 months. During this time any rough tastes will be smoothed out and the wine will improve in bouquet and flavour.

This recipe makes 1 gallon (4.5 litres) of wine. For larger quantities simply multiply the quantities of ingredients except for the Yeast and Winefine. One sachet of each of these will be sufficient for any quantity between 1 and 5 gallons.

Chapter 17. Top 30 Cocktail and Mixer Recipes:

This section illustrates some interesting bar mixers and cocktails that you may wish to try out in your home bar to demonstrate your mixology skills. If you make your own spirits and liqueurs, then you have a cost-effective source of drinks to use as a base for these recipes.

The recipe list contains classic cocktails but also includes some modern cocktail and mixer innovations. Modern cocktails encompass a wide range of inventive and creative drinks that have emerged in recent years. These cocktails often push the boundaries of traditional mixology by incorporating unique ingredients, innovative techniques, and imaginative presentations.

Before attempting to recreate these recipes, you should refer to the earlier section of this book – 'Making Liqueurs and Spirit Based Drinks', and 'The Art of Mixology - Making Cocktails and Mixers', for more information.

Aperol Spritz:

The Aperol Spritz is a popular and refreshing Italian cocktail that has gained widespread popularity in recent years. It is known for its bright orange colour, light and bubbly profile, and slightly bitter taste. The Aperol Spritz is perfect for sipping on warm summer days or as an apéritif before a meal. It has become the trendy drink to been seen with in the après-ski bars.

Ingredients:

2 oz (60 ml) Aperol
3 oz (90 ml) Prosecco (or other dry sparkling wine)
Splash of soda water
Orange slice, for garnish
Ice

Instructions:

Fill a large wine glass or a highball glass with ice cubes.
Add the Aperol to the glass.
Pour in the Prosecco.
Top with a splash of soda water.
Stir gently to combine.
Garnish with an orange slice.
Optionally, you can also add a green olive as a garnish.

The Aperol Spritz is typically served in a wine glass or a highball glass filled with ice, allowing the drink to stay cool and refreshing. The combination of Aperol's bitter orange flavour, the fizziness of the Prosecco, and the effervescence of the soda water creates a refreshing and balanced cocktail that's perfect for any occasion.

Bloody Mary:

The Bloody Mary is a simple cocktail with a rich history and a reputation as a brunch staple. It is known for its bold and savoury flavours, often enjoyed as a hangover cure or a morning pick-me-up. While its exact origins are debated, the Bloody Mary is believed to have been created in the 1920's by Fernand Petiot, a bartender at Harry's New York Bar in Paris. According to legend, Petiot originally concocted a drink called the "Bucket of Blood," which consisted of vodka and tomato juice. Over time, the recipe evolved, and additional ingredients such as Worcestershire sauce, hot sauce, lemon juice, and spices were added to create the Bloody Mary as we know it today.

Ingredients:

1 1/2 oz (45 ml) vodka
3 oz (90 ml) tomato juice
1/2 oz (15 ml) fresh lemon juice
1 dash Worcestershire sauce
2-3 dashes hot sauce (such as Tabasco)
Pinch of celery salt
Pinch of black pepper
Ice
Celery stalk, lemon wedge, and/or other garnishes (such as olives, pickles, or cocktail shrimp)

Instructions:

Fill a shaker with ice cubes.
Add the vodka, tomato juice, fresh lemon juice, Worcestershire sauce, hot sauce, celery salt, and black pepper to the shaker.
Shake well until chilled.
Strain the mixture into a glass filled with ice.
Garnish with a celery stalk, lemon wedge, and/or other garnishes of your choice.
Optionally, you can rim the glass with celery salt or seasoning for extra flavour.

Feel free to adjust the ingredients and proportions to suit your taste preferences. Some people prefer their Bloody Marys spicier, so you can add more hot sauce or even horseradish for an extra kick. Additionally, you can customise the garnishes to make your Bloody Mary unique and visually appealing.

Cosmopolitan:

The Cosmopolitan is a popular cocktail known for its vibrant pink colour and refreshing taste. It is made with vodka, triple sec, cranberry juice, and freshly squeezed lime juice. It is often referred to as a "Cosmo," and is a cocktail that gained widespread popularity in the 1990s and early 2000s, thanks in part to its association with the television show "Sex and the City."

Ingredients:

1 1/2 oz (45 ml) vodka
1/2 oz (15 ml) Orange Liqueur (such as Triple Sec, Cointreau)
1/2 oz (15 ml) cranberry juice
1/2 oz (15 ml) fresh lime juice
Lime twist or wedge, for garnish

Instructions:

Fill a shaker with ice cubes.
Add the vodka, orange liqueur, cranberry juice, and fresh lime juice to the shaker.
Shake the mixture vigorously until well-chilled.
Strain the mixture into a chilled martini glass.
Garnish with a lime twist or wedge.
Optionally, you can also add a splash of simple syrup for added sweetness.
Serve immediately.

The Cosmopolitan is known for its balance of sweet and tart flavours, with the cranberry juice providing a fruity note and the lime juice adding a refreshing citrus kick.

Daiquiri:

The Daiquiri cocktail has a rich history that dates back to the late 19th century and originates from the Caribbean Island of Cuba. The cocktail's name is derived from the small mining town of Daiquirí near Santiago de Cuba, where American mining engineer Jennings Cox is credited with its creation around the year 1898. Cox improvised the drink when he ran out of gin while entertaining American guests. He mixed together local ingredients, including Cuban rum, lime juice, and sugar, creating a refreshing and flavourful cocktail that was an instant hit with his guests. The Daiquiri quickly gained popularity among American expatriates in Cuba and soon spread to other parts of the world. It is a simple, yet elegant drink made with rum, lime juice, and simple syrup.

Ingredients:

2 oz (60 ml) white rum
3/4 oz (22 ml) fresh lime juice
1/2 oz (15 ml) simple syrup

Instructions:

Fill a shaker with ice cubes.
Add the white rum, fresh lime juice, and simple syrup to the shaker.
Shake the mixture vigorously until well-chilled.
Strain the mixture into a chilled cocktail glass, such as a martini glass.
Optionally, you can garnish the Daiquiri with a lime wheel for an extra touch of citrus.

The Daiquiri is known for its refreshing and balanced flavour, with the rum providing a smooth base, the lime juice adding tartness, and the simple syrup providing just the right amount of sweetness. It is a versatile cocktail that can be enjoyed on its own or customised with variations such as flavoured syrups or different types of rum.

Daiquiri (Frozen Strawberry Daiquiri):

The Frozen Strawberry Daiquiri is a delicious variation of the classic Daiquiri, perfect for hot summer days or for serving up a refreshing and fruity cocktail at a weekend barbeque.

Ingredients:

2 oz (60 ml) white rum
1 oz (30 ml) fresh lime juice
1 oz (30 ml) simple syrup (adjust to taste)
1 cup (about 6 oz or 170 grams) frozen strawberries
1 cup (about 8-10) ice cubes
Additional strawberries for garnish (optional)

Instructions:

Add the white rum, fresh lime juice, simple syrup, frozen strawberries, and ice cubes to a blender.
Blend the mixture until smooth and creamy. If the consistency is too thick, you can add a splash of water or additional lime juice to thin it out.
Taste the Frozen Strawberry Daiquiri and adjust the sweetness or tartness by adding more simple syrup or lime juice if desired.
Once you have achieved the desired consistency and flavour, pour the Frozen Strawberry Daiquiri into glasses.
Garnish each glass with a strawberry slice on the rim or skewered on a cocktail stick.
Serve immediately.

This Frozen Strawberry Daiquiri is bursting with fruity flavour and has a wonderfully smooth texture, making it a perfect choice for cooling down on a hot day or for adding a touch of tropical flair to any occasion.

Dark and Stormy:

The Dark and Stormy is a classic mixer that combines dark rum with ginger beer and lime juice. It is a refreshing and flavourful drink with a hint of spice from the ginger beer. The Dark and Stormy cocktail is said to have originated in Bermuda. It is widely believed that the cocktail was created by sailors in the Royal Navy, who were stationed in Bermuda. Legend has it that the mixer was born when sailors mixed Gosling's Black Seal rum, which was readily available in Bermuda, with ginger beer, a popular beverage among sailors due to its ability to combat seasickness.

The name, "Dark and Stormy," is thought to be inspired by the drink's appearance, with the dark rum resembling storm clouds and the ginger beer representing the stormy sea. Additionally, the drinks refreshing, bold flavours make it a fitting choice for sailors and beachgoers alike, adding to its popularity in Bermuda and beyond. The mixer is very popular in the States, in particular, the Great Lakes of Michigan, where it is associated with sailing clubs.

Ingredients:

2 oz (60 ml) dark rum
4 oz (120 ml) ginger beer
1/2 oz (15 ml) fresh lime juice
Lime wedge, for garnish

Instructions:

Fill a highball glass with ice cubes.
Pour the dark rum over the ice.
Squeeze the lime juice into the glass.
Top off the glass with ginger beer, leaving some space at the top.
Stir gently to combine the ingredients.
Garnish with a lime wedge.

Optionally, you can also add a dash of Angostura bitters for extra flavour complexity.
Serve immediately.

Elderflower Gin Fizz:

The Elderflower Gin Fizz is a delicious and refreshing modern cocktail that combines the floral sweetness of elderflower cordial with the crisp botanicals of gin, creating a light and effervescent drink perfect for any occasion. The floral notes of the elderflower cordial pair harmoniously with the herbal and citrus undertones of the gin, while the effervescence from the soda water adds a refreshing fizz that dances on the palate.

Ingredients:

2 oz Gin
1/2 oz Elderflower Cordial
3/4 oz Fresh Lemon Juice
1/2 oz Simple Syrup
Soda Water
Ice
Edible Flower (for garnish)
Slice of Lemon (for garnish)

Instructions:

Add the gin, elderflower cordial, lemon juice, and simple syrup with ice in a shaker.
Shake vigorously for 30 seconds then strain into a highball glass filled with ice. Top with soda water and stir gently. Garnish with an edible flower.

Whether enjoyed on a warm summer day or as an aperitif, the Elderflower Gin Fizz is a modern cocktail that captures the essence of contemporary mixology with its combination of unique flavours, fresh ingredients, and stylish presentation. Make a note to make this cocktail in late Spring when the elderflowers are abundant. There is a recipe earlier in this book to make your own elderflower cordial.

Espresso Martini:

The Espresso Martini is a relatively modern cocktail, created in the late 20th century. The cocktail's creation is attributed to the late bartender Dick Bradsell, who was working at the Soho Brasserie in London during the 1980s. It was invented when a model approached Bradsell and asked for a drink that would "wake me up and then f*** me up." In response, Bradsell combined vodka, coffee liqueur (typically Kahlúa), and freshly brewed espresso to create the cocktail we now know as the Espresso Martini.

The drink quickly gained popularity, particularly among the fashionable crowd in London's Soho district, and it soon became a staple of cocktail menus around the world. The Espresso Martini's appeal lies in its combination of rich, bold coffee flavour with the smoothness of vodka and the sweetness of the coffee liqueur. It is a sophisticated and indulgent cocktail that is perfect for a luxurious after-dinner treat.

Ingredients:

1 1/2 oz (45 ml) vodka
1 oz (30 ml) coffee liqueur (such as Kahlúa)
1 oz (30 ml) freshly brewed espresso coffee, cooled to room temperature.
1/2 oz (15 ml) simple syrup (optional, for added sweetness)
Coffee beans, for garnish (optional)

Instructions:

Fill a shaker with ice cubes.
Add the vodka, coffee liqueur, and freshly brewed espresso to the shaker.
If preferred, add simple syrup to the shaker for added sweetness.
Shake the mixture vigorously until well-chilled.
Strain the mixture into a chilled martini glass.
Optionally, garnish with a few coffee beans floated on top of the cocktail.
Serve immediately.

The Espresso Martini is known for its rich and velvety texture, with the coffee providing a robust flavour that is perfectly complemented by the smoothness of the vodka and the sweetness of the coffee liqueur.

French 75:

The French 75 has a history that dates back to World War I. The cocktail is named after the French 75mm field gun, known for its powerful kick, which is likened to the kick of the cocktail itself. It is a delicious and elegant drink that combines gin, champagne, lemon juice, and sugar, resulting in a refreshing and bubbly concoction.

Ingredients:

1 1/2 oz (45 ml) gin
3/4 oz (22 ml) fresh lemon juice
1/2 oz (15 ml) simple syrup
2 oz (60 ml) champagne
Lemon twist, for garnish

Instructions:

Fill a shaker with ice cubes.
Add the gin, fresh lemon juice, and simple syrup to the shaker.
Shake well until chilled.
Strain the mixture into a chilled champagne flute.

Top with champagne.
Garnish with a lemon twist.

The French 75 is known for its effervescence and bright citrus flavour, making it a perfect celebratory cocktail or a refreshing option for a brunch or afternoon gathering.

Gimlet:

The Gimlet is a classic cocktail with a history dating back to the early 20th century. It is a simple yet refreshing drink made with gin or vodka and lime juice, typically served straight up in a cocktail glass or on the rocks. The Gimlet is known for its crisp, tangy flavour.

Ingredients:

2 oz (60 ml) gin or vodka
3/4 oz (22 ml) fresh lime juice
1/2 oz (15 ml) simple syrup
Lime wheel or twist, for garnish

Instructions:

Fill a shaker with ice cubes.
Pour the gin or vodka, lime juice, and simple syrup into the shaker.
Shake well until chilled.
Strain the mixture into a chilled cocktail glass filled with ice or straight up into a martini glass.
Garnish with a lime wheel or twist.

The Gimlet is a versatile cocktail that can be adjusted to suit individual tastes. Some variations may include using different proportions of gin or vodka, adjusting the sweetness level by varying the amount of simple syrup, or even using flavoured syrups for a unique twist.

Mai Tai:

The Mai Tai is a classic cocktail that originated in the 1940s, most notably associated with Polynesian-style bars and tiki culture. It is widely believed to have been created by Victor J. "Trader Vic" Bergeron, a renowned restaurateur and mixologist, at his Trader Vic's restaurant in Oakland, California. According to popular legend, the Mai Tai was first concocted in 1944 when Bergeron created the drink for some friends visiting from Tahiti. After tasting it, one of the friends supposedly exclaimed "Maita'i roa ae!" which means "very good" or "out of this world" in Tahitian. This exclamation supposedly gave the cocktail its name, "Mai Tai."

The original recipe for the Mai Tai typically includes rum (usually a blend of aged Jamaican rum and rhum agricole from Martinique), lime juice, orange liqueur (such as orange curaçao), and orgeat syrup (a sweet almond syrup). It's typically served over crushed ice and garnished with a mint sprig and a slice of lime.

Ingredients:

2 oz (60 ml) aged Jamaican rum.
1 oz (30 ml) Martinique Rhum Agricole
0.75 oz (22 ml) fresh lime juice
0.5 oz (15 ml) orange curaçao
0.25 oz (7 ml) orgeat syrup
Mint sprig and lime wedge, for garnish.

Instructions:

Fill a shaker with ice cubes.
Add the Jamaican rum, Martinique rhum agricole, lime juice, orange curaçao, and orgeat syrup to the shaker.
Shake well until chilled.
Fill a glass with crushed ice.

Strain the cocktail into the glass over the crushed ice.
Garnish with a mint sprig and a lime wedge.
Optionally, you can float a small amount of dark rum on top for added flavour and presentation.

Mai Tai is a versatile cocktail, and there are many variations and interpretations of this drink. Feel free to adjust the recipe according to your taste preferences, and don't be afraid to experiment with different rums and additional ingredients to create your own unique twist on this classic cocktail.

Manhattan:

One popular story suggests that the Manhattan was invented in the 1870s at the Manhattan Club in New York City, where it was created for a banquet hosted by Lady Randolph Churchill, the mother of Sir Winston Churchill. The cocktail quickly gained popularity and became a staple of New York City's social scene. The Manhattan is made with whiskey (usually rye or bourbon), sweet vermouth, and bitters, and garnished with a cherry.

Ingredients:

2 oz (60 ml) rye or bourbon whiskey
1 oz (30 ml) sweet vermouth
2 dashes Angostura bitters
Maraschino cherry, for garnish

Instructions:

Fill a cocktail shaker with ice cubes.
Add the whiskey, sweet vermouth, and Angostura bitters to the shaker.
Shake until well-chilled.
Strain the mixture into a chilled cocktail glass (such as a martini glass).
Garnish with a maraschino cherry.

The Manhattan is known for its smooth and complex flavour, with the whiskey providing a rich and smoky base, complemented by the sweet and herbal notes of the vermouth and the aromatic bitterness of the bitters. While the classic Manhattan recipe remains popular, there are also several variations of the cocktail that have emerged over the years. For example, a "Perfect Manhattan" includes equal parts sweet and dry vermouth, while "Rob Roy" substitutes Scotch whisky for the rye or bourbon. Additionally, variations using different types of bitters or flavoured liqueurs have also become popular among cocktail enthusiasts.

Margarita:

The Margarita is a classic cocktail that originated in Mexico. It is a refreshing and tangy drink made with tequila, triple sec (orange liqueur), and lime juice, often served with a salted rim. The Margarita quickly gained popularity in the United States during the mid-20th century. It became associated with Mexican culture and cuisine, thanks in part to the rising popularity of Mexican restaurants and the spread of tourism to Mexico. The Margarita's refreshing taste and versatility made it a hit among cocktail enthusiasts, leading to its widespread adoption in bars and restaurants across the country.

Ingredients:

2 oz (60 ml) tequila
1 oz (30 ml) orange liqueur (such as Triple Sec, Cointreau or Grand Marnier)
1 oz (30 ml) fresh lime juice
Salt, for rimming the glass.
Lime wedge, for garnish

Instructions:

Begin by rimming the edge of a margarita glass with salt. To do this, rub a lime wedge around the rim of the glass to moisten it, then dip the rim into a plate of salt to coat it.
Fill the glass with ice cubes.
In a shaker filled with ice, combine the tequila, orange liqueur and fresh lime juice.
Shake the mixture vigorously until well-chilled.
Strain the mixture into the prepared glass filled with ice.
Garnish with a lime wedge.
Optionally, you can also add a splash of orange juice or agave syrup for added sweetness.
Serve immediately.

The Margarita is a versatile cocktail that can be customised to suit your taste preferences. It can be shaken or blended, on the rocks or frozen, sweet, or tart.

Martini:

The Martini is one of the most iconic and classic cocktails in the world. It is known for its simplicity, elegance, and versatility. Traditionally, a Martini is made with gin and dry vermouth, garnished with either a lemon twist or an olive. However, variations exist, including the Vodka Martini, which substitutes vodka for gin. James Bond, the iconic fictional spy created by author Ian Fleming, is known for his sophisticated tastes, including his preference for the Vodka Martini. In the original novels, Bond famously orders his Martinis with the instruction, "Shaken, not stirred." This phrase has become synonymous with the character. This recipe makes a classic Gin Martini.

Ingredients:

2 1/2 oz (75 ml) gin
1/2 oz (15 ml) dry vermouth
Lemon twist or olive, for garnish

Instructions:
Fill a shaker with ice cubes.
Pour the gin and dry vermouth into the shaker.
Shake until chilled.
Strain the mixture into a chilled martini glass.
Garnish with a lemon twist or olive.
For a Vodka Martini, simply substitute vodka for gin in the recipe. Some people prefer their Martini "dry," meaning with less vermouth, while others prefer it "wet," with more vermouth. The garnish can also be adjusted according to personal preference.

The Martini is a timeless classic that has been enjoyed for generations. It's simple yet sophisticated flavour profile has made it a favourite among cocktail enthusiasts worldwide.

Mint Julep:

The Mint Julep is a Southern cocktail that's synonymous with the Kentucky Derby, where it has been the official drink since 1938. It is a refreshing and aromatic cocktail, perfect for sipping on a hot day. The Mint Julep traditionally features bourbon, mint, sugar, and crushed ice.

Ingredients:

2 oz (60 ml) bourbon
1/2 oz (15 ml) simple syrup
4-6 fresh mint leaves, plus more for garnish
Crushed ice

Instructions:

Place the mint leaves and simple syrup in the bottom of a julep cup or glass.
Gently muddle the mint leaves to release their oils and flavours.
Fill the cup with crushed ice, packing it down firmly.
Pour the bourbon over the ice.
Stir gently to combine and chill the drink.
Garnish with a sprig of fresh mint.

The Mint Julep is known not only for its refreshing taste but also for the presentation. Traditionally served in a silver or pewter cup, the frosty exterior of the cup adds to the overall experience of enjoying this classic cocktail. Whether you're watching the Kentucky Derby or simply enjoying a warm day, the Mint Julep is a good choice for any occasion.

Moscow Mule:

The Moscow Mule is a cocktail that originated in the United States during the 1940s. It is known for its refreshing combination of vodka, ginger beer, and lime juice, and is usually served in a distinctive copper mug.

Ingredients:

2 oz (60 ml) vodka
4 oz (120 ml) ginger beer
1/2 oz (15 ml) fresh lime juice
Lime wedge, for garnish

Instructions:

Fill a copper mug (or a highball glass) with ice cubes.
Pour the vodka over the ice.
Squeeze the lime juice into the mug.
Top off the mug with ginger beer, leaving some space at the top.
Stir gently to combine the ingredients.
Garnish with a lime wedge.

Optionally, you can also add a sprig of fresh mint for extra garnish. Serve immediately.

The Moscow Mule is known for its crisp and refreshing flavour, with the spicy ginger beer complementing the smoothness of the vodka and the tartness of the lime juice.

Negroni:

The Negroni cocktail has a fascinating history that dates back to the early 20th century and is rooted in Italy. The exact origin story of the Negroni is a matter of some debate, and there are several popular theories surrounding its creation. One widely accepted story attributes the invention of the Negroni to Count Camillo Negroni, a Florentine aristocrat, who is said to have ordered an Americano cocktail with a stronger kick. Legend has it that in the early 20th century, Count Negroni requested his bartender at the Caffè Casoni in Florence to replace the soda water in his Americano with gin, creating the Negroni as we know it today. The Negroni is made with equal parts gin, sweet vermouth, and Campari, garnished with an orange peel.

Ingredients:

1 oz (30 ml) gin
1 oz (30 ml) sweet vermouth
1 oz (30 ml) Campari
Orange peel, for garnish

Instructions:

Fill a cocktail shaker with ice cubes.
Add the gin, sweet vermouth, and Campari to the shaker.
Shake until well-chilled.
Strain the mixture into a rocks glass filled with ice cubes.

Squeeze the oils from an orange peel over the drink by gently twisting it over the glass to release its aroma, then drop the peel into the glass as garnish.
Optionally, you can also add a splash of soda water or club soda for a lighter version of the cocktail.

The Negroni is known for its bittersweet flavour, with the gin providing a botanical base, the sweet vermouth adding richness and depth, and the Campari contributing a distinct bitterness and vibrant red colour.

Old Fashioned:

The Old Fashioned is a classic cocktail that dates back to the 19th century, making it one of the oldest known mixed drinks. It is a simple yet sophisticated cocktail that combines the flavours of whiskey (typically bourbon or rye), sugar, bitters, and a hint of citrus.

Ingredients:

2 oz (60 ml) bourbon or rye whiskey
1 sugar cube or 1/2 oz (15 ml) simple syrup
2-3 dashes Angostura bitters
Orange twist or cherry, for garnish

Instructions:

This cocktail is traditionally served in a short tumbler glass known as an "Old Fashioned glass" or "rocks glass." This type of glass is short and wide-bottomed, allowing room for a large ice cube or ice sphere. The wide rim also provides space for muddling ingredients if using a sugar cube, and it allows for easy stirring of the cocktail.
Muddle the sugar cube (or simple syrup) in the glass, with the bitters until the sugar is dissolved.
Add a large ice cube to the glass.
Pour the bourbon or rye whiskey over the ice.
Stir gently to combine the ingredients.
Garnish with an orange twist or cherry.

Optionally, you can also add a splash of soda water or club soda for a lighter version of the cocktail.
Serve immediately.

The Old Fashioned is known for its smooth and robust flavour, with the whiskey providing a rich and complex base, complemented by the sweetness of the sugar and the aromatic bitterness of the bitters.

Painkiller:

The Painkiller cocktail is a tropical and refreshing drink that originates from the British Virgin Islands. It's known for its creamy texture and delightful blend of flavours, including rum, pineapple juice, coconut cream, and orange juice. Pussers Rum is the traditional choice for the commercial painkiller.

Ingredients:

2 oz (60 ml) dark navy rum
4 oz (120 ml) pineapple juice
1 oz (30 ml) cream of coconut (such as Coco Lopez)
1 oz (30 ml) orange juice
Freshly grated nutmeg, for garnish
Pineapple wedge or cherry, for garnish (optional)

Instructions:

Fill a shaker with ice cubes.
Add the dark rum, pineapple juice, cream of coconut, and orange juice to the shaker.
Shake the mixture vigorously until well-chilled and combined.
Strain the mixture into a glass filled with ice cubes.
Grate fresh nutmeg over the top of the cocktail for garnish.
Optionally, garnish with a pineapple wedge or cherry for an extra tropical touch.
Serve immediately.

The Painkiller is known for its creamy texture, tropical flavours, and hint of spice from the freshly grated nutmeg. It is an interesting alternative to the Pina Colada and a perfect drink for sipping on a sunny afternoon.

Paloma:

A Paloma is a refreshing and tangy cocktail that originates from Mexico. It is typically made with tequila, lime juice, and grapefruit soda, often served over ice in a highball glass. The combination of tart lime, the slightly bitter-sweet flavour of grapefruit, and the smoothness of tequila creates a well-balanced and flavourful drink. Some variations of the Paloma may include a salted rim on the glass for added flavour contrast and garnished with a wedge of grapefruit or lime for visual appeal.

Ingredients:
2 oz (60 ml) tequila
1/2 oz (15 ml) lime juice
Grapefruit soda
Salt (for rimming the glass, optional)
Grapefruit wedge or slice (for garnish, optional)

Instructions:

Rim a highball glass with salt by running a lime wedge around the rim and dipping it into a plate of salt (optional).

Fill the glass with ice.
Pour the tequila and lime juice into the glass.
Top off with grapefruit soda, filling the glass almost to the top.
Give the drink a gentle stir to mix the ingredients.
Garnish with a grapefruit wedge or slice (optional).
Optionally, you can also add a lime wedge for an extra burst of citrus flavour.
Serve and enjoy your refreshing Paloma!

The Paloma is known for its bright and lively flavours, making it a popular choice for warm weather or as a refreshing sipper any time of year.

Piña Colada:

The Piña Colada is a classic tropical cocktail that evokes images of sun-soaked beaches, swaying palm trees, and relaxation. Its origins can be traced back to Puerto Rico in the mid-20th century, and its sweet, coconut flavour has made it a favourite among cocktail enthusiasts around the world. The Piña Colada has had a significant cultural impact over the years and remains one of the most recognisable cocktails in the world. It is celebrated annually on National Piña Colada Day on July 10th. It is a creamy and refreshing blend of white rum, coconut cream, and pineapple juice.

Ingredients:

2 oz (60 ml) white rum
3 oz (90 ml) pineapple juice
2 oz (60 ml) coconut cream
1 cup (about 8-10) ice cubes
Pineapple wedge and/or maraschino cherry, for garnish (optional)

Instructions:

In a blender, combine the white rum, pineapple juice, coconut cream, and ice cubes.
Blend the mixture until smooth and creamy.
If the consistency is too thick, you can add more pineapple juice or rum to thin it out.
Pour the blended mixture into a tall glass.
Garnish with a pineapple wedge and/or maraschino cherry, if desired.

Optionally, you can also serve the Piña Colada in a hollowed-out pineapple for an extra tropical presentation.

While the classic Piña Colada recipe remains popular, there are also several variations of the cocktail that have emerged over the years. For example, a "Frozen Piña Colada" is made by blending the ingredients with additional ice to create a slushy consistency, while a "Virgin Piña Colada" is made without alcohol for a non-alcoholic version of the cocktail.

Porn Star Martini:

The Porn Star Martini is a modern and popular cocktail known for its exotic flavours and playful presentation. It is a fruity and sweet cocktail with a hint of tartness, typically served with a side shot of Prosecco (or other sparkling wine. The cocktail is believed to have been created in London during the early 2000s by bartender Douglas Ankrah.

Ingredients:

2 oz (60 ml) vanilla vodka
1 oz (30 ml) passion fruit syrup
1/2 oz (15 ml) vanilla syrup
1/2 oz (15 ml) fresh lime juice
Champagne or Prosecco, (served alongside the cocktail)
Passion fruit slice or half a passion fruit, for garnish

Instructions:

Fill a shaker with ice cubes.
Add the vanilla vodka, passion fruit puree or juice, vanilla syrup, and fresh lime juice to the shaker.
Shake well until chilled.
Strain the mixture into a chilled martini glass.
Serve the cocktail with a shot of prosecco (or sparkling wine) on the side.

Garnish with a passion fruit slice or half a passion fruit floating on top of the cocktail.

The Porn Star Martini is known for its fruity and tropical flavours, balanced with the sweetness of vanilla and the acidity of lime. The addition of the prosecco shot on the side adds a fun and celebratory touch to the cocktail, making it perfect for special occasions or a night with friends.

Pousse Café:

This cocktail stands as a testament to the elegance and creativity of mixology. This stunning layered drink not only tantalises the taste buds but also captivates the eyes with its vibrant colours and intricate layers. The origins of the Pousse Café can be traced back to the 19th century, where it emerged as a popular after-dinner drink in European cafes. The term "Pousse Café" translates to "push coffee" in French, although the drink contains no coffee whatsoever. Instead, it refers to the traditional practice of "pushing" one layer of liqueur on top of another using the back of a spoon.

At its core, a Pousse Café is a layered cocktail composed of multiple liqueurs with varying densities, resulting in distinct layers of colour and flavour. The key to achieving the signature layered effect lies in the careful pouring technique and the use of liqueurs with different specific gravities. This is a great cocktail for testing out your mixology skills.

Ingredients:

Crème de Menthe (green)
Crème de Cacao
Brandy

Instructions:

Prepare Your Glassware: Choose a narrow, stemmed glass for serving the Pousse Café. A tall, thin glass like a cordial glass or a Pousse Café glass is ideal for showcasing the layers.

To create distinct layers, you'll need to pour each ingredient carefully over the back of a spoon into the glass. Start with the heaviest liqueur and work your way up to the lightest. In this case, the order will be Crème de Menthe, followed by Crème de Cacao, and finally Brandy.

Pour about 1/3 to 1/2 ounce of Crème de Menthe into the bottom of the glass.

Using the back of a spoon, gently pour the Crème de Cacao over the spoon so that it sits on top of the Crème de Menthe. This will help create a clear separation between the layers.

Finally, pour the Brandy over the back of the spoon to create the top layer.

Once all the layers are poured, your Pousse Café is ready to be served. Serve it with a small spoon or straw, allowing your guests to enjoy each layer individually or to mix them together for a unique flavour experience. You can garnish the Pousse Café with a twist of lemon or orange peel for a touch of citrus aroma.

Tips for Success:

Pour each layer slowly and with precision to avoid mixing the colours.

Use liqueurs with contrasting colours and densities for the best visual effect.

Chill the liqueurs beforehand to help slow down the mixing process and maintain the layers.

Practice makes perfect! Layering cocktails like the Pousse Café takes practice, so don't be discouraged if your first attempt isn't perfect.

Once you have mastered the basic recipe, you can enjoy experimenting with different liqueurs and extra layers to create your own unique variations of this classic cocktail!

Mojito:

The Mojito is a classic Cuban cocktail known for its refreshing combination of flavours, including mint, lime, rum, sugar, and soda water. It gained popularity in Cuba during the early 20th century, particularly among the working class and sugar cane workers. Its popularity continued to grow throughout the 20th century, and it became a staple of Cuban cocktail culture. The Mojito's association with Cuba and its vibrant flavours made it a favourite among tourists visiting the island, further fuelling its popularity on a global scale. It is a drink that's perfect for hot summer days or as a light and refreshing lead-in for barbeques.

Ingredients:
2 oz (60 ml) white rum
1/2 oz (15 ml) fresh lime juice
1/2 oz (15 ml) simple syrup (or 2 teaspoons of granulated sugar)
6-8 fresh mint leaves, plus extra sprigs for garnish
Soda water (or sparkling water)
Ice cubes.
Lime wedge, for garnish
Optional: additional mint leaves and lime slices for garnish

Instructions:

In a highball glass, muddle the mint leaves and lime juice together gently using a muddler or the back of a spoon. Be careful not to over-muddle, as this can release bitter flavours from the mint.
Add the simple syrup (or sugar) to the glass and stir until the sugar is dissolved.
Fill the glass with ice cubes.
Pour the white rum over the ice.
Top off the glass with soda water, leaving some space at the top.
Stir gently to combine the ingredients.

Garnish with a lime wedge and a sprig of fresh mint. You can also add additional mint leaves and lime slices for extra garnish.

The Classic Mojito is perfect for sipping on a hot summer day or as a refreshing cocktail any time of year. Adjust the sweetness or tartness to your preference by varying the amount of sugar or lime juice. While the classic Mojito recipe remains popular, there are also several variations of the cocktail that have emerged over the years. For example, a "Berry Mojito" adds fresh berries to the traditional recipe for a fruity twist, while a "Coconut Mojito" incorporates coconut rum or coconut cream for a tropical taste.

Sex on the Beach:

Sex on the Beach is a popular and fruity cocktail known for its tropical flavours and vibrant appearance. It is typically served over ice in a highball glass and garnished with a slice of orange and/or a cherry. The exact origins of the Sex on the Beach cocktail are uncertain, but it gained popularity in the 1980s and has remained a favourite ever since.

Ingredients:

1 1/2 oz (45 ml) vodka
1/2 oz (15 ml) peach schnapps
2 oz (60 ml) cranberry juice
2 oz (60 ml) orange juice
Ice
Orange slice and/or cherry, for garnish

Instructions:

Fill a shaker with ice cubes.
Add the vodka, peach schnapps, cranberry juice, and orange juice to the shaker.
Shake well until chilled.
Fill a highball glass with ice cubes.
Strain the mixture into the glass over the ice.
Garnish with an orange slice and/or cherry.

The Sex on the Beach cocktail is known for its sweet and fruity flavour profile, with the peach schnapps adding a hint of tropical sweetness and the cranberry and orange juices providing tartness and acidity. It is a refreshing and easy-to-drink cocktail that's perfect for sipping on a hot day or enjoying at a social gathering.

Sidecar:

The Sidecar has a long history, dating back to the early 20th century. It is a simple yet sophisticated drink that features brandy or cognac as its base spirit, along with orange liqueur and lemon juice. It is served chilled in a cocktail glass with a sugar rim (or without, depending on personal preference).

Ingredients:

2 oz (60 ml) brandy or cognac
1 oz (30 ml) orange liqueur (such as Cointreau or triple sec)
3/4 oz (22 ml) fresh lemon juice
Optional: Sugar for rimming the glass
Lemon twist, for garnish

Instructions:

Prepare the glass by moistening the rim with a lemon wedge and dipping it into sugar to coat the rim. Set aside.
Fill a shaker with ice cubes.

Pour the brandy or cognac, orange liqueur, and lemon juice into the shaker.
Shake well until chilled.
Strain the mixture into a chilled cocktail glass.
Garnish with a lemon twist.

The Sidecar is a well-balanced cocktail with a tangy citrus flavour from the lemon juice, balanced by the sweetness of the orange liqueur and the richness of the brandy or cognac.

Tequila Sunrise:

The Tequila Sunrise is a vibrant and visually striking cocktail that has become a classic in the world of mixology, to showcase layering skills. Its origins can be traced back to the 1930s and 1940s, but it rose to prominence in the 1970s, thanks in part to its association with the rock band The Eagles and their hit song "Tequila Sunrise." It is a simple, yet elegant cocktail made with just a few ingredients.

Ingredients:

2 oz Tequila
4 oz Orange Juice
1/2 oz Grenadine
Ice cubes.
Orange slice and a cherry for garnish

Instructions:

Fill a highball glass with ice cubes to the top.
Pour 2 oz of tequila into the glass.

Add 4 oz of orange juice into the glass, pouring it gently over the ice and tequila.

Using a spoon, carefully pour 1/2 oz of grenadine into the glass. Pour it slowly over the back of the spoon or along the side of the glass. This will create the signature sunrise effect as the grenadine sinks to the bottom of the glass.

Allow the grenadine to settle, creating distinct layers of colour in the glass. Garnish the drink with an orange slice and a cherry for a decorative touch.

Feel free to adjust the proportions of the ingredients to suit your personal taste preferences. Some people prefer a sweeter drink and may add a bit more grenadine, while others may prefer a stronger tequila flavour and may add an extra splash of tequila.

Vesper:

The Vesper cocktail is a classic cocktail made famous by Ian Fleming's James Bond novel, "Casino Royale." In the book, Bond orders the Vesper Martini, specifying its ingredients and preparation. It is a potent and sophisticated cocktail with a unique flavour profile.

Ingredients:

3 oz (90 ml) London dry gin
1 oz (30 ml) vodka
1/2 oz (15 ml) Lillet Blanc (a French aperitif wine)
Lemon twist, for garnish

Instructions:

Fill a shaker or mixing glass with ice cubes.
Add the gin, vodka, and Lillet Blanc to the shaker or mixing glass.
Stir well until chilled.
Strain the mixture into a chilled martini glass.
Garnish with a lemon twist.

The Vesper Martini is a strong and aromatic cocktail, with the gin providing botanical depth, the vodka adding neutrality and smoothness, and the Lillet Blanc contributing sweetness and complexity.

Lillet Blanc is made from a blend of Bordeaux wines, primarily Semillon and Sauvignon Blanc, which serve as the base. The wine is then fortified with citrus liqueurs and flavoured with a variety of botanicals, herbs, and spices, including bitter orange peel, cinchona bark (the natural source of quinine), and other secret ingredients. The exact recipe is a closely guarded secret known only to the Lillet family.

The Vesper is traditionally served straight up in a martini glass and garnished with a lemon twist, although some variations may call for a different garnish or preparation method.

It is worth noting that the Vesper Martini is not for everyone, as it packs quite a punch due to its high alcohol content. However, for those who appreciate bold and sophisticated cocktails, the Vesper Martini is a true classic with a fascinating history.

Whiskey Sour:

The Whiskey Sour is a classic cocktail known for its balanced combination of whiskey, lemon juice, and simple syrup, garnished with a cherry and/or orange slice. the cocktail dates back to the 18th century and has roots in naval history. One prevailing theory suggests that the Whiskey Sour was originally created as a variation of the British Navy's grog, a mixture of rum, water, sugar, and citrus juice. Sailors would often add citrus juice to their rum to help prevent scurvy during long sea voyages. As American colonists began to experiment with different spirits, whiskey became a popular substitute for rum in cocktails, leading to the creation of the Whiskey Sour.

Ingredients:

2 oz (60 ml) whiskey (bourbon or rye)
3/4 oz (22 ml) fresh lemon juice
1/2 oz (15 ml) simple syrup
Cherry and/or orange slice, for garnish

Instructions:

Fill a shaker with ice cubes.
Add the whiskey, fresh lemon juice, and simple syrup to the shaker.
Shake the mixture vigorously until well-chilled.
Strain the mixture into a rocks glass filled with ice cubes.
Garnish with a cherry and/or orange slice.
Optionally, you can also add a dash of Angostura bitters for extra flavour complexity.
Serve immediately.

The Whiskey Sour is known for its tart and refreshing flavour, with the whiskey providing a smooth and smoky backdrop to the bright citrus notes of the lemon juice.

White Russian:

The White Russian has a creamy texture and smooth, indulgent flavour. It gained widespread popularity in the 1970s and experienced a resurgence in popularity in the 1990s, thanks in part to its appearance in the cult classic film "The Big Lebowski. The cocktail is simple to make, requiring just a few ingredients, and is often enjoyed as a dessert cocktail or a nightcap.

Ingredients:

2 oz Vodka
1 oz Coffee Liqueur (such as Kahlúa)

1 oz Single Cream or Full Fat Milk
Ice cubes.

Instructions:

Fill an old-fashioned glass or a rocks glass with ice cubes.
Pour the vodka and coffee liqueur over the ice in the glass.
Stir gently to combine the ingredients.
Slowly pour the cream or milk over the back of a spoon so that it floats on top of the vodka and coffee liqueur mixture.

Garnish with a sprinkle of ground nutmeg or a coffee bean for added flavour and presentation.

The White Russian has become more than just a cocktail; it is a cultural icon that symbolises indulgence, relaxation, and fun. It is easy to make and so is a good choice when you are starting out on your mixology journey.

A Black Russian version of the cocktail can be made by omitting the cream (or milk) from the recipe.

Future Trends in Mixology:

Trends in mixers and cocktails can vary from year to year and from region to region, but themes that are emerging in the world of mixology include:

Craft Gin and Tonics: With the resurgence of craft gin distilleries, gin and tonics have become more popular, often featuring artisanal gins infused with unique botanicals and paired with premium tonic water and garnishes like herbs, citrus, or berries.

Low-ABV Cocktails: As more people seek moderation in their alcohol consumption, low-alcohol or low-ABV cocktails have gained popularity. These cocktails feature ingredients like vermouth, sherry, or fortified wines mixed with soda water or non-alcoholic mixers for a lighter option.

CBD Cocktails: Cannabidiol (CBD) has emerged as a trendy ingredient in cocktails, offering potential relaxation and stress-relief benefits. CBD-infused cocktails can include a variety of spirits and mixers, often paired with botanical flavours such as lavender or chamomile.

Sustainable Cocktails: With a growing focus on sustainability and environmental consciousness, bartenders are incorporating eco-friendly practices and ingredients into their cocktails. This may include using locally sourced and seasonal ingredients, reducing waste, and utilizing sustainable spirits and mixers.

Bitter Cocktails: Bitter flavours have been making a comeback in cocktails, with ingredients such as amaro, Campari, and other herbal liqueurs taking centre stage. Bitter cocktails can range from classic Negronis and Boulevardiers to inventive creations that balance bitterness with sweet and savoury elements.

Frozen Cocktails: Frozen cocktails are enjoying a surge in popularity, with bartenders putting their own twists on classic frozen drinks such as Piña Coladas, Margaritas, and Daiquiris. These icy drinks are perfect for hot summer days or barbeques.

Mocktails: As the demand for non-alcoholic options grows, mocktails have become more sophisticated and diverse. Bartenders are crafting creative and flavourful non-alcoholic cocktails using fresh juices, herbs, spices, and house-made syrups to cater to those looking for alcohol-free alternatives.

Cocktail trends are continually evolving, so it is worth exploring new ingredients, techniques, and flavour combinations to stay up to date with the latest trends in mixology.

Glossary of Winemaking Terms:

It can sometimes seem like another language when winemakers are discussing their hobby. Therefore, it is worth knowing some of the terms and acronyms that are frequently used:

Acid- An essential element of winemaking. Supports fermentation and contributes to the final taste. Acid levels are usually expressed as a pH value. Key acids used in winemaking are citric, tartaric, malic, and acid blend.

Aeration – The process of introducing as much oxygen into the must as possible as the yeast is introduced. Yeast requires oxygen at the start of the process to support fermentation. Usually this is achieved by agitation/vigorous stirring with a paddle or long handled spoon. Some commercial winemakers use aeration stones to bubble gas into the wine.

Aerobic Fermentation – This means fermentation with air. The initial fermentation of some fruits in buckets covered with cloth is designed to help extract flavours and break down fruits. Usually, this process takes no longer than five days.

Ageing- A crucial aspect of winemaking that involves allowing the wine to mature and develop its flavours over time. Wine will benefit from ageing, and the process can lead to increased complexity, smoother textures, and a more integrated overall profile.

Airlock- A device used in winemaking and fermentation processes to allow carbon dioxide gas produced during fermentation to escape from a fermentation vessel while preventing oxygen and contaminants from entering.

Anaerobic Fermentation – This means fermentation without air. Once airlocks are fitted to fermenters the must will ferment without air. As fermentation progresses it is important to restrict air content to avoid exposure of the wine to oxygen. At the start of the winemaking process oxygen is your friend, towards the end it is your enemy.

ABV – Alcohol by Volume. This is the final strength of the wine. As a guide, white wines have a lower ABV of around 10-11% and reds are slightly stronger (11-14%). An accurate measure can be made by taking a hydrometer reading at the start of the process before adding yeast (OG). Make a note, and then take a second hydrometer reading at the end of fermentation (FG). A more precise calculation can then be made to determine the actual ABV of your wine.

Aroma- Refers to the collection of scents or smells perceived when smelling wine. The aroma is an essential component of the overall sensory experience and plays a significant role in how we perceive and enjoy wine. It encompasses a wide range of olfactory sensations, providing depth and complexity to the drinking experience.

Attenuation- Attenuation refers to how well a strain of yeast converts sugars into alcohol. The attenuation rate of yeast is usually listed as a percentage. Visible signs of attenuation commencing are the appearance of yeast foam on the surface of your wine and airlock activity as CO_2 is released.

Balance- Refers to the harmonious integration and proportion of various elements, such as sweetness, acidity, bitterness, alcohol, and aroma in the final wine. Achieving balance is essential for creating a wine that is enjoyable, with no single component dominating or overwhelming the overall sensory experience.

Body- Refers to the perceived thickness, fullness, or viscosity of wine in the mouth. It is one of the sensory attributes that contributes to the overall mouthfeel of wine. Measuring body involves assessing how the mead coats your palate and the overall weight or substance perceived during consumption.

Bouquet- the complex and aromatic combination of scents that are perceived when smelling wine. The bouquet encompasses a wide range of aromas, which can originate from the grapes, fermentation process, yeast, any added fruits, or spices, and, in some cases, ageing or oak influences.

Blow-Off Tube- This is a tube fitted in place of an airlock, which extends into a water vessel. It is designed to allow more CO_2 to be released during the first vigorous part of the fermentation. During the first few days yeast krausen can be forced through the airlock and a blow-off tube is sometimes fitted to avoid this issue.

Brewing Sugar- This is Dextrose Monohydrate. Dextrose brewing sugar, often referred to as "corn sugar" or "glucose" is recommended in place of household white sugar "sucrose" if you are required to add extra sugar to recipes or kits. Dextrose is easier to dissolve than white sugar and 100% fermentable. Brewing sugar tends to ferment faster, more consistently, and is higher yielding compared to normal household sucrose-based sugars.

Brix- A scale used to measure the concentration of dissolved solids, primarily sugar, in a liquid. The Brix scale is commonly used in brewing, winemaking, and the production of various syrups and juices. Brix represents the percentage by weight of sugar in a solution. A solution with 10 degrees Brix, for example, contains 10 grams of sucrose in 100 grams of solution. It is measured using a Refractometer.

Carbonation- The process of introducing dissolved CO2 into wine to make sparkling wine. May be achieved by a natural process, through secondary fermentation, or forced carbonation using a CO2 canister and regulator.

Carbon Dioxide- The gas released during fermentation. 50% of the sugar is converted to alcohol during fermentation, and 50% into carbon dioxide. It can be seen bubbling through airlock chambers, and is an indication that fermentation is progressing.

Colloidal Suspended Particles- Colloidal particles in wine refer to tiny, suspended particles that are dispersed in the liquid but don't settle due to their small size. They can contain proteins, tannin, pectin, polysaccharides, and yeast cells. They can affect the clarity and taste of wine. Fining and filtering will usually remove these particles.

Enzyme- Protein, pectin, or starch molecules joined to an organic compound. Enzymes play a crucial role in winemaking, facilitating various biochemical reactions that influence the fermentation process, flavour development, and overall quality of the wine. They can be counter-productive n clearing wines after fermentation. Finings, Pectinaze, and Amylaze are used to minimise the impact of enzymes on the clearing process.

Fermentation- The process of converting sugar and oxygen into ethanol-based alcohol and carbon dioxide, by yeast.

Fermenter- A vessel to contain wine during the fermentation process. Fermenters may be a plastic or stainless-steel bucket style with snap on lid, or a glass or plastic, with a mouth suitable to accommodate a bung and airlock. Usually in sizes 1 gallon to 5 gallons (5-23 litres).

Filtration- The last part of the winemaking process before bottling and is essential to achieve a professional finish. Filter systems allow wine to pass through porous pads which remove all dead yeast cells and other suspended particles. The presence of these particles might otherwise be tasted in the final wine and would affect the clarity and appearance. Wine Filters are either gravity based or electric pumped. Although pumped filters are quicker, they are more expensive and not efficient for smaller batch sizes up to 5 gallons. Their higher operational pressure can also force some of the smaller particles through the porous filter pad. The best option for home winemakers is a gravity/syphon-based system such as the Harris Vinbrite Filter. The filter is very easy to use and is highly effective for clearing batches up to 5 gallons. The wine is simply syphoned through the pad and the flow rate is controlled to ensure an effective contact time of the wine on the pad. The flow is not designed to be fast. Many winemakers start the filtering process before going to bed and allow it to complete overnight. Any small amounts of residual sediment at the bottom of the fermenter can be filtered to retrieve as much usable wine as possible. There is a myth that filtering detrimentally affects the flavour of the wine. This is false. Filtering only removes solid suspended colloidal particles, such as proteins and dead yeast. Their presence could be detected as off-tastes and would certainly adversely affect the final appearance and clarity of the wine. Virtually all commercial winemakers use filters, and for good reason. You should too.

FG (Final Gravity)- Gravity of wine after fermentation has completed and all the available sugar has been attenuated.

Finings- Finings can be added to wine to help clearing and to improve the efficiency of filtering. Traditionally, finings have been made from isinglass but there are other types such as Chitosan and vegan friendly finings, such as Kieselsol.

Fortification- The process of adding higher ABV alcohol to wines to increase their strength. Brandy and Vodka are often used to fortify wines.

Gravity- A measure of density of wine (effectively the amount of sugar in it). This is measured on a hydrometer or refractometer.

Hydrometer- An instrument used for measuring the level of sugar in a wine. It is often used in combination with a trial jar to give a visual scale reading.

Krausen- This is the foamy, frothy head that forms on top of a fermenting wine or other fermentable beverage during the active fermentation phase. It is a visible sign of the vigorous production of carbon dioxide and the expansion of yeast activity in the fermentation vessel.

Lees- Also known as sediment, this is the dead yeast, fruit pulp, and colloidal particles that fall to the bottom of the fermenter during and after fermentation.

Maceration- The soaking of grape skins, (and sometimes fruits), in the must after crushing. This process extracts colour, tannins, aroma compounds, and other phenolic compounds from the grape solids into the juice, ultimately influencing the finished wine.

Mixology- The art and science of creating cocktails. It involves the skilful blending of different ingredients, including spirits, liqueurs, mixers, fruits, herbs, and spices, to craft balanced and flavourful drinks.

Mouthfeel- The sensory experience and textural qualities perceived in the mouth while drinking wine. It encompasses various sensations, including viscosity, carbonation, astringency, and overall texture. Mouthfeel plays a crucial role in the overall enjoyment and perception of a wine's quality.

Muddler- a bartender's tool used for muddling, which is the process of gently crushing or bruising ingredients to release their flavours and essential oils. Typically made of wood, metal, or plastic, a muddler consists of a handle and a flat or textured end. The flat end is used to crush ingredients such as herbs, fruits, or sugar cubes in the bottom of a glass or mixing vessel to extract their flavours and aromas.

Must- The term 'must' is derived from the Latin term vinum mustum, meaning 'young wine'. Must is the name given to the honey and water mix. In some wines, the must will also contain fruit pulp, and the skins of the grapes. Must is fermented by yeast in your fermenter to produce alcohol. CO_2 will be given off during fermentation, which normally passes through an airlock.

OG (Original Gravity)- This is sometimes referred to as SG or Starting Gravity. It is the hydrometer reading that is taken immediately before adding the yeast and indicates the amount of sugar that is available to be converted into alcohol by the yeast.

Oxidation- Refers to a chemical reaction where compounds in the wine interact with oxygen, leading to changes in flavour, aroma, and colour. While oxygen is essential at the start of the brewing process, excessive exposure to oxygen after fermentation can result in undesirable characteristics in the finished wine.

Pectin- A naturally occurring substance found in the cell walls of fruits, particularly in their skins and seeds. Pectin can lead to haze or cloudiness in the final wine, as it may form a gel-like substance. Adding Pectinaze to wines will breakdown pectin and assist the clearing process.

pH- The level of acid in wine. The pH of wine can vary depending on several factors, including the type of grape used, the water composition, the presence of fruits or other ingredients, and the fermentation process. The pH of wine typically ranges from around 2.8 to 3.8, although there can be some variation depending on factors such as grape variety, winemaking techniques, and aging processes. White wines tend to have a slightly higher pH than red wines, typically falling in the range of 3.0 to 3.4, while red wines often have a pH ranging from 3.3 to 3.8.

Phenols- Phenols can be desirable and undesirable. They play a role in the flavour and aroma profile of wine, particularly when they are derived from various ingredients, fermentation processes, or ageing conditions. They are a broad class of organic compounds that include aromatic rings with hydroxyl groups. Phenolic compounds can undergo transformations during ageing. Over time, some phenolic flavours may mellow or evolve, contributing to the overall complexity and character of the wine.

Pitching- The action of introducing yeast into the must.

Polysaccharides- Complex sugars that are found in honey and grape cell walls and are released during fermentation. These compounds contribute to the mouthfeel and texture of wine but can also lead to haziness if present in excessive amounts.

Primary Fermentation- The initial vigorous fermentation that occurs soon after pitching yeast. It usually takes 3-5 days and is the stage where fruit pulp is broken down by the action of fermentation.

Racking- The process of syphoning wine from any sediment and fruit residue, into a secondary fermenter.

Refractometer- A device used to measure the refractive index of a substance, which can provide information about the concentration or composition of a solution. In the context of winemaking, they are sometimes used instead of hydrometers to measure the sugar content in liquids.

Sanitisation & Sterilisation-Sanitisation is the most important element of home winemaking. The process is undertaken immediately before using equipment. The golden rule is that anything your wine touches should be sanitised. Sanitisation reduces any potential sources of microbial spoilage to irrelevant levels, which will minimise the risk of anything spoiling your wine. Today, no-rinse sanitisers such as Suresan are mostly used as they are highly effective, will not damage stainless steel equipment, and are kind to clothes and skin. Suresan can also be used to sanitise household items such as gym water bottles etc. To compliment good sanitisation practice, it is important to clean all equipment thoroughly after use, and before it is stored. Cleaning refers to removing yeast/sediment marks, dirt, and other visible stains. This is the same level as washing crockery and cutlery. Everything you use during a brew should be spotlessly clean and free of stains or marks and stored dry. When cleaning plastic items avoid using hard scouring pads, or anything that might scratch the surface, as those small scratches are an ideal place for microbes to hide. If buckets or other equipment become scratched or split (including syphon tubes) it is best to replace them. A thorough washing is a precursor to sanitising, as sanitising agents alone will not be able to remove built up grime and deposits on equipment that harbour bacteria.

Sterilisation is a third process of killing all living organisms on a surface, such as surgical instruments in a dental surgery or hospital. This is not a level that is necessary or routinely undertaken in winemaking. Sanitising your equipment is the best way to ensure that even at the microbial level there shouldn't be enough microbes to cause any infection. However, if you have been unlucky and have experienced an infection, it is recommended that you fill your fermenter with water and adding a dose of Steri-Cleen, which is 99.9% effective in killing bacteria and microbial cells. Immerse all equipment into the solution and soak for a minimum of 4 hours. Be careful to avoid the solution touching clothes as it will take the colour and may irritate skin. Thoroughly rinse equipment with cold water afterwards to remove traces of the steriliser. Steri-Cleen can also be used for deep cleaning equipment and glassware. If necessary, it can be mixed with an oxi-based household cleaner for removing stubborn marks and stains.

Secondary fermentation- Refers to the transfer of the wine from the primary fermentation vessel to a secondary vessel after the initial vigorous fermentation has taken place, and where fruit pulp has been strained off. It is also used to describe the natural carbonation process for sparkling wine when sugar or Brew Fizz Carbonation Drops are added to bottles.

Sediment- Yeast debris (dead yeast cells) and other particles will fall onto the bottom of the fermenter during the fermentation process. This is known as sediment. At the end of fermentation, it is recommended that your wine is syphoned from the sediment. Further sediment will subsequently fall as a result of adding finings and the clearing process. Your syphon tube should be fitted with a rigid sediment trap to avoid transferring sediment into bottles and secondary fermenters.

Specific Gravity (SG)- A scale used to monitor the progress of fermentation and to estimate the alcohol content of the wine. Before fermentation begins, the specific gravity of the must is measured using a hydrometer. As fermentation progresses and sugars are converted into alcohol by yeast, the specific gravity decreases because alcohol is less dense than water.

Starting Gravity. This is another term for Original Gravity and means the same thing.

Starter- A Yeast Starter is a culture made from a sachet of yeast by adding nutrients, warm water, and acid. The aim of a starter is to boost the number of yeast cells that are introduced to the must.

Sulphite- Sulphites, specifically sulphur dioxide (SO2), are commonly used in winemaking. They act as antioxidants, helping to prevent the oxidation of the wine. They also function as antimicrobial agents, inhibiting the growth of undesirable microorganisms such as bacteria and wild yeasts. This helps maintain the stability and quality of the wine.

Sweetness- The residual sugar left after fermentation has completed. This can be indicated by final gravity readings on a hydrometer. Dry Wine (0.996-1.005), Medium Wine (1.005-1010), Sweet Wine (1.010-1.015+).

Tartness- The tangy flavour profile that is often attributed to the presence of acids, typically organic acids, in the wine. Tartness can be a desirable characteristic in certain styles of wine, adding complexity and balancing sweetness. The perception of tartness is subjective and can vary depending on factors such as the type of grape used, the fermentation process, and any additional fruits included in the recipe.

Tannin- Polyphenolic compounds found in various plants, including fruit skins, nuts, and oak chunks. They play a role in the production and ageing of wine. Tannins contribute to the overall sensory profile of wine, affecting its mouthfeel, astringency, and ageing potential.

Yeast- A single cell organism that multiplies to support fermentation and convert sugars into alcohol, producing CO2 as a bi-product.

Scales and Conversion Tables:

This book provides temperature in degrees Celsius with (degrees Fahrenheit shown in brackets). The equation for converting Celsius to Fahrenheit is $F=9/5 \times C+32$.

Degrees Celsius	Degrees Fahrenheit
0	32
5	41
10	50
15	59
20	68
25	77
30	86
35	95
40	104
45	113
50	122
55	131
60	140
65	149
70	158
75	167
80	176
85	185
90	194
95	203
100	212

Volume is provided in millilitres or litres, with UK fluid ounces or gallons shown in brackets. Note: American volume scales differ from UK. There are slight variations in the sizes of pints between the United States and the United Kingdom. The US pint is equal to 473.176 millilitres, while the UK pint is equal to 568.261 millilitres. The litre is a metric unit, and 1 litre is equal to 1,000 millilitres.

A conversion can be easily calculated if the recipes are being followed in United States.

UK Gallons	UK Pints	US Pints	Millilitres
1	8	8.658	4,546
2	16	17.316	9,092
3	24	25.974	13,638
4	32	34.632	18,184
5	40	43.291	22,730

1 UK gallon = 160 UK fluid ounces

1 UK fluid ounce ≈ 0.05 UK pints

1 UK fluid ounce ≈ 28.4131 millilitres

1 US gallon = 128 US fluid ounces

1 US fluid ounce ≈ 0.0625 US pints

1 UK pint ≈ 1.20095 US pints

1 US fluid ounce ≈ 28.4131 millilitres

Weight is provided in grams or kg, with UK ounces or lbs shown in brackets.

Ounces	Pounds (lbs)	Grams (g)	Kilograms (kg)
1	0.0625	28.3495	0.02835
2	0.125	56.699	0.0567
4	0.25	113.398	0.1134
8	0.5	336.796	0.2268
16	1	453.592	0.4536

US and UK imperial weight scales are the same. The metric to imperial weight conversion factor is *pounds = Grams/453.592*. This is based on the fact that 1 pound is approximately equal to 453.592 grams. Divide the weight in grams by this conversion factor to obtain the weight in pounds.

1 ounce = 28.3495 grams

1 pound = 16 ounces

1 pound = 453.592 grams

1 kilogram = 1,000 grams

Hydrometer Temperature Correction:

Wine Temperature (Degrees Centigrade)	Wine Temperature (Degrees Fahrenheit)	Adjustment
10	50	-0.6
15	59	No correction needed
20	68	+0.9
25	77	+2.0
30	86	+3.4
35	95	+5.0
40	104	+6.8

Specific Gravity/Plato/Balling Conversion Chart:

Specific Gravity (SG)	Plato (°P)	Balling (°Brix)	Specific Gravity (SG)	Plato (°P)	Balling (°Brix)
1.000	0	0	1.054	13.5	13.5
1.002	0.5	0.5	1.056	14	14
1.004	1	1	1.058	14.5	14.5
1.006	1.5	1.5	1.060	15	15
1.008	2	2	1.062	15.5	15.5
1.010	2.5	2.5	1.064	16	16
1.012	3	3	1.066	16.5	16.5
1.014	3.5	3.5	1.068	17	17
1.016	4	4	1.070	17.5	17.5
1.018	4.5	4.5	1.072	18	18
1.020	5	5	1.074	18.5	18.5
1.022	5.5	5.5	1.076	19	19
1.024	6	6	1.078	19.5	19.5
1.026	6.5	6.5	1.080	20	20
1.028	7	7	1.082	20.5	20.5
1.030	7.5	7.5	1.084	21	21
1.032	8	8	1.086	21.5	21.5
1.034	8.5	8.5	1.088	22	22
1.035	9	9	1.090	22.5	22.5
1.036	9.5	9.5	1.092	23	23
1.038	10	10	1.094	23.5	23.5
1.040	10.5	10.5	1.096	24	24
1.042	11	11	1.098	24.5	24.5
1.044	11.5	11.5	1.100	25	25
1.045	12	12	1.102	25.5	25.5
1.046	12.5	12.5	1.104	26	26
1.048	13	13	1.106	26.5	26.5
1.050	7.5	0	1.108	27	27
1.052	8	0.5	1.110	27.5	27.5

This chart provides a basic reference for converting between specific gravity, Plato (°P), and Balling (°Brix) readings. It is important to note that these conversions are approximate and may vary slightly depending on factors such as temperature and sugar composition.

Sugar Addition Chart for Grape Wines:

Starting SG	Starting ABV	Desired ABV	Amount of Sugar to Add (lbs)	Amount of Sugar to Add (grams)
1.040	5.0%	6.0%	0.084	38.1
1.045	6.0%	7.0%	0.106	48.1
1.050	7.0%	8.0%	0.128	58.1
1.055	8.0%	9.0%	0.151	68.5
1.060	9.0%	10.0%	0.174	79.0
1.065	10.0%	11.0%	0.197	89.5
1.070	11.0%	12.0%	0.220	100.0
1.075	12.0%	13.0%	0.243	110.5
1.080	13.0%	14.0%	0.267	121.1
1.085	14.0%	15.0%	0.291	131.8
1.090	15.0%	16.0%	0.315	142.9
1.095	16.0%	17.0%	0.339	154.0
1.100	17.0%	18.0%	0.363	165.0
1.105	18.0%	19.0%	0.388	176.5
1.110	19.0%	20.0%	0.413	187.5

This chart indicates the amount of sugar to be added to a gallon of wine to increase the alcohol by volume (ABV) from a starting specific gravity (SG 1.040 to 1.110).

To calculate the amount of sugar needed to increase the alcohol by volume (ABV) in a gallon of wine from a starting specific gravity (SG) to a target specific gravity, you can also use the following formula:

$$\text{Sugar to be added (lbs)} = \frac{(\text{Target SG} - \text{Starting SG}) \times 131.25}{\text{Starting SG} \times (2.0665 - \text{Starting SG})}$$

Where:
Starting SG is the starting specific gravity of the wine.
Target SG is the desired specific gravity after the addition of sugar.

131.25 is a constant representing the amount of potential alcohol (in % ABV) that can be produced per pound of sugar per gallon of liquid. 2.0665 is a constant representing the potential alcohol of pure sugar in water.

How to use the formula:

Determine the starting specific gravity (SG) of the wine.
Determine the target specific gravity (SG) you want to achieve after adding sugar.
Plug the values into the formula to calculate the amount of sugar to be added in pounds.
Optionally, convert the result to grams if needed.
For example, let's say the starting SG is 1.080, and you want to increase it to a target SG of 1.090:

$$\text{Sugar to be added (lbs)} = \frac{(1.090 - 1.080) \times 131.25}{1.080 \times (2.0665 - 1.080)}$$

$$\text{Sugar to be added (lbs)} = \frac{0.010 \times 131.25}{1.080 \times 0.9865}$$

$$\text{Sugar to be added (lbs)} = \frac{1.3125}{1.06212}$$

$$\text{Sugar to be added} = 1.2316 \text{ lbs}$$

Approximately 1.236 pounds of sugar should be added to one gallon of wine, therefore, to increase the ABV from a starting SG of 1.080 to a target SG of 1.090.

To convert the result from pounds to grams, you can use the conversion factor that 1 pound is approximately equal to 453.6 grams. So, you would multiply the result obtained in pounds by this conversion factor to get the equivalent amount in grams.

Continuing from the previous example:

1.236 x 453.6 = 560.8576

So, approximately 560.8576 grams of sugar should be added to one gallon of wine to increase the ABV from a starting SG of 1.080 to a target SG of 1.090.

Index:

Foreword	iii
Acid Blend	44
Acid Reducer	45
Acidity	116
Adapting Wine Kits	59-63
Advanced Winemaking Techniques and Equipment	116
Ageing and Maturing Wine	108
Ageing Vessels	23
Airlock	17
Air Still	145
Ammonium Sulphate	37
Amylaze	47
Aperol Spritz	314, 315
Apple Cider	106, 107
Apple Wine	170-172
Apricot Wine	173-175
Banana Wine	176-178
Basics of Home Winemaking	10
Beetroot Wine	179-181
Benefits of Making Wine at Home	9
Black Russian Cocktail	346
Blackberry Wine	182-184
Blackcurrant Wine	185-186
Blending Wines	96-107
Blending Wines made from Craft Country Wines	104-107
Bloody Mary Cocktail	315, 316
Blueberry & Apple Wine	187-189
Bottle Closures	85, 112

Bottle Washer	112
Bottling and Labelling your Wine	111
Brewing Sugar	50
Campden Tablets	47, 48
Caraway Seed & Tea Wine	190-192
Carrot Wine	193-195
Caustic Soda	17
Cava	87, 88
Cherry Brandy Liqueur Chocolates	200
Cherry Brandy Liqueur	199, 200
Cherry Wine	196-198
Christmas Spiced Metheglin	269, 270
Citric Acid	13, 41, 42
Cloudy Wine	119, 120, 133
Cosmopolitan Cocktail	317
Crab-Apple Wine	128, 129
Daiquiri Cocktail	318, 319
Damson Liqueur Chocolates	211
Damson Port	207-209
Damson Vodka Liqueur	210, 211
Damson Wine	204-206
Dandelion Wine	212-214
Dark and Stormy Mixer	320
Demijohn	16
Developing Mixology Skills	156
Dextrose Monohydrate	50
Diammonium Phosphate	36, 37
Digital Hydrometers	124, 125
Dispensing Wine from Kegs	127-130
Dry Oaked Mead	262, 263
Elderberry Wine	215-217
Elderberry Port	218-220
Elderflower Cordial	227, 228
Elderflower Gin Fizz	213, 214

Elderflower Prosecco	224-226
Elderflower Wine	221-223
Enzybrew 10	17
Equipment Required to Make Wine	14
Espresso Martini Cocktail	322, 323
Essential Inventory	15
Extended Maceration	48, 49
Fermentation Vessel	9
Fig & Date Dessert Wine	229-231
Filter	15, 22, 115
Final Thoughts on Craft Winemaking	163
Forced Carbonation	89, 90, 127
French 75 Cocktail	323, 324
Frozen Strawberry Daiquiri Cocktail	319
Fusels	138-140
Future Trends in Mixology	347
Gimlet Cocktail	324
Glossary of Winemaking Terms	349-357
Golden Syrup	51, 52
Gooseberry Wine	232-234
Grape Juice Recipes	254-256
Grape Wine (Orange Wine)	241-243
Grape Wine (Provençal Rosé Wine)	247-249
Grape Wine (Red)	244-246
Grape Wine (White Zinfandel Rosé Wine))	250-253
Grape Wine (White)	238-240
Growing your own Vines	68-73
Heat Pad	22, 56
Hedgerow Wine	257-259
History of Winemaking at Home	3
Honey	61, 62
How to Make a Wine Kit	56-59
Hydrometer	18-20
Invert Sugar	51, 76

Lactic Acid	17, 43, 44, 135
Lactose	52
Mai Tai Cocktail	325, 326
Making Cider	92
Making Mead	80
Making Sparkling Wines	84
Making Spirit Based Drinks and Liqueurs	145
Making Wine from Grapes	42
Making Wine from Kits	68
Making Wine from your own Grapes	73
Malic Acid	43, 44
Malolactic Fermentation	43, 44, 75, 135
Manhattan Cocktail	326, 327
Margarita Cocktail	327, 328
Martini Cocktail	328, 329
Mead Infusions	51
Measuring Utensils	13
Melomel	50
Metheglin	51
Mint Julep Cocktail	329, 330
Mojito Mixer	225, 226
Moscow Mule Mixer	330, 331
Mulled Wine	271-273
Negroni Cocktail	331, 332
Nitrogen	35, 36, 128, 129
Novatwist Caps	59, 115
Odours	132
Old Fashioned Cocktail	323, 333
Orange Wine	274, 275
Oxygen	29, 35, 65
Painkiller Cocktail	333, 334
Paloma Cocktail	334, 335
Parsnip Sherry	276-278
Peach Wine	279, 280

Pear Wine	281, 282
Pectin Reduction	118
Pectin Test Kits	119, 120
Pectolytic Enzyme	45, 46
Pellicle Formation	140, 141
Perry	283-285
Pina Colada Cocktail	335, 336
Plum Wine	286-288
Popped Corks	137
Porn Star Martini Cocktail	336, 337
Post-fermentation Haze	134
Pot Still	146
Potassium Sorbate	48, 49
Pousse Café Cocktail	337, 338
Prizewinning Craft Wine Recipes	165
Prosecco	90, 91
Pure Brew	25, 40
Pyment	81, 82
Raspberry Wine	289, 290
Redcurrant Wine	291-293
Refractometers	125-127
Rhubarb Wine	294-296
Rice & Raisin Wine	297-299
Rose Petal & Raspberry Rosé Wine	303-305
Rosehip Wine	300-302
Sack Mead	31, 81, 264
Sanitisation	17
Scales and Conversion Tables	358-364
Sediment	11, 133, 134
Serving Wine	142-144
Sex on the Beach Cocktail	340-341
Sidecar Cocktail	341, 342
Sloe Gin Liqueur	309-310
Sloe Wine	306-308

Sparkling Gooseberry Fizz	235-237
Sparkling Mead	266-268
Speeding up the Bottling Process	112
Starch Reduction	119
Starch Test Kits	120
Steri-Cleen	17, 134
Strawberry Wine	311-313
Stuck Fermentation	131, 132
Succinic Acid	45
Sugar	49
Sustainability and Biodiversity in Winemaking	160
Syphoning Equipment	18
T500 Still	145-148
Tartaric Acid	42, 43
Tequila Sunrise Cocktail	342, 343
The Art of Mixology	151
The Experience of Making Wine at Home	1
The Process for Making Basic Craft Wines	64
Thermometer	20
Top 30 Cocktail Mixer Recipes	314
Traditional Mead	81, 82, 260, 261
Troubleshooting Common Issues	131
Vesper Cocktail	343, 344
Vinegar	134
Whiskey Sour Cocktail	344, 345
White Russian Cocktail	345, 346
Wine Chemistry	13, 14
Wine Filtration	121-123
Wine Press	23-26
Wine Tannin	40, 41
Winemakers Test Kits	120, 121
Yeast	26-35
Yeast Nutrient	35-40

Printed in Great Britain
by Amazon